INTERIOR DESIGN VISUAL PRESENTATION

A Guide to Graphics, Models, and Presentation Techniques

THIRD EDITION

MAUREEN MITTON

JOHN WILEY & SONS, INC.

Library of Congress Cataloging-in-Publication Data:

Mitton, Maureen.
  Interior design visual presentation : a guide to graphics, models, and presentation techniques / Maureen Mitton. — 3rd ed.
      p. cm.
  Includes index.
  ISBN 978-0-471-74156-5 (pbk.)
  1. Interior decoration rendering. 2. Interior decoration--Design. 3. Graphic arts. I. Title.
  NK2113.5.M58 2007
  729.028—dc22
                                        2007026433

Printed in the United States of America

10 9 8 7 6 5 4 3

INTERIOR DESIGN
VISUAL PRESENTATION

For
Roger, Anna, and Luc

CONTENTS

ACKNOWLEDGMENTS

This book, like the other editions, compiles the work of many hands (and keyboards) and conversations. It has been made possible by the generous contributions of numerous people, to whom I would like to express my gratitude.

First, I must acknowledge my current and former students, who have taught me volumes and who continue to give me the energy to keep going. This edition includes work by the following talented and hardworking, current and former students:

Tiffany Baca, Nicole Banaszewski, Laura Blanchard, Nina Bruss (Bouten), Tina Bucher, Ciarah Coenen, Laura Eysnogle, Ellie Feenstra, Stephanie Holmblad, Megan Gruner, Amber Liestman, Jenna Michels, Laura Purcell, Sunny Reed, Vicky Salzsieder, and Mary Wawra.

I must thank all of the former students who contributed work to earlier editions: Kristy Bokelman, Dan Effenheim, Denise Haertl, Anne Harmer, Theresa Isaacson, Leanne Larson, Anne (Cleary) Olsen, Ardella Pieper, Cory Sherman, Angela Skaare, Justin Thomson, and Randi Steinbrecher. And I thank former exchange students, Laura Sudbrock and Ilka Schnelle, whose works are included in this edition, as well as Jessica Tebbe and Dirk Olbrich, whose works were featured in previous editions.

I have been amazed and touched by the generosity of members of the design community who shared time and contributed projects. Traci Lesneski and the staff at Meyer, Scherer & Rockcastle, Ltd. (MS&R) generously allowed me to review projects and contributed excellent project work. The staff at Cuningham Group Architecture contributed time and a range of projects and process work. Jim Smart of Smart Associates graciously contributed work for this and previous editions.

Conversations with my friend Lynn Barnhouse were instrumental in helping to develop the first and second editions. This and previous editions include generous contributions of time and work by Jane Rademacher; Thom Lasley; Thomas Oliphant; Jim Moeller, at Arthur Shuster Inc.; Craig Beddow, of Beddow Design; Janet Lawson, of Janet Lawson Architectural Illustration; Robert Lownes, of Design Visualizations; and Harris Birkeland.

A special thanks to Matthew Saunders, a gifted illustrator and designer for his significant contributions: His skills in digital and manual rendering and drawing enrich this edition immensely.

Melissa Brewer contributed new CAD drawings as well as Photoshop contributions; this book would not have been possible without her. Her talents, insights, and great attitude made many good things possible—as usual. I am especially grateful for her prompt help with many last minute requests.

I must acknowledge and thank my current and former University of Wisconsin–Stout colleagues. Courtney Nystuen, a wonderful teacher and architect, contributed in many ways to all editions. Kristine Recker Simpson and Jack Zellner contributed work to this and the previous edition. Additionally some typically excellent student work from Ms. Recker Simpson's courses has been included in this edition. Shelley Pecha kindly (and quickly) contributed to this edition. Bill Wikrent and the staff (including Andrew Bottolfson and Katie Hladilek) at Learning Technology Services contributed all of the photography included, unless otherwise noted.

Thank you to Margaret Cummins and Lauren Poplawski at John Wiley & Sons. Also special thanks to Ava Wilder and Brent Savage at Wiley, and Jeff Baker, all of whom are responsible for the beautiful appearance of this edition.

My parents Robert and Margaret Mitton and my siblings, Michele, Marilyn, and Mark, provided emotional support at a very difficult time and I appreciate this greatly. All of their contributions made this edition possible and I am very thankful for the help and kindness of so many.

INTRODUCTION

The first edition of this book was intended as a primer on interior design visual communication, one that presented a range of styles and techniques. The goal with that and each later edition has been to provide students and practitioners with up-to-date information on visual presentation techniques. Like earlier editions, this book identifies methods used in the visual presentation of interior spaces and articulates them in written and visual language. Various phases of the design process are discussed in order to reveal the connection between process and presentation. Some often overlooked basic principles of graphic design and portfolio design are also discussed.

Research for this edition made clear the significant role computer-generated imagery plays in current practice and in the academic world. Despite this, hand drawing continues to be a useful tool, particularly in producing perspective drawings and in visual note-taking. Quickly created perspective drawings offer the benefit of providing designers with a visualization tool early in the design process, prior to the time finalized design drawings are complete. In addition, skills learned in drawing by hand transfer directly to computer modeling. The ability to create quick perspec-

tive sketches in client conferences and in team meetings is a highly useful tool; this is something that I have heard many times from those hiring designers. For these reasons, numerous examples of quick sketching techniques are included.

This book covers methods of manual drawing and presentation that can be found, at least in part, elsewhere—with the exception of estimated perspective sketching. Estimated sketching requires "eyeballing" perspectives, a method that I have found works well for students, although many educators find it horrifying. In addition to estimated sketching, information on more traditional methods of perspective drawing is included.

As this edition goes into production, designers are using computers for most drafting, three-dimensional modeling, rendering, image manipulation, and composition of presentations. Hardware and software may vary, but presentation has gone digital to a large degree. While this book does not go into a great detail about any particular software, it is meant to provide a brief discussion of the most widely used programs and to provide specific details about some software as it relates to presentation. For example, while this book provides very little in-depth coverage of

Adobe Photoshop®, it does provide some instruction related specifically to rendering using Photoshop—which is common in current practice. Therefore, a working knowledge of some basic software programs is required in addition to the instruction provided in this book.

This book offers a only a cursory description of most three-dimensional modeling software with the exception of a basic introduction to SketchUp software. My reasoning here is that I have found SketchUp to be the most intuitive of modeling software (although it certainly has limitations) and it allows for easy and quick success. This ease allows for use of SketchUp early in the design process, as well as at many points along the way, making it much like handsketching.

At this time, many designers continue to present projects using traditional presentation boards and those are covered in detail in this edition. Information is also provided about digital presentations methods, as many designers are creating completely digital and virtual presentations. Clearly we are at a time of transition, where new methods are employed by some and "traditional" methods are favored by others—both are covered in detail in this edition.

As with earlier editions, many of the examples included here were executed by undergraduate design students. I've included these because I want students to see real examples of developing skills. It is important for all designers to develop drawing and sketching skills. Drawing and modeling building should not be reserved for the final presentation of fully developed designs. Instead, sketching, drawing, and model building must be acknowledged as ways of seeing and exploring throughout the design process—from beginning to final presentation. I admit my desire to get interior designers to draw (and draw and draw). It is

the best way to learn to visualize and develop good work.

Examples of work done by professional illustrators, digital illustrators, and model makers are also included in order to demonstrate what is being done in current practice by specialists. The work is beautiful and highly professional, and it depicts what top professionals can produce. We can learn from this work and allow it to influence our design drawings and in-process presentations.

Many chapters begin with information about specific materials and tools. Each provides written instructions in the text as well as step-by-step illustrated instructions. In teaching, I've found that some students learn best by reading, while others learn by following brief graphic guides. My goal is to provide instruction for a variety of learning styles. The examples and projects presented here vary in scope from small residential student projects to huge public interior spaces designed by professionals; this is a means of acquainting readers with the range of projects professional designers are involved in.

In completing this edition I came to some conclusions. One is that while much has changed since the first edition—particularly related to digital technology—so many things have stayed consistent, particularly regarding the process of design and the complex yet flexible type of thinking required of a professional designer. This continues to be a profession populated by bright, creative individuals who are required to call upon a broad range of talents and skills in everyday practice. While technology has made many things easier and faster, today's designers are required to know more and to possess more skills than at any time previously. I hope this book will help today's designers in their acquisition of some of the many skills required in current practice.

1

ORTHOGRAPHIC DRAWINGS

Interior design is a multifaceted and ever-changing discipline. The practice of interior design continues to evolve due to technological as well as societal changes.

The sentences above were written roughly ten years ago, in the introduction to the first edition of this book, and continue to hold true today. Digital technology continues to influence and to work as a change agent in the ongoing evolution of design practice. Today's practicing interior designers use software for drafting, three-dimensional modeling programs, digital rendering programs, digital imaging software, as well as a range of word processing, spreadsheet, and presentation programs.

In addition to undergoing constant, rapid technological advancement, the profession of interior design has grown in terms of scope of work, specialization, and the range of design practiced. The growth of the profession, combined with efforts toward development of educational standards, registration, and licensing, have increased its legitimacy as a serious professional discipline.

Constant change in society and in one's profession can be overwhelming and a bit frightening, and for that reason it is useful

to consider the elements that remain constant in an evolving profession. In many ways, the design process itself remains constant—whether practiced with a stick in the sand, a technical pen, or a powerful computer and software. There are many stories about designers drawing preliminary sketches on cocktail napkins or the backs of paper bags, and these stories lead us to a simple truth.

Professional designers conduct research, take piles of information, inspiration, and hard work, and wrap them all together in what is referred to as the DESIGN PROCESS, to create meaningful and useful environments. A constant and key factor in interior design is the fact that human beings—and other living creatures—occupy and move within interior spaces. To create interior environments, professional designers must engage in a process that involves research, understanding, idea generation, evaluation, and documentation. These are significant constants that exist in a changing world.

For the most part this book covers the process designers engage in and the related presentation techniques used in DESIGN COMMUNICATION. These processes and basic concepts are consistent, whether generated manually or by computer. Some examples included here were created

1-1

manually, whereas others were computer generated. Regardless of how drawings and graphics are generated, they are part of a process of discovery, exploration, and creation.

This chapter covers what is often referred to as *drafting*, as well as other forms of two-dimensional graphics; this specific type of drawing is required for all projects that will be constructed. The term DRAFTING refers to measured drawings done with specialized tools and equipment. The truth is that not all drawings used in the process of interior design are drawn with the aid of drafting tools or computers. Often those drawings created in the preliminary stages of the design process are rough sketches and involve little use of drafting tools or equipment. As designs are refined, there is clearly a need for highly accurate, measured, and detailed drawings, and these are drafted with tools.

This chapter presents the materials, equipment, and tools used for manually drafted and freehand design drawings, as well as an overview of the most common drawings used in interior design practice. The information presented in this chapter is meant as an overview, not a definitive drawing or drafting reference. Subsequent chapters cover the other forms of drawings and design graphics used in sketching, and other forms of idea generation.

MATERIALS, TOOLS, AND EQUIPMENT FOR MANUAL DRAFTING

The graphics and drawings used in interior design practice vary, ranging from conceptual sketches and rough layouts to measured technical drawings. The materials, tools, and equipment used to create the variety of drawings and graphics are numerous and ever proliferating. The media and tools selected must be appropriate to the task at hand. This means that their proper selection requires careful consideration of the drawing type and use, as well as an understanding of the available products. Currently most schools and design firms create the majority of design drawings digitally, using COMPUTER-AIDED DESIGN (CAD) programs. However, some students begin the study of drafting by creating drawings manually; for that reason a description of manual drawing tools and equipment follows. Figure 1-1 illustrates commonly used manual drafting and drawing materials and equipment, which are discussed as follows.

Drawing Surfaces

The type of drawing surface selected directly affects the quality of the drawn image. Some surfaces accept pencil and ink readily and allow for clear, consistent imagery. Transparent papers allow for diazo reproduction (blueprinting) and can be used as an overlay to continue a drawing by transferring details from one sheet to another. Drawings produced on nontransparent surfaces are reproduced by photocopying, digital reproduction (scanning), or photographic processes.

TRACING PAPER is the most common paper surface for sketching in-process design drawings and graphics. Known in various parts of the country as *trace*, *flimsy*, and *bumwad*, this paper is highly transparent and relatively inexpensive. Tracing paper is available in cut sheets and in rolls in a variety of sizes. Rolls of tracing paper work well for interior design drawing because of the varying sizes of drawings required. Tracing paper is available in white, buff, and canary (yellow). Most designers have a personal color preference based on previous experience. Some designers use tracing paper to create actual presentation sketches (used to communicate with a client or end-user) while others use them only for personal exploration.

Because tracing paper is relatively inexpensive, it can be used to develop preliminary sketches and for in-process drawings. This allows for exploration through the creation of many sketches and the generation of many ideas. Tracing paper also works very well overlaid on drawings for transfer and refinement of images. Often many layers of tracing paper are overlaid as a design is refined or as a complicated perspective drawing is constructed. Images on tracing paper can be reproduced easily by being photocopied or being scanned for inclusion in design presentations.

While this is done less commonly in current practice, final design drawings created manually and intended for diazo reproduction are drawn on DRAFTING VELLUM, a transparent paper available in a variety of finishes and weights (thicknesses) and most often white. Drafting vellum should have a high rag or cotton content, giving it a rich finish, strength, and good stability. It is excellent for line work generated with graphite pencils. Good-quality diazo prints can be run from drafting vellum originals. Vellum is also photocopied, scanned, and photographed with excellent results.

In addition to vellum, PLASTIC DRAFTING FILMS are used for final drawings and for some design presentations. Plastic (and polyester) drafting films are expensive, tear resistant, and generally do not react to fluctuations in temperature or humidity (as do many paper surfaces). They accept ink beautifully and allow for easy ink erasure. These films require the use of special pencils. Drafting film originals produce excellent diazo prints and photocopies. For years prior to the use of CAD, plastic film and ink drawings were considered the finest for reproduction.

A range of ART PAPERS is available; the papers are made with a variety of materials and come in many colors, sizes, and finishes. Some of these papers can be used as a drawing surface or as a background or visual element included within a presentation; a range of paper types is discussed in Chapter 5, beginning on page 145.

ADHESIVE REPRODUCTION FILM, also called *appliqué film* and often referred to generically as *sticky back*, is used on vellum or bond drawings. Typed or printed images can be drawn or photocopied onto adhesive reproduction film. The film is then carefully measured and cut and applied to the vellum or bond paper.

Manually generated design drawings can be reproduced on large-format photocopying machines. However, CAD-generated drawings—printed or plotted on bond paper—are the most commonly used in current practice. It is also worth noting that many designers and design firms scan hand drawings and combine them with additional graphics using imaging software such as Photoshop or page layout software such as InDesign® to create digital presentations such as those in discussed in Chapter 5, page 157 (Digital Rendering).

Line- and Mark-Making Implements

Lines and marks record spatial information in interior design drawings and graphics. Control of line thickness and the type of stroke used are important and convey specific information. Thus, the implement used to create lines and marks is a key factor in manually created design drawings.

GRAPHITE is mixed with clay and other elements to produce what are commonly called *lead* pencils. Graphite pencils, used in design drawing, are available in a range of hardnesses based on the mixture of clay to graphite. Graphite pencils and replaceable "leads" are coded with a standard rating system: H stands for hard, B stands for black (the softer leads). The number found next to the H or B refers to the level of hardness. For example, a 6B is softer than a 2B; an 8H is very hard. F-rated leads are at the center of the range, and HB leads are slightly harder than Bs. The softer leads are used in sketching and rendering, whereas

H, 2H, and sometimes F leads are most commonly used in drafting.

The graphite described above is used in a variety of mark-making implements. WOODEN DRAWING PENCILS involve a graphite mixture encased in wood and are sharpened like standard wooden writing pencils. MECHANICAL PENCILS are hollow instruments that hold very fine graphite leads. These are sold in a variety of lead widths to create a range of line weights. LEAD HOLDERS are hollow implements that accept thicker leads than mechanical pencils. Although lead holders do not allow for any variety in lead widths, they do accept a range of lead types in terms of softness. Lead holders require the use of a specialized sharpener, known as a LEAD POINTER.

Specialized colored drafting pencils and leads can be used to develop drawings prior to hard-lining them. NONPHOTO-BLUE colored pencils do not reproduce when photographed; however, they sometimes reproduce when photocopied. NONPRINT colored pencils do not reproduce in diazo prints. When appropriate, both types of pencil can be used to lay out drawings prior to completion.

One of the significant advantages of using graphite pencils is the ease of erasing. Harder leads are often the most difficult to erase, whereas soft pencil marks are easily lifted with gray kneaded erasers or pink erasers. Plastic and film erasers can be used to remove marks made with harder leads. A metal ERASER SHIELD is used to protect the drawing surface from unwanted erasing. DRY CLEANING PADS, containing art gum powder that sifts onto drawing surfaces, are available to keep drawings clean.

TECHNICAL PENS have tubular points and refillable ink reservoirs. They are available in a range of point sizes that allow for absolute control of line weight. Because they employ black ink and metal points, technical pens create the finest line work of any drawing implement. They must be used with the appropriate ink, as specified by the manufacturer.

DISPOSABLE TECHNICAL PENS combine a tubular support with a felt tip and are available in a range of point sizes. These pens require no maintenance or cleaning, making them easy to use. Although disposable pens have been known to skip, causing inconsistent line work, they have improved a great deal recently and are becoming very popular.

FELT-TIP PENS are available in a range of styles and point sizes; they are often used in sketching, exploration, and rendering. Felt-tip pens are not generally used for refined drafted drawings or working drawings.

Erasing ink marks is rather difficult and requires special erasers. Hard plastic erasers can remove ink. However, an ELECTRIC ERASER with the appropriate eraser insert is most useful in removing ink. Electric erasers are very effective but must always be used with an eraser shield. Ink marks on film are erased more easily than those on vellum. Sharp razor blades are sometimes used to scrape ink away from drawing surfaces.

A quality DRAWING BOARD is required for the creation of successful drawings. Serious students must purchase a top-quality drawing board if possible. The board should accommodate a minimum paper size of 24 inches by 36 inches. Drawing boards should be covered with a specialized vinyl drawing surface, sold at drafting and art supply stores. The vinyl surface helps to improve line consistency.

T SQUARES are used in conjunction with the edge of the drawing board to provide an accurate horizontal line or right angle for drawings. PARALLEL RULERS can be attached to drawing boards using a system of screws, cables, and pulleys. This creates the sliding straightedge that is the standard in profes-sional practice. Triangles are used with a T square to create vertical and angled lines. Adjustable and 45/45-degree and 30/60-degree triangles are readily available. Triangles should be fairly clear, easy to see through, and as substantial as possible. An inking triangle with raised edges is required when using ink. It is also useful to have a tiny triangle on hand as an aid in lettering. Triangles should never be used as a cutting edge; this will ruin them. A cork-backed metal ruler is the best edge for cutting.

DRAFTING TAPE or PRECUT DRAFTING DOTS are used to attach drawings to drawing boards. Unlike standard masking and household tape, drafting tape and dots are easy to remove from both the paper and the drawing board. A DRAFTING BRUSH is used to remove eraser debris from the drawing surface.

Measured interior design drawings require the use of a proportional scale. This allows for large areas to be reduced in size to fit on relatively small drawings. An ARCHITECTURAL SCALE is the standard scale ruler used in interior design drawing. In the United States, standard architectural scales employ imperial units, that is feet and inches. Standard architectural scales are marked incrementally with numbers running from left to right, with a number or fraction to the right or left of the incremental lines that indicate scale. For example, in ¼-inch scale the ruler is marked so that each ¼-inch measures 1 foot in scale. Architectural scales have inches marked below the zero marking; these are used to measure elements that are not exact to the foot. In transferring measurements, great care should be taken to record accurate dimensions. Scale rulers should never be used to draw against, as this would result in poorly drawn lines and damaged rulers. More information on the actual scales used for specific types of drawings can be found later in this chapter.

FIGURE 1-2
When an object is enclosed in a glass box, each plane of the box can serve as a picture plane. The view through the top plane (picture plane) creates a plan view, in this case a roof plan.

FIGURE 1-3
The view through the picture plane enclosing the side of the box is called an *elevation*.

FIGURE 1-4
A section is a view of an object with the picture plane slicing neatly through it.

FIGURE 1-5
A floor plan is a view of the building from above with a horizontal plane sliced through it and removed to expose the thickness of the walls.

Figures 1-2 through 1-5 drawn by Ciarah Coenen

An ENGINEER'S or ENGINEERING SCALE is used for measuring larger scale items, typically related to building sites, roads, topographical features and other items such as water and sewer lines. In the United States these scales are based on imperial units—that is feet. These scales are marked incrementally with numbers running from left to right only, with a number given at the left of the incremental lines that indicates scale. These scales measure in parts to the inch, such as 1 inch equals 10 feet, or one inch equals 20 feet and so on up to 60 feet—on standard scales. In using an engineer scale, each value given requires that you multiply the value by 10. For example, using the portion of the scale where 1 inch equals 10 feet; where the 1 is written actually measures 10 feet, and where the 2 is written equals 20 feet. Individual increments marked by small lines along the ruler (without numbers written next to them) represent individual feet—for example, two small line marks to the right of 2 represents 22 feet.

METRIC SCALES are standard throughout most of the world (with the exception of the United States) and represent meters (m) and centimeters (cm) or millimeters (mm). Much like the aforementioned engineer's scale, these scales are based on ratios, such as 1:50, where 1 millimeter would scale to represent 50 millimeters. More information on the actual scales used for specific types of drawings can be found later in this chapter. It is worth noting that the simplified modern version of the metric system is properly called the International System of Units, symbolized by *SI*, according to the U.S. Metric Association; this system includes other units of measurement as well.

TEMPLATES are most commonly constructed of plastic and are used much like stencils to draw various shapes, including circles, ellipses, furnishings, and fixtures.

The more expensive templates—constructed of heavy, durable plastic—are worth the extra money. Furniture and fixture templates work well to quickly lay out and plan spaces. However, in presentation drawings furniture and fixtures drawn from templates can appear artificial and monotonous.

FRENCH CURVES are drawn against as an aid in producing curved lines. FLEXIBLE CURVES, also known as snakes, are also used as an aid in drawing curved lines. These have flexible spines that can be bent to accommodate the desired curve. These also work well for transferring curves from one drawing surface to another. A COMPASS is used for drawing accurate circles and arcs and is useful in situations where a template does not contain a circle of the required size. It is worthwhile to purchase a good compass that adjusts easily and accepts drawing leads and ink heads.

UNDERSTANDING ORTHOGRAPHIC PROJECTION DRAWINGS

The practice of interior design requires the creation and use of various types of drawings. These can be divided into three broad categories based on purpose. The first type of drawing allows the designer to explore ideas (known as *ideation*) and work conceptually, often in the form of sketches. The second type allows the designer to communicate to others, including members of the design team, the client, end users, consultants, and other professionals (presentation drawings). A third type of drawing conveys the technical information required for construction (construction documents or working drawings). This book focuses on the first two types of drawing: those used for exploration and presentation or for graphic communication of ideas.

Unlike ideation sketches, presentation drawings and construction documents

1-2

1-3

1-4

1-5

must use certain standard drawing conventions to clearly communicate and delineate the proposed design; these generally involve drafting in scale. Unlike fine art drawing, design drawing requires adherence to conventions, proportional scale, and accuracy of line. Design drawings are highly standardized so that they carry universal meaning. Or, as one early reviewer of this book put it, "Design drawing is much like a language; the drawings must convey the designer's meaning clearly."

While this publication does not cover them in any detail, highly technical construction drawings are always drafted in scale, either manually or using CAD, and they employ many of the concepts covered in this chapter. They are, however, quite distinct and follow very specific conventions and because of this should be studied in detail by interior design students—toward that end, the References section of this chapter lists two books that describe and illustrate construction drawings clearly for students. Various examples of technical

LEGEND

WALLS IN REMODELING SITUATIONS

EXISTING WALLS TO REMAIN | WALLS TO BE REMOVED | NEW WALLS

NEW CONSTRUCTION

INT. WALLS — 4 1/2"± ACTUAL / 4" NOMINAL

EXT. WALLS — 7"± ACTUAL / 6" NOMINAL

OBJECT LINE

HIDDEN FEATURE AND/OR FEATURE THAT IS ABOVE THE PLAN CUTTING PLANE (E.G. SOFFITS, BALCONY EDGE, ETC)

CENTER LINE

PROPERTY LINE

BREAK LINE

SUITABLE DIMENSION LINES

DOOR SWINGS

DOOR SWINGS - CLOSET DOORS

BI-FOLD DOORS

SUITABLE WINDOW SYMBOLS

1-6a

FIGURE 1-6a

Common graphic notations used in orthographic projection drawings.

construction drawings can be found at the end of this chapter in Figures 1-17a through 1-17d and Figures 1-18a through 18-c.

The design drawings most commonly used in scaled delineation of interior environments are *floor plans*, *interior elevations*, *sections*, and *reflected ceiling plans*. These drawings, called ORTHOGRAPHIC PROJECTIONS, are created by projecting information about an object onto an imaginary plane known as the PICTURE PLANE. This direct projection of an object's dimensions allows orthographic projections to retain shape and proportion, making these drawings accurate and precise.

Orthographic projection creates fragmentary views of an object, resulting in the need for multiple drawings. This means that because of their fragmentary nature orthographic projections become parts of

a system and are mutually dependent on one another. By their nature, orthographic projections appear flat and lack the three-dimensional quality of perspective drawings. One way to visualize orthographic projection is to imagine an object enclosed in a transparent box. Each transparent plane of the enclosing box serves as the picture plane for that face of the object

The view through the top plane of the enclosing box is called a PLAN. In a plan view only those elements seen when looking directly down at the object are drawn. Figure 1-2 depicts a roof plan.

The views through the picture planes that form the sides of the enclosing box are called ELEVATIONS. Elevations depict only what is visible when viewed directly through the picture plane. Figure 1-3 is an exterior elevation.

GRAPHIC SYMBOLS

———— — —— ℄ CENTER LINE

———— — — — ℗ PROPERTY LINE

— — — — — — — HIDDEN, OR EXISTING CONSTRUCTION TO BE REMOVED, OR FUTURE

——————╱\——— BREAK LINE

DIMENSIONS:

10'-0"	8'-0"	HATCH MARK
10'-0"	8'-0"	ARROW
10'-0"	8'-0"	DOT

△1 (NO./DWG)— DETAIL INDICATOR

△1 ▲(NO./DWG)— SECTION INDICATOR

△1 ▲(NO./DWG) INTERIOR ELEVATION VIEW INDICATOR

⊕ EL— CONTROL ELEVATION INDICATOR

ROOM NAME
[NO.] ROOM IDENTIFIER

(NO.) COLUMN LINE OR GRID INDICATOR

DWG ◓— MATCH LINE (DWG = DRAWING NUMBER FOR CONTINUATION)

⬡ NO. WINDOW IDENTIFIER

[NO.] NOTE IDENTIFIER

[NO.]┬ WALL TYPE IDENTIFIER

(NO.) EQUIPMENT IDENTIFIER

(NO.) DOOR/OPENING IDENTIFIER

╱EL ✛ EXISTING ELEVATION IDENTIFIER

╱EL▭ ✛ NEW (FINISH) ELEVATION IDENTIFIER

1-6b

FIGURE 1-6b
Graphic symbols used for references and notes. Items shown with a 1 near them are reference symbols that include a number on top of another number. The number on top refers to the drawing number and the lower number refers to the sheet the drawing may be found on.

A SECTION portrays a view of the object or building with a vertical plane sliced through it and removed. One way of understanding section views is to imagine that a very sharp plane has been inserted into the object or building, cutting neatly into it and revealing the structure and complexity of the object's form (see Figure 1-4).

A FLOOR PLAN, also known as a horizontal section, portrays a view of the building with a horizontal plane sliced through it and removed, exposing the thickness of the walls and the elements below the cut line such as floor finishes and furniture (see Figure 1-5).

Orthographic projection drawings are clearly an abstraction of reality and use specific conventions to delineate space and materials. Unlike some other forms of drawing, orthographic projection drawings require adherence to conventions, proportional scale, and accuracy of line; these design drawings are highly standardized so that they carry universal meaning. Therefore, items such as walls, doors, windows, property boundaries, references to other

FIGURE 1-6c

Graphic symbols used for lighting and electrical information.

Figures 1-6a through 1-6c drawn by Melissa Brewer

drawings and other items are represented by very specific graphic symbols or combinations of lines. Figures 1-6a, 1-6b, and 1-6c illustrate some graphic notations used in these types of drawings such as wall lines, door and window symbols, as well as reference and notation symbols.

ORTHOGRAPHIC PROJECTION DRAWINGS FOR INTERIOR ENVIRONMENTS

The special orthographic projection drawings used in delineation of interior environments are based on the concepts mentioned to this point. These drawings impart information particular to interior construction.

Floor Plans

As stated, floor plans can also be called HORIZONTAL BUILDING SECTIONS, this is because they are drawn as though a horizontal cut has been made in the building (typically between 3 feet 6 inches and 5 feet 6 inches above the floor) as shown in Figure 1-7. Cutting into the building at this location exposes the thickness of walls and other structural elements, and shows windows, doors, and can show floor finishes and furnishings—all of which are located below the location of the cut.

In the United States, floor plans are most often drawn at a scale of ⅛" = 1'0" or ¼" = 1'0", although this varies according to project conditions. Larger-scale floor

1-7

plans are useful for presentation of complex or highly detailed spaces. Smaller-scale floor plans are required for large projects and are also used as key plans in complex presentations. In creating floor plans using metric measurements, a scale of 1:50 is relatively common; it is somewhat similar to ¼" = 1'0" scale (that would be 1:48 to be exact). Architectural drawings—other than small-scale interior related drawings, such as the floor plans mentioned—are commonly drawn using a metric scale of 1:100.

In drawing floor plans it is important to convey significant spatial relationships with consistent graphic conventions. Various line weights are used to convey depths and qualities of form. In standard floor plans the boldest line weight is used to outline those elements that have been cut through and are closest to the viewer (such as full-height wall lines). An intermediate line weight is employed to outline objects that

lie below the plane of the cut but above the floor plane, such as fixtures, built-ins, and furnishings. A finer line weight is used to outline surface treatment of floors and other horizontal planes, such as tile and wood grain. Objects that are hidden, such as shelves, or above the plane of the cut are dashed or ghosted in; this must be done in a manner that is consistent throughout the presentation.

Figures 1-8a and 1-8b are examples of town-house floor plans drawn using AutoCAD software and employing standard conventions and reference symbols. Figures 1-8c is an enlarged portion of the floor plan included to show detailed information.

Standard doors are generally drawn open at 90 degrees to the wall and are often shown with the arc of their swing. The door frame and the space it requires must be considered in the drawing of the door system (this means the dimensions of the frame must be

LOWER LEVEL PLAN

1-8a

FIGURE 1-8a

Town-house lower-level floor plan employing standard drafting conventions.

1. Boldest lines indicate the location of cut, meaning full-height walls are bold. Lower walls may be shown with lighter line weights (1a).

2. Fixtures, cabinetry, and finish materials are drawn with progressively lighter lines as they recede from the cut location.

3. Elements that are above or below the cut line—such as cabinets (3a) and soffits—or hidden such as dishwashers, are indicated with dashed lines.

4. Standard doors are drawn open at 90 degrees with the arc of swing shown; the full swing can be shown ensure that nothing impedes the full swing of the door.

5. Specialized doors, such as smaller closet doors (shown), bi-fold doors, sliding doors, and pocket doors, are drawn in a way that indicates size and construction.

6. Window glass and sill lines are shown, often with a lighter-weight line than walls.

7. Stairs are drawn as broken off past the line of the cut; a special breakline is used.

8. A title, north arrow, and scale notation are required on all plans. Because this drawing was reduced, a standard written scale was omitted; instead, a graphic scale device is included.

9. This is a section reference symbol. The arrow indicates the direction of the view of the section.

10. This is an elevation reference symbol. The arrow indicates the direction of the elevation view. The number indicates the particular drawing that is referenced.

11. Flooring materials may be shown as required (using a light line weight).

12. This is a centerline, indicating the centerline of the shared wall in the town house.

considered). Doors other than standard such as smaller swinging closet doors, bi-fold, sliding and pocket types are drawn in a manner that is consistent with their construction as shown in Figure 1-6a. Windowsills are typically outlined, often with a lighter line weight at the sill only. Window frames and sheets of glass are shown in various details as scale allows. Stairs are generally shown as broken off past the height of the plane of the cut; this is signified with a special cut or breakline as shown in Figure 1-8a. An arrow should be included to indicate the direction of the stairs from the level of the floor plan, with the word UP or DOWN (DN) adjacent to the directional arrow.

A title, a north arrow, and some type of scale notation should be included on all

BEDROOM

STUDIO

(ROOF)

DN

BEDROOM

BATH

(OPEN)

A

UPPER LEVEL PLAN

0 2 4 8

1-8b

floor plans. Scale notation can be stated numerically, for example: $\frac{1}{4}$" = 1'0". Current practice often requires the use of a graphic scaling device, which allows for reduction, enlargement, and electronic transmission of the drawings.

Symbols relating the floor plan to additional orthographic views or details are often drawn on the floor plan and serve as cross-references.

Successful floor plan presentation drawings require a thorough understanding of drafting conventions. Presentation floor plans may be drawn fastidiously with tools or drawn freehand. Regardless of the style of drawing, presentation floor plans must be accurate and drawn to the appropriate scale so that they communicate the design and can be used by the designer as the project moves forward. Presentation floor plans are enhanced by the use of tone, value, color, and other graphic devices. The graphic enhancement of floor plans is discussed in greater detail in Chapter 5, page 151. Additional examples of plans for commercial projects may be found at the end of this chapter beginning with Figures 1-17a and 1-18a.

Interior Elevations

Just as exterior elevations are created to reveal exterior elements and features, interior elevations reveal the interior features of a building. One way to understand the creation of interior elevations is to imagine ourselves inside the room we are drawing. Imagine standing inside a room facing one wall directly, with a large sheet of glass (the picture plane) inserted between the viewer and the wall. The interior elevation can then be created by outlining (projecting onto the picture plane) the significant features of the wall. Each wall of the room can be drawn in elevation by means of projecting what is visible as the viewer faces that wall directly as illustrated in Figure 1-9.

Interior elevations are used extensively in professional practice. Successful elevations

1-8c

must clearly depict all interior architectural elements in a consistent scale. Interior elevations are typically drawn in a scale ranging from ¼" = 1'o" to 1" = 1'o". Elevations drawn to depict accessories, equipment, cabinetry, fixtures, and design details are often drawn at ⅜" = 1'o" or ½" = 1'o". Millwork and other highly complicated elevations are often drawn at ½" = 1'o" or larger.

All elevations require the use of differing line weights to clearly communicate spatial relationships. Typically, any portion of walls cut through and those closest to the viewer are drawn using a bold line weight. Receding elements become progressively lighter in line weight as they move farther from the picture plane. Some designers draw the line representing the ground line as the boldest, with those lines representing the top and sides of the wall drawn just slightly lighter in weight. Figure 1-10 depicts kitchen elevations for the town-house project.

Drawing interior elevations by hand or digitally can be difficult for beginning students to master and requires a clear understanding of the concepts involved. To this end, a plan and elevations for another project can be found in Appendix 3; additional drawing examples may also be found at the end of this chapter (see Figures 1-17a, 1-17d, 1-18a, and 1-18c).

Interior elevations are an excellent vehicle for developing and refining interior details as illustrated by Figures 1-11a and 1-11b, which are interior elevations depicting very different design schemes for the same lobby space.

Like floor plans, elevations used for design presentations vary greatly from those used for construction. Elevations used for construction drawings must necessarily contain significant dimensions as well as appropriate technical information as illustrated at the end of this chapter (see

FIGURE 1-9
In drawing interior elevations, the picture plane is inserted between the viewer and wall(s). What is visible through the picture plane is drawn in elevation.

① ELEVATION

② ELEVATION

FIGURE 1-10

1. Portions of walls cut into or closest to viewer are bold.

2. Receding elements are drawn with progressively lighter lines.

3. In elevations including cabinetry and or millwork, details such as countertops, door frames, and hardware should be included.

4. Interior elevations require titles, reference symbols (names or numbers), and scale notation.

ELEVATION (A)

1-11a

ELEVATION (A)

1-11b

FIGURE 1-11a
This elevation delineates a traditional wood-paneling design treatment for a hotel lobby. Because this drawing was reduced, a graphic scale notation was used in place of written information.

FIGURE 1-11b
This elevation delineates a completely different design approach for the hotel lobby shown in Figure 1-11a. Because this drawing was reduced, a graphic scale notation was used in place of written information.

Figures 1-17d and 1-18c). Those used for presentations can be drawn more freely and often contain less technical information but must be drawn accurately and in consistent scale. Figure 1-12 is a preliminary elevation sketch created to convey design elements for a professionally designed project.

For elevations to work well in visual presentations, they must be clearly keyed, noted, or referenced to the floor plan. Regardless of the referencing method used, titles must be included beneath all elevations and scale should always be noted. Elevations used for presentations are enhanced by the use of tone, value, color,

and other graphic devices, many of which are discussed in Chapter 5.

Sections

As described earlier, a building section is a view created as though a vertical plane has cut through the building and been removed. Unlike interior elevations, which depict only what occurs inside the interior; sections can expose the structure of the building. In drawing sections, it is important to include the outline of the structural elements as well as the internal configuration of the interior space. Sections require varied line weights as a means of describing

SILK SCREEN

READER BOARD
SUSPENDED FROM DOME

CONCRETE COLUMNS

SPORTS BOOK BACK WALL BEYOND
CENTER "PARTY ROOM"

SILK SCREEN IMAGES OF ATHLETES
(SILHOUETTES)

SUSPENDED MONITORS
W/ READER BOARD
BELOW.

CAN WALK
BELOW
SCREEN 7'-0"

ICE DRINK RAIL

SECTION THROUGH "PARTY ROOM"
SCALE: 1/4" = 1'-0"

MAIN FLAT SCREEN - HIGH RESOLUTION (CAN BE SEEN @ ENTRY)

1-12

depths and spatial relationships. It is typical to show what is cut through, and therefore closest to the viewer, in the boldest line weight; receding features and details are drawn using progressively lighter line weights.

It is important to consider carefully the most useful location (or locations) of the building to show in section. The section should be cut through the building as a single continuous plane. Sections should expose and convey important interior relationships and details such as doors, windows, changes in floor level, ceiling heights, and, in some cases, finish material locations.

Design and presentation sections differ greatly from construction sections. Construction sections require technical information to communicate information about building systems. In contrast, design sections and presentation sections focus on form, finish materials, and definition of interior space. For sections to work well in visual presentations, they must be clearly keyed, noted, or referenced to the appropriate floor plan. Generally, sections are referenced to the floor plan with use of a

symbol that denotes the locations of the vertical cut. Figure 1-13 is an example design section for the town-house project.

Reflected Ceiling Plans

REFLECTED CEILING PLANS are often used in conjunction with floor plans, elevations, and sections to communicate interior design. Reflected ceiling plans communicate important information about the design of the ceiling, such as materials, layout and locations of light fixtures, items such as sprinklers, diffusers, grilles, and ceiling heights. A reflected ceiling plan is drawn as though a giant mirror were on the floor reflecting the elements located on the ceiling. The use of reflective imagery allows for the ceiling plan to have exactly the same orientation as the floor plan.

There is a distinction between ceiling plans used for presentation and those used for construction. Typically, ceilings plans created for construction are highly technical and include a great deal of information. Reflected ceiling plans used in design presentations can be simplified to include basic ceiling lighting information, ceiling heights, and finish materials as shown in

FIGURE 1-12

A preliminary elevation study for a professional project, drawn on tracing paper with markers.

By Cuningham Group Architecture, P.A.

FIGURE 1-13

Building section for the town-house project.

1. Boldest lines indicate location of cut.

2. Receding elements are drawn with progressively lighter lines.

3. Sections require titles, reference symbols (names or numbers), and scale notation.

FIGURE 1-14

Simple reflected ceiling plan for town-house project.

1. Ceiling heights are noted and enclosed in a symbol.

2. Light fixture locations are noted with various symbols and are keyed to a legend.

3. Finish materials such as gypsum board, wood, and ceiling tiles are indicated in scale.

4. Reflected ceiling plans require titles, north arrows, and scale notation.

Note: Reflected ceiling plans require legends (keyed to symbols used); in this example, the legend has been omitted.

Figure 1-14. Precisely measured, complex technical ceiling plans are required for construction (as illustrated at the end of this chapter in Figure 1-17c).

Together, floor plans, elevations, sections, and ceiling plans communicate information about the quality of an interior environment. Because these drawings are abstracted, fragmented versions of three-dimensional form, they depend on one another to communicate effectively.

The orthographic projections covered in this chapter relate directly to the communication and design of interior space. Differing versions of orthographic projections are used for construction and presentation, but they are used in one form or another on virtually all projects.

Additional types of orthographic drawing are used to communicate the features of buildings and building sites. Site plans, foundation plans, demolition plans, roof plans, framing plans, exterior elevations, wall sections, and design details are also used in the design of buildings. Designers of interior space must be knowledgeable about the nature of these drawings, how they are created, and how they relate to the interior architecture of a building.

Lettering

Traditionally, in the days before CAD, floor plans, elevations, and sections contained notes and dimensions written in a standardized style of hand lettering. However, changes in technology allow for creation of

FIGURE 1-15
Hand-lettering reference.

HAND LETTERING BASICS

HORIZONTAL AND VERTICAL GUIDELINES ARE REQUIRED FOR ACCURATE AND CONSISTENT HAND LETTERING.

USE ALL CAPITAL LETTERS, WITH NO STEMS BELOW OR ABOVE GUIDELINES.

VERTICAL STROKES (STEMS) SHOULD BE PERFECTLY VERTICAL AND NOT SLANTED. USE A SMALL TRIANGLE AS A GUIDE IN CREATING PERFECT VERTICALS.

MOST LETTERS HAVE A SQUARE SHAPE A B C D E

SPACE BETWEEN LETTERS IS MINIMAL AND IS VISUALLY ASSESSED, NOT MEASURED WITH RULERS.

AN 'O" OR "C" SIZE SPACE SHOULD BE LEFT BETWEEN WORDS, LEAVE A SLIGHTLY LARGER SPACE BETWEEN SENTENCES

TYPICALLY VERTICALS ARE THIN WHILE HORIZONTAL STROKES ARE THICK. THIS IS DONE IN PENCIL BY CREATING A CHISEL POINT AND ROLLING THE PENCIL FROM THE THIN TO THICK SIDE.

THE BEGINNING AND END OF EACH LETTER STROKE CAN BE EMPHASIZED TO INCREASE LEGIBILITY. STROKES SHOULD LOOK LIKE THIS: BEGIN ———————— END

WHILE INDIVIDUAL LETTERING STYLES VARY, CONSISTENCY MUST BE MAINTAINED WITHIN THE DOCUMENT OR DRAWING.

THE FOLLOWING ARE HAND LETTERING STYLES THAT VARY SLIGHTLY:

A B C D E F G H I J K L M N O P Q R S T U V W X Y Z
1 2 3 4 5 6 7 8 9 10
A B C D E F G H I J K L M N O P Q R S T U V W X Y Z
1 2 3 4 5 6 7 8 9 10
A B C D E F G H I J K L M N O P Q R S T U V W X Y Z 1 2 3 4 5 6 7 8 9 10

1-15

LOWER LEVEL PLAN

1-16a

FIGURE 1-16a

Dimensioned lower-level floor plan for town-house project, employing standard conventions for locating interior and exterior dimensions outside of the plan boundaries.

1. Dimension lines and leader lines should be lighter than wall lines or objects measured.

2. Horizontal written dimensions sit above the dimension lines, so they are underlined by the dimension line as shown, or are written in a break in the dimension line.

3. Note location of dimensions: they should not read by rotating the sheet counterclockwise (as in reading from the left side of the sheet) and one absolutely should not have to turn the sheet upside down to read these dimensions.

4. Leader lines run from the building location being dimensioned to the dimension lines. Leader lines should not touch the building; instead, they should be drawn slightly away.

5. Dimensions are written in feet and inches unless less than one foot.

6. Dimensions measured from center-lines must be clearly indicated. Windows are commonly measured to centerlines or rough openings as shown.

7. Exterior walls (and plumbing walls) are shown as nominal 6" thick (actual: 6½" to 7½").

8. Interior walls are shown as nominal 4" thick (actual: 4½" typically).

type that can be applied to hand-drawn orthographic projections. Lettering and type can be computer generated, printed on adhesive reproduction film (sticky back), and applied to drawings and presentation boards. Lettering is also created by specialized machines (lettering machines) that print on adhesive-backed tape that can be applied to drawings. Lettering machines can be used to produce type in a range of sizes, styles, and colors. In addition, all of the commonly used CAD programs allow for consistent, standardized type to be readily applied to the appropriate location on a drawing.

Even with these changes in technology, it is useful to develop the ability to hand-letter in a consistent standardized style. Many designers still create quick sketches,

BEDROOM

FIGURE 1-16b
Portion of a dimensioned upper-level floor plan for town-house project, delineating conventions for interior "paint to paint" or "finish to finish" dimensions.
Note: This example has dimension numbers and line "tic marks" that are larger than is standard; in this case this was done so that the drawing size could be reduced for publication.
Figures 1-16a through 1-16b design by Courtney Nystuen, drawn by Melissa Brewer

preliminary design details and some presentation drawings by hand, and for the sake of visual consistency, developing skills related to hand lettering is crucial.

There are some basic rules for lettering design drawings, as well as some stylistic elements that influence letterform. Guidelines are required for all lettering locations. Horizontal guidelines create the lines on which the lettering rests. Consistent spacing between the lines of lettering is required. Vertical guidelines must be drawn so that the lines of type are aligned consistently. Lettering for design drawings is typically all capitals, allowing all letters to fit within a single pair of guidelines, with no tips or tails above or below the guidelines. Letters should have perfectly vertical strokes; the vertical strokes should not slant to the left or to the right. A tiny lettering triangle is used as a straightedge in making vertical strokes. Figure 1-15 is a hand-lettering reference.

Dimensions

Dimensions, required on most construction drawings, are sometimes necessary on drawings used for presentation purposes. Their inclusion is based on the project and the presentation audience. When included dimensions must be accurate, complete, readable, and are generally listed in feet and inches; for example $2'4"$ is written, rather than $28"$, except for those dimensions that are less than a foot; for example, $11"$ (or $0'11"$). Dimensions should be placed on "top" of the dimension line, so that they are "underlined" by the dimension line, and should be placed to as to not require being read by rotating the sheet counterclockwise (reading from left to right) or upside down.

Generally, for standard construction, dimensions and dimension lines are placed outside of the object (such as the building) as shown in Figure 1-16a. In terms of organizing a series of dimensions;

ASIAN BISTRO — ENLARGED FINISH PLAN
ROOM 1850

2
A743   SCALE: 1/4"=1'-0"

1-17a

FIGURE 1-17a

Floor plan for a professional restaurant design project. This is part of a set of construction documents (Figures 17b through 17d are part of this set).

specific dimensions are placed close to the particular object they are related while the overall distances are placed in the position farthest from the construction (as shown in Figure 1-16a).

Openings such as windows and doors are dimensions to centerlines or to rough frame opening (R.O.); with the exception of masonry openings (M.O.), which are not drawn to centerlines. Another rule of thumb for dimensions is to dimension things once and only once; repetition from one drawing to another can lead to discrepancy errors.

Dimensions typically run from the outside of exterior walls to the centerline of interior walls: where interior tolerances are critical, dimensions can be run from the face of the finished wall to the face of the other finished wall (paint-to-paint so to speak), as shown in Figure 1-16b. This type of dimension can be employed for interior design projects created within existing architecture—for example, when dimensioning walls for an interior renovation of an existing office or retail space, it is common to dimension only the paint-to-paint dimensions rather than exterior to center

ASIAN BISTRO — ENLARGED FLOOR PLAN
ROOM 1850

SCALE: 1/4"=1'-0"

1-17b

dimensions, as shown in Figure 1-16b. Additional examples of dimensioned drawings can be found at the end of this chapter in Figures 1-17b, 1-17d, 1-18b, and 1-18c.

Computer-Aided Design (CAD): Ongoing Advances

Until very recently, Autodesk's AutoCAD® was the most widely used CAD program in commercial interior design and architectural firms in the United States. AutoCAD is a vector graphics drawing program, in which primitive elements such as lines,

polylines, arcs, and text serve as the foundation for more complex objects. Current AutoCAD versions allow for two-dimensional and three-dimensional design and drafting and can serve as a base for industry specific products such as Architectural Desktop®. AutoCAD LT® is a scaled-down, less costly version of AutoCAD, which does not include full three-dimensional drawing capabilities as well as certain presentation graphics, sheet set management, and other elements.

Autodesk Revit® Building software is quickly becoming a new CAD industry

FIGURE 1-17b
A dimensioned floor plan for the project featured in the previous figure.

ASIAN BISTRO — ENLARGED REFLECTED CEILING PLAN
ROOM 1850
SCALE: 1/4" = 1'-0"

1-17c

FIGURE 1-17c
A reflected ceiling plan for the project featured in the previous figure.

favorite for commercial interior design and architectural practice. Revit is Building Information Modeling (BIM) software that allows for parametric modeling and drafting. An advantage of BIM software is its ability to create coordinated, consistent, computable information about a building project. This means that changes made in one view are automatically integrated into related drawings and schedules. In contrast to AutoCAD, which at this time requires that drawings are "X-referenced" for this to occur.

Other types of CAD software used by design firms throughout the world include MicroStation (owned by Bentley), which generates two-dimensional and three-dimensional vector graphic objects and elements. ArchiCAD® (owned by Graphisoft) is also used in architectural, facilities management, and interior design practice and employs "smart," data-enhanced, parametric objects; these in turn help to create the basic structure and elements that come together to create the building.

Designers and sales professionals specializing in kitchen and bath design as well as those involved in residential design and furniture sales use a software program

SOUTH ELEVATION @ ASIAN BISTRO
ROOM 1850
SCALE: 1/4"=1'-0"

SOUTH ELEVATION @ ASIAN BISTRO
ROOM 1850
SCALE: 1/4"=1'-0"

PT-28 TYP.

PT-27 TYP.

STAINLESS STEEL HOOD
BY KITCHEN CONSULTANT

PENDANT LIGHTS –
SEE ELECTRICAL

RESTAURANT SIGNAGE BY SIGNAGE
CONSULTANT, ALL SIDES. FINAL DESIGN
AWAITING OWNER PROVIDED
RESTAURANT IDENTITY.

DG-2, INSTALL PANELS WITH
SEAM AT CENTER OF WALL

STNB-14

SP-5

1-17d

called 20-20 Design. This software allows for two-dimensional drawing and planning as well as the generation of three-dimensional views that can be used for client presentations and can incorporate manufacturers' specific product information into drawings.

There are a number of software programs used specifically for three-dimensional modeling and rendering; some of these are discussed in Chapter 4, page 133.

Clearly, things continue to evolve in terms of software and hardware used in

design and design presentations. With that said, it is important to note that the conceptual basis for orthographic drawings and drafting conventions is the same whether created by hand or through the use of electronic tools. The meaning communicated in a floor plan is the same whether the drawing is created by hand or with the use of any within a range of CAD programs and for that reason this book covers the concepts behind the drawings rather than supplying detailed information about the software used to create them.

FIGURE 1-17d

Elevations for the project featured in the previous figure.
Figures 1-17a through 1-17d by Cuningham Group Architecture, P.A.

1-18a

FIGURE 1-18a
Floor plan for a professional restaurant design project. This is part of a set of construction documents (Figures 18b and 18c are included in this set).

STEAKHOUSE ENLARGED FLOOR PLAN
ROOM 1840
SCALE: 1/4" = 1'-0"

1-18b

REFERENCES

(Contains both works cited and recommended reading. Annotations where appropriate.)

Ching, Frank. *Architectural Graphics*. New York: John Wiley & Sons, 1996.

——. *A Visual Dictionary of Architecture*. New York: John Wiley & Sons, 1995.

Forseth, Kevin, and David Vaughn. *Graphics for Architecture*. New York: John Wiley & Sons, 1998.

Kirkpatrick, Beverly, and James Kirkpatrick. *AutoCAD for Interior Design and Space Planning Using AutoCAD® 2005*. Upper Saddle River, NJ: Prentice Hall, 2005.

Kilmer, Otie, Rosemary Kilmer, and Stephen Hanessian. *Construction Drawings and Details for Interiors: Basic Skills*. Hoboken, N.J.: John Wiley & Sons, 2001. *A good introduction to drafting concepts and to drawings for construction documents.*

Liebling, Ralph. *Architectural Working Drawings*, 4th edition. Hoboken, N.J.: John Wiley & Sons, 1999. *Contains some valuable information about drafting and drawings for construction documents.*

Porter, Tom. *Architectural Drawing*. New York: Van Nostrand Reinhold, 1990.

FIGURE 1-18b
A dimensioned floor plan for the project featured in the previous figure.

FIGURE 1-18c

Elevations for the project featured in the previous figure.

Figures 1-18a through 1-18c by Cuningham Group Architecture, P.A.

Smith, C. Ray. *Interior Design in 20th Century America: A History*. New York: Harper & Row, 1987.

U.S. Metric Association (USMA). *FAQ: Frequently Asked Questions About the Metric System*. http://lamar.colostate.edu/~hillger/faq.html, 2006 (December).

2 THE DESIGN PROCESS AND RELATED GRAPHICS

It is imperative that students of design understand that *design communication* and *design process* are directly tied together due to the fact that the reasons for communication may change as the project advances. A clear understanding of the process of design allows for the appropriate form of communication to be employed at the appropriate time with a successful outcome. Toward that end, this chapter covers the design process and related design communication methods.

The complexity of the design process requires that at various points along the way designers communicate aspects and outcomes of the process to clients and consultants. Like professionals, students must present in-process projects to team members, instructors, and guest critics. Visual presentations must vary to accommodate the process of design and to communicate both process and outcome.

In *Interior Design Illustrated*, Francis Ching identifies three basic stages of design process: analysis, synthesis, and evaluation. According to Ching, ANALYSIS involves defining and understanding the problem; SYNTHESIS involves the formulation of possible solutions; and EVALUATION involves a critical review of the strengths and weaknesses of the proposed solutions.

These three basic stages of design process are used by design practitioners in a variety of disciplines. Industrial designers, graphic designers, exhibition designers, and others often engage in a similar process. Of course, the design disciplines vary a great deal in terms of professional practice and final outcome. For this reason, actual interior design process and project phases are quite distinct and are more elaborate than the three basic stages may indicate.

For purposes of contractual organization, the process of design engaged in by architects and interior designers in the United States has been divided into five basic project phases: (1) PROGRAMMING, (2) SCHEMATIC DESIGN, (3) DESIGN DEVELOPMENT, (4) CONSTRUCTION DOCUMENTATION, and (5) CONTRACT ADMINISTRATION. These phases are derived from the American Institute of Architects (AIA) Owner-Architect Agreement for Interior Design Services and the American Society of Interior Designers (ASID) Interior Design Services Agreement. Both of these documents serve as contracts for design services and reflect the current design process and project management in the United States.

Figure 2-1 identifies generally accepted project phases and visual presentation methods.

PROJECT PHASE	TYPICAL TASKS AND ACTIVITIES	TYPICAL MEANS OF VISUAL PRESENTATION
Programming also known as *pre-design*	**In-depth analysis and documentation of needs, requirements goals, and objectives.** Can include: identification of space and adjacency requirements analysis; asset assessment; specialized needs assessments; codes and accessibility research; identification of conceptual and thematic issues, as well as analysis of architectural or site parameters; and analysis of scheduling and budget.	Most often written information compiled in a programming report. Often includes problem identification, diagrams, charts, matrices, and may include some orthographic drawings and early fit studies. May include preliminary scheduling graphics.
Schematic Design also known as the preliminary design phase	**Preliminary conceptual, spatial, and technical design of project.** Includes preliminary space planning often using relationship diagrams matrices, bubble diagrams, blocking diagrams, stacking and fit plans, as well as initial furnishings, fixtures, and equipment design/layout. Development of projects conceptual and thematic issues. Color, material, and finish studies. Preliminary code review. Preliminary budgetary information.	Graphic presentation of preliminary design; can include relationship diagrams; blocking and fit plans; preliminary space plan(s); preliminary furnishing and equipment layouts; preliminary elevations and sections; preliminary 3-D drawings; preliminary color and materials studies; and study models. Presentation may also include graphic presentation of conceptual and thematic issues using sketches, diagrams, and mixed media.
Design Development	**Refinement of finalized design.** Includes space plan and design of interior construction elements and details. Often involves incorporation of lighting, electrical, plumbing, and mechanical systems design, as well as data and telecommunication systems integration. Often includes millwork design and detailing. Also includes color, materials, and finish selection. Design and specification of furnishings, fixtures, and equipment, as well as refinement of budgetary and scheduling information.	Finalized, refined design presentation incorporating all necessary components of design. Graphic presentation of finalized design can include conceptual diagrams; space plan(s); and plan(s) for furnishings, fixtures and equipment, as well as elevations; sections, ceiling plans; 3-D drawings; colors, materials, and finish samples; scale models and mock-ups. Multimedia presentations can incorporate all of the above elements plus sound and animation.
Construction Documentation	**Preparation of drafted, working drawings and/or contract documents.** Includes preparation of drawings, schedules, details, and specifications, as well as coordination and integration of consultant's documents. Can include preparation of specialized equipment and furnishings documents for bidding by purchasing agents. May include purchasing documents.	Preparation of contract documents. Often includes submission to general contractor(s) and purchasing agents for bid and to appropriate agencies for plan check.
Contract Administration	**Guide and review construction and installation. Can include periodic site visits and creation of progress reports.** Coordination and review of shop drawings and sample submittals. May include clarification and interpretation of drawings, as well as possible review of billing and payment. Preparation of punch list. May include move coordination and supervision of furnishings, fixtures, and equipment installation.	Communication with contractors, agencies, and clients is primarily written and verbal. May include scheduling, budgetary, and administrative graphics.

2-1 Adapted from: AIA Owner-Architect Agreement for Interior Design Services and the ASID interior Design Services Agreement.

William Peña, Steven Parshall, and Kevin Kelly, writing in *Problem Seeking*, identify the actual design process as taking place in the first three project phases. They state that "programming is part of the total design process but is separate from schematic design." The authors go on to link schematic design and design development as the second and third phases of the total design process. This chapter is intended as an exploration of the three phases of the design process identified by Peña, Parshall, Kelly, and others and as a study of the drawings and graphics used to communicate, document, inform, and clarify the work done during these phases.

PROGRAMMING

The experienced, creative designer withholds judgment, resists preconceived solutions and the pressure to synthesize until all the information is in. He refuses to make sketches until he knows the client's problem . . .
Programming is the prelude to good design.
—William Peña, Steven Parshall, and Kevin Kelly in *Problem Seeking*, 1987

Programming, also known as *pre-design* or strategic planning, involves detailed analysis of the client's (or end user's) needs, requirements, goals, budgetary factors, and assets, as well as analysis of architectural or site parameters and constraints. Information gathered about the user's needs and requirements is often documented in written form, whereas architectural or site parameters are often communicated graphically through orthographic projection. These two distinct forms of communication, verbal and graphic, must be brought together in the early stages of design.

Some firms employ professionals to work as programmers and then hand the project over to designers. It is also common for project managers and designers to work on project programming and then continue to work on the design or management of the project. It could be said that programmers and designers are separate specialists, given the distinctions between programming (analysis) and design (synthesis). However, many firms and designers choose not to separate these specialties or do so only on very large or programming-intensive projects.

In practice, programming varies greatly from project to project. This is due to variation in project type and size and to the quantity and quality of information supplied by the client (or end user). In some cases clients provide designers with highly detailed written programs. In other situations clients begin with little more than general information or simply exclaim, "We need more space, we are growing very fast," or "Help, we are out of control." In situations such as the latter, research and detective work must be done to create programming information that will allow for the creation of successful design solutions.

It is difficult to distill the programming process used in a variety of projects into a brief summary. Clearly, the programming required for a major metropolitan public library is very different from that required in a small-scale residential renovation. It is important, therefore, to consider what all projects relating to interior environments share in terms of programming.

All projects require careful analysis of space requirements for current and future needs, as well as analysis of work processes, adjacency requirements, and organizational structure (or lifestyle and needs-assessment factors in residential design). Physical inventories and asset assessments are required to evaluate existing furniture

FIGURE 2-1
Project phases and related visual presentation methods.

and equipment as well as to plan for future needs. Building code, accessibility, and health and safety factors must also be researched as part of the programming process.

In addition to this primarily quantitative information, there are aesthetic requirements. Cultural and sociological aspects of the project must also be identified by the designers. All of these should be researched and can be documented in a programming report that is reviewed by the client and used by the project design team. When possible, it is important to include a problem statement with the programming report. The problem statement is a concise identification of key issues, limitations, objectives, and goals that provide a clearer understanding of the project. With the programming report complete, the designers

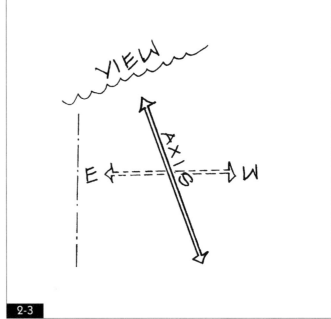

FIGURE 2-2
A diagram showing the relationship between the various spaces in a dwelling. A diagram showing the possible relationships within a building site.

FIGURE 2-3
A diagram showing the possible relationships within a building site.

FIGURE 2-4
A diagram showing the relationship between entrances, exhibition spaces, and an information desk.

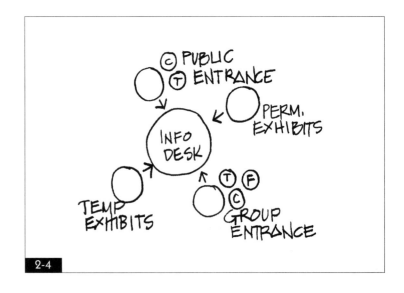

can begin the job of synthesis and continue the design process.

DIAGRAMS AND PROGRAMMING ANALYSIS GRAPHICS

Prior to continuing on with a discussion of programming, it is necessary to describe the use and importance of diagrams and visual notes, especially in the preliminary phases of design. Norman Crowe and Paul Laseau have defined in *Visual Notes for Architects and Designers* (1995), a diagram as "a simple, rapid method for representing the underlying structure or relationships in either a physical setting, physical design or in the process by which something operates. Diagrams help make sense out of a complex whole . . ."

Diagrams can be considered "graphic thinking" (Laseau, *Graphic Thinking for Architects and Designers*, 2001) and can serve as a mechanism for distilling written project information graphically in ways that are useful to the designer or design team. Many diagrams serve as a sort of visual brainstorming allowing visual information to be recorded quickly during design ideation and sorted through later. Put another way: diagrams are a useful way to get ideas outside of our heads and onto paper for later refinement and use.

Many of the types of diagrams designers use can serve as a bridge between information uncovered in the programming phase of a project and the creation of ideas generated in the schematic or preliminary design phase. Most diagrams employ symbols to serve as abstract representation of information or ideas. These include abstract representation of: relationships (see Figure 2-2), size and area (see Figure 2-3), and context (see Figure 2-4).

In addition to diagrams and graphic analysis being used for idea generation clients, consultants, and designers may also require them as a way of understanding and gaining insight into programming data and information. Diagrams, charts, matrices, and visual imagery are comprehended with greater ease than pages of written documentation. It is useful to develop ways of sorting and simplifying programming information so that it can be easily assimilated.

Many designers find it useful to obtain early programming data and incorporate it into graphic worksheets. Using a flip-chart pad, brown kraft paper, or other heavy paper, the programmers can create large, easy-to-read graphic documents. These sheets are created so that they may be understood easily by the client and can therefore be approved or commented on. Often, the eventual project designers find these sheets useful as a means of project documentation.

The book *Problem Seeking* (Peña, Parshall, and Kelly, 1987) provides an additional technique for the graphic recording of information generated in the early stages of programming, using a device known as analysis cards. Analysis cards allow for easy comprehension, discussion, clarification, and feedback. The cards are drawn from interview notes and early programming data. Based on the notion that visual information is more easily comprehended than verbal, the cards contain simple graphic imagery with few words and concise messages.

Residential projects generally require less intensive programming graphics. Programming is a significant element of the residential design process; however, the relationships, adjacencies, and organization of the space are often simplified in relation to large commercial and public spaces. For this reason the following discussion focuses primarily on commercial design, where a significant amount of visual

FIGURE 2-5

Programming information for the sample project.

ECO
TOYS Programming Information

Company History:
Eco Toys is a young, dynamic company. Larry Leader, the company president started the company in 1985. The company designs and produces toys for preschoolers, using recycled plastic products. Eco Toys has enjoyed tremendous success and growth in the last five years. Owing to recent growth, the company must move to larger, better organized design and marketing offices.

Company Structure and Organization:
The president is at the center of all company operations and constantly interacts with all members of his staff. Mr. Leader depends a great deal on his assistant Steve Stable. Although Mr. Leader is in touch with all levels of operation, he has set up the company in a horizontal organizational structure. This means that all members of the Eco Toys staff have equal status and power and are seen as important contributors to the organization. The design of the space should reflect the organizational structure of the company.

General Requirements:
Because of the non hierarchical organizational structure, all workstations must be exactly the same size. As a means of encouraging team meetings and sharing within departments small (8' x 8') individual workstations have been requested. As a result of complicated egress conditions, the existing door locations must be retained.

Department Information and Requirements:

Entry/Reception: Very public, must visually represent company's mission. Requires reception desk with work surface and transaction counter, task seating. Guest seating for 6. Must allow space for movement of children into toy test center. Must be near conference room, toy test center and close to marketing dept.
Conference Room: Very public and attractive, seating for 10 at tables with additional seating available. Requires multimedia center. View if possible. Immediately adjacent to toy test center (with visual connection), close to reception, and near marketing dept.
Toy Testing Center: Open and flexible space for use by 4 - 6 preschool age children. Must be visually connected to conference room and adjacent to entry and conference room.
Design Dept.: 2 designers and 2 assistants. All individual work spaces must accommodate CADD station, plus layout space, 2 file drawers, and handy reference storage. Adjacent to model shop; a messy, noisy, enclosed space -120 sq. ft. min. Adjacent to engineering dept. Nearby team meeting space with casual seating for 4, room for plotter, display area, and filing.
Marketing Dept.: 2 marketing managers and 1 assistant. All individual work spaces must accommodate a P.C., 2 file drawers, and handy reference storage. Must have adjacent team space with table and seating for 5. Must be near conference room, toy test and reception area.
Engineering Dept.: 2 engineers. All individual work spaces must accommodate CADD station, and lay-out space, two file drawers, and handy reference storage. Must be adjacent to design dept. and near design team space.
Accounting Dept.: 2 accountants. Individual work spaces must accommodate a P.C. and printer, 2 file drawers, and handy reference storage. Requires some privacy and no major interaction with other departments, with the exception of the President.
President: Pres. plus assistant (2 total); must accommodate P.C. and printer, 2 file drawers, and handy reference storage. President to have small conference table (to seat 4). Near all depts. and break room.
Break Room: Generous counter space, base and wall cabinets, sink, refrig., microwave, and commercial coffee makers. Seating for 8 minimum.
Copy/Mail: Room for copy machine and adjacent 5 lineal ft. of collating space, room for 16 mailboxes, paper, and supply storage. Convenient to corridor.
Storage: Generous heavy-duty shelving. Must be enclosed and private, requires shelving and ventilation for Local Area Computer Network.

2-5

FIGURE 2-6

Floor plan for the sample project.
By Leanne Larson

2-6

FIGURE 2-7
Examples of diagrams for the
sample project.

communication of programming information is often required. A sample project will
be used to illustrate some of the design
process concepts covered in this chapter.
Figure 2-5 contains programming information for a sample project. Figure 2-6 is a
floor plan for the sample project and Figure
2-7 illustrates some program-based diagrams for the project.

PROGRAMMING MATRICES

Matrices are another useful tool in programming, incorporating a wealth of information into an easily comprehended visual
tool. An ADJACENCY MATRIX is commonly
used as a means of visually documenting
spatial proximity, identifying related activities and services, and establishing priori-
ties. Adjacency matrices vary in complexity
in relation to project requirements. Large-
scale, complex projects often require highly
detailed adjacency matrices. Figures 2-8
and 2-9 illustrate two types of adjacency
matrix.

A CRITERIA MATRIX can distill project
issues such as needs for privacy, natural
light, and security into a concise, consistent format. Large-scale, complex design
projects may require numerous detailed,
complex matrices, whereas smaller, less
complex projects require more simplified
matrices. Criteria matrices are used in
residential design projects and in the programming of public spaces. Smaller projects allow for criteria matrices to be
combined with adjacency matrices. Figure
2-10 illustrates a criteria matrix that
includes adjacency information. Special
types of matrix are used by designers on
particular projects. A blank version of this
criteria matrix, illustrated here, can be
found in Appendix 2 (see Figure A-1).

Programming graphics, such as project
worksheets, diagrams, and a variety of
matrices, are widely used in interior design
practice. These are presented to the client
or end user for comment, clarification, and
approval. Many of these graphics are
refined, corrected, and improved upon
during the programming process and are
eventually included in the final programming report.

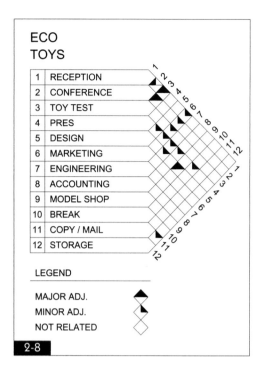

ECO TOYS

1	RECEPTION
2	CONFERENCE
3	TOY TEST
4	PRES
5	DESIGN
6	MARKETING
7	ENGINEERING
8	ACCOUNTING
9	MODEL SHOP
10	BREAK
11	COPY / MAIL
12	STORAGE

LEGEND

MAJOR ADJ. ▲

MINOR ADJ. ◢

NOT RELATED ◇

2-8

ECO TOYS

	RECEPTION	CONFERENCE	TOY TEST	PRES.	DESIGN	MARKETING	ENGINEERING	ACCOUNTING	MODEL SHOP	BREAK	COPY / MAIL	STORAGE
RECEPTION	·	●	●	○	○	◐	○	○	X	○	○	○
CONFERENCE	●	·	●	○	○	◐	○	○	X	○	○	○
TOY TEST	●	●	·	○	○	◐	○	○	X	○	○	○
PRES.	○	○	○	·	◐	◐	◐	◐	○	◐	○	○
DESIGN	○	○	○	◐	·	○	◐	○	●	○	○	○
MARKETING	◐	◐	◐	◐	○	·	○	○	○	○	○	○
ENGINEERING	○	○	○	◐	◐	○	·	○	○	○	○	○
ACCOUNTING	○	○	○	◐	○	○	○	·	○	○	○	○
MODEL SHOP	X	X	X	○	●	○	○	○	·	○	○	○
BREAK	○	○	○	◐	○	○	○	○	○	·	○	○
COPY / MAIL	○	○	○	○	○	○	○	○	○	○	·	○
STORAGE	○	○	○	○	○	○	○	○	○	○	○	·

LEGEND

● MAJOR ADJACENCY

◐ MINOR ADJACENCY

○ NOT CLOSELY RELATED

X UNDESIRABLE

2-9

FIGURE 2-8
Simple adjacency matrix for the sample project.
By Melissa Brewer

FIGURE 2-9
Another type of adjacency matrix for the sample project.
By Melissa Brewer

SCHEMATIC DESIGN

With the programming phase completed, designers may begin the work of synthesis. Another way of stating this is that with the problem clearly stated, problem solving can begin. The creation of relationship diagrams is often a first step in the schematic design of a project. Relationship diagrams serve a variety of functions that allow the designers to digest and internalize the programming information. Relationship diagrams also allow the designer to begin to use graphics to come to terms with the physical qualities of the project.

One type of relationship diagram explores the relationship of functional areas to one another and uses information completed on the criteria and adjacency matrices. This type of one-step diagram can be adequate for smaller commercial and residential projects. Larger-scale, complex projects often require a series of relationship diagrams. Diagrams of this type do not generally relate to architectural or site parameters and are not drawn to scale. Most specialized or complex projects require additional diagrams that explore issues such as personal interaction, flexibility, and privacy requirements.

Bubble Diagrams

As relationship diagrams begin to incorporate and account for necessary require-

FIGURE 2-10

A combination criteria and adjacency matrix, computer generated. Appendix 2 includes a blank version of this, for student use.
By Leanne Larson

	ECO TOYS	Adjacencies	# of Dept Members	Seating Req's	Public Access	Privacy	Plumbing	Data/Phone	Special Req's	Comments
1	Reception	② ③ 6	1	6 min	●			●	Y	Visually rep mission; used by adults & children; "dynamic & playful"
2	Conference	① ③ 6		10+	●			●	Y	"Dynamic & playful"; multimedia center; multiple lap-top /computers
3	Toy Test	① ②		4-6	●			○	Y	Used by preschoolers; open, flexible, playful
4	President	5 6 7 8 10	2	4				●	Y	PC, printer, 2 file drawers, ref storage for each 8' x 8' work space
5	Design	⑨ ⑦	4	4 min				●	Y	CADD, lay-out, 2 file drawers, ref storage for each 8' x 8' work space
6	Marketing	① ② 3	3	5 min				●	Y	PC, printer, 2 file drawers, ref storage for each 8' x 8' work space
7	Engineering	⑤	2					●	Y	CADD, lay-out, 2 file drawers, ref storage for each 8' x 8' work space
8	Accounting	4	2			●		●	Y	PC, printer, 2 file drawers, ref storage for each 8' x 8' work space
9	Model Shop	⑤				○	●	○	Y	Messy & noisy; enclosed
10	Break Room	4		8 min			●	○	Y	Relaxing & inviting; gen counters; refrig, microwave, sink, coffee makers req
11	Copy/Mail							○	Y	5 lineal feet collating space; 16 mailboxes; storage
12	Storage					●			Y	Generous heavy-duty shelving; ventilation

2-10

ments and adjacencies, they can become refined into what are generally referred to as BUBBLE DIAGRAMS. Bubble diagrams take the project one step further in the schematic design process. Often bubble diagrams relate approximately to the actual architectural parameters (the building space) in rough scale. In addition, they often incorporate elements identified in criteria and adjacency matrices through the use of graphic devices keyed to a legend. Figures 2-11a, 2-11b, and 2-11c are a sequence of bubble diagrams for the sample project.

It is important to note that a primary purpose of these early schematic diagrams is to generate a number of options. Brainstorming many ideas is highly advisable. Designers with years of experience use brainstorming techniques, as should students of design. Successful design requires sparks of creativity in every phase, and these sparks are fostered by nurturing idea generation. Rarely does the first try (or even the first several) create a masterpiece or a workable solution. It is often the combination of several diverse schemes that eventually generates a good solution.

FIGURES 2-11a AND 2-11b
Preliminary bubble diagrams
for the sample project.

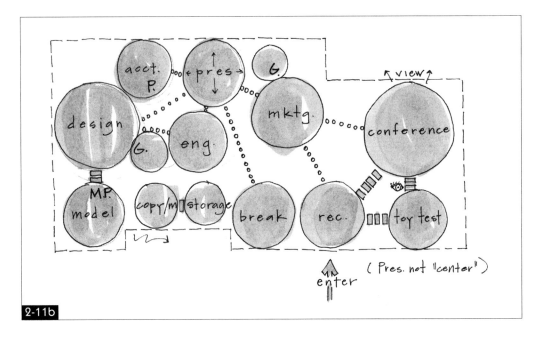

Blocking Diagrams

Bubble diagrams are part of a continuous process of refinement. One diagram may have useful components that can be combined with elements of another. As this process of refinement continues, designers often proceed to BLOCKING DIAGRAMS.

Before design students move to blocking diagrams, they benefit from the creation of space studies, also known as *area prototype sketches*. Each area or function is sketched in scale with furniture and equipment included, and these sketches can be used for purposes of approximation in the blocking diagram. Space study sketches are also helpful in the design of systems furniture, allowing students to explore possibilities and gain insight into the use of these

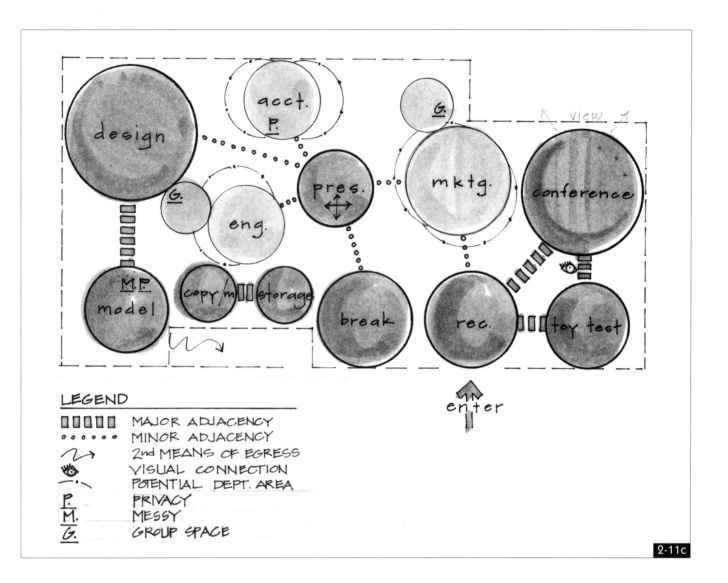

LEGEND

▯▯▯▯▯	MAJOR ADJACENCY
○○○○○○	MINOR ADJACENCY
↝	2nd MEANS OF EGRESS
👁	VISUAL CONNECTION
⌐·⌐	POTENTIAL DEPT. AREA
P.	PRIVACY
M.	MESSY
G.	GROUP SPACE

2-11c

products. See Figures 2-12a, 2-12b, and 2-12c for examples of space studies.

Blocking diagrams can be generated on tracing paper taped over a scaled, drafted floor plan of the existing or proposed building. In rare cases projects do not involve the use of existing architectural parameters because the interior space will dictate the final building form. In these cases, bubble diagrams and blocking plans are sometimes the genesis for the eventual building plan. It is increasingly common for designers to begin the blocking plan process on CAD and take the project through the rest of the design process using CAD. Some designers find that space planning on CAD is frustrating and therefore plot out a CAD drawing and work over it with tracing paper.

As stated, blocking diagrams are generally drawn to scale and relate directly to the architectural parameters or the existing building plan. Blocking plans are generally drawn with each area or function represented by a block of the appropriate square footage; circulation areas are often blocked in as rectilinear corridors. Figures 2-13a, 2-13b, and 2-13c are blocking diagrams.

Some experienced designers move quickly to blocking diagrams, foregoing the

FIGURE 2-11c
Final successful bubble diagram for the sample project.

FIGURES 2-12a, 2-12b, AND 2-12c
Space studies for the sample project.

ECO
TOYS
GROUP SPACE STUDIES

DESIGN: "LIVING RM"

MARKETING: "PUZZLE TABLE"

PRES.: "LIVING RM"

DESIGN: "COMBINATION"

MARKETING: "ROUND PLUG IN"

PRES.: "LIVING RM 2"

DESIGN "PUZZLE TABLE"

MARKETING "RECT. PLUG IN"

PRES.: "TRADITIONAL"

2-12c

use of bubble diagrams, whereas others dislike the blocky, confining nature of blocking diagrams. Many designers develop a personal system of schematic diagrams that is a combination of bubble and blocking diagrams. The approach and graphic quality of schematic diagrams used by individual designers vary greatly, yet the underlying purpose is consistent. Designers use these diagrams to move from verbal and simplified graphic notation toward true scale and the eventual realization of architectural form.

Fit Plans and Stacking Plans

A FIT PLAN can be considered a further refinement of the blocking diagram. Basically the fit plan is a test determining whether the requirements and needs clarified in programming fit into a given space. In some cases, fit plans are drawn up when a client reviews a piece of real estate or a potential site. In other cases, fit plans are drawn up to indicate the way a proposed office tower may eventually be laid out. These types of fit plans are generated for both real estate professionals and end users.

In still other situations, the fit plan is part of the final stage of the space-planning process. For this reason, fit plans often contain furniture and equipment accurately drawn to scale as a means of testing the space plan for fit and for client review.

A STACKING PLAN is used when a project occupies more than one floor of a building.

**FIGURES 2-13a, 2-13b,
AND 2-13c**
Blocking diagrams for the sample project. Note that these
blocking diagrams focus on the
layout of individual work spaces
as the other spaces are fixed.

blocking diagram #1

2-13a

blocking diagram #2

2-13b

blocking diagram #3

2-13c

Often the interrelationships of departments or work-group locations are examined in a stacking diagram. Generally, stacking diagrams are created early in the design process as a means of evaluating the use of each floor before refined space planning is done.

Conceptual Design

The schematic design phase is often a time when designers explore symbolic representation for the conceptual foundation of a project. Although relationship, bubble, and blocking diagrams represent functional and spatial requirements, they sometimes do little to illuminate the conceptual nature of a project. It is often useful to employ an abstract diagram or graphic device to represent the conceptual qualities of a project.

One means of illustrating conceptual project themes is the use of a design PARTI. Frank Ching, in *A Visual Dictionary of Architecture* (1995), defines a parti as "the basic scheme or concept for an architectural design represented by a diagram." A design parti can take a wide range of forms, from a highly simplified graphic symbol to a more complex plan diagram. Some designers use a conceptual diagram such as a parti as an aid in bringing together the functional and conceptual components of a design. The parti, or another conceptual diagram, can be used throughout the design process as a conceptual anchor for the project. Designers sometimes employ the parti extensively, and it may be the foundation for the design and appear as a logo or project icon on all presentation graphics.

A formal design parti is not sought for all design projects. Most projects do, however, include a considerable number of thematic issues. Views, geography, climate, building context and site, functional requirements, and cultural issues may contribute to the project on a conceptual level. Often the existing building form provides project constraints in the design of interior environments. Most designers find it useful to articulate and explore conceptual and thematic issues early in the schematic phase of a project Some designers find it useful to create three-dimensional conceptual studies in the form of models (see Chapter 6). In professional practice the methods of presentation of conceptual components of a project are varied and highly personal, and involve both verbal and graphic notations.

For purposes of organization, space planning and conceptual development are discussed separately here. However, in design practice these elements are brought together in the early stages of project design. Bubble diagrams often incorporate conceptual elements, and a design parti can serve as an organizational anchor in the space-planning process. It is important to see the schematic or conceptual design phases as a continuous process of refinement whereby all elements are brought together. Figures 2-14a and 2-14b are conceptual sketches that might be generated during the drawing of blocking diagrams.

As the project evolves and blocking diagrams make way for a schematic space plan, it is often helpful to consider the totality of the design through the use of preliminary elevations. Preliminary elevations, much like early perspective studies, allow for more complete understanding of the total volume of a space. Preliminary elevations can be used as a means of ideation or idea generation, and therefore it is useful to attempt more than one approach as the elevations are undertaken. Two such preliminary elevations of varying approaches for the design shown in the blocking diagram in Figure 2-14b can be found in Figure 2-15.

Mood and Inspiration Boards

In developing an aesthetic or conceptual direction for a project, some designers

2-14a

2-14b

FIGURES 2-14a AND 2-14b
Conceptual blocking diagrams for the sample project.

ELEVATION #1

LOBBY   INSET   LOGO   HALLWAY
SAME HT AS WALL→?
GLASS SHELF
WOOD
DISPLAY: WOOD/GLASS?
HT?
DISPLAY (SIDE)

ELEVATION #2

SUSPENDED? DRYWALL?
PAINT?
LOBBY   LOGO   HALLWAY
METAL TURNBUCKELS?   WOOD OR MESH?
METAL/TURNBUCKELS?
CAP? WOOD? METAL?
5'0"? 6'0"
HT?
DISPLAY SHELF WOOD, METAL?
DISPLAY (SIDE)

2-15

create MOOD BOARDS or inspirational boards. These boards perform a function similar to visual notation, as these are another form of visual language that can help set the visual direction of the project.

The term *mood board*, which evolved from the world of advertising and branding has been defined by the Association for Qualitative Research as "[a] form of visual stimulus material, usually comprising large boards covered with images (often cut from magazines) and designed to represent a mood, atmosphere or feeling." In advertising and product development, these boards are presented to research subjects and focus groups as a type of stimulus material.

Interior designers do not always share these boards with clients and end users. Some use them in-house to develop and define an aesthetic direction for the project, while others use them to communicate

this direction, early on, to clients or end users. In most cases, this type of board serves as a preliminary mechanism to get a feel or visual direction for the project very early on. Different firms have differing names for these boards and varying ways for crafting and developing them.

While the name, mechanics, and audiences may vary, most designers create the boards with the same idea in mind. Generally, the idea is to create these boards in a way that allows them to remain unspecific about the final actual materials, the details, and the furnishings, and yet setting a direction for the way the materials will look or feel, for perhaps a general color palette, and to include any other defining visuals (usually in a vague manner) for the project.

Occasionally the boards are used in conjunction with a preliminary presentation of materials samples to communicate a

FIGURE 2-15
Two preliminary elevations of varying approaches for the design shown in the blocking diagram in Figure 2-14b.

2-16a

2-16b

FIGURE 2-16a
Mood or inspiration board for the sample project, made with a cut-and-paste collage technique.

FIGURE 2-16b
Mood or inspiration board for the sample project, made using Photoshop and color sampling the images to create a potential palette. A color mood board is shown in Figure C-1a on page 53.

project's evolution. Figures 2-16a and 2-16b illustrate mood or inspiration boards for sample project. Figures C-1a and C-1b on page 53 illustrate the evolution of colors, materials and furnishings from mood board to early sample presentation board (detailed information about preparing material sample boards can be found in Chapter 7).

These boards may be made using traditional collage technique, whereby printed images from a variety of sources are neatly cut and pasted onto a surface such as foam board or Gatorfoam® board, as shown in Figure 2-16a. Or they can be composed using graphic imaging software such as Photoshop, InDesign, or Quark as illustrated in Figure 2-16b. This type of software allows for images to be cropped, enlarged, and reduced easily. In addition, most graphic imaging software offers the ability to "pick" or "sample" colors from images and to ise these to create a digital palette.

LEGEND

A	ACCOUNTING	E	ENGINEERING
B	BREAK	F	FLEX SPACE
C	CONFERENCE	M	MARKETING
CM	COPY/MAIL	MG	MARKETING GROUP
D	DESIGN	R	RECEPTION
DM	DESIGN/MODEL	T	TESTING
DG	DESIGN GROUP		

ECO TOYS
concept

PRELIMINARY FLOOR PLAN

0'   4'   8'   16'

2-17a

Schematic Design Presentation Graphics

The preliminary design(s) created in this process of continual refinement must be evaluated by the designer or design team, as well the client, for the project to continue successfully. Presentation of the preliminary design may be highly informal or formal, depending on the nature of the project. In all cases it is useful to consider the purpose of the presentation as well as its audience. The audience for a preliminary presentation may include the client, consultants, real estate professionals, and those with financial interests in the project. Prior to the creation of any presentation, it is worthwhile to take time to assess the audience for the presentation; identifying and understanding this audience is imperative to the quality of the communication.

In addressing members of the design team or design consultants, a presentation may consist of rough sketches and multiple

FIGURE 2-17a AND 2-17b
Schematic presentation for the sample project.

ELEVATION Ⓐ

ELEVATION Ⓑ

ELEVATION Ⓒ

ECO TOYS Ⓖ concept

PRELIMINARY ELEVATIONS

0' 4' 8'   16'

2-17b

layers of paper. Designers and most consultants are familiar with orthographic drawings and can wade through some confusing and messy drawings and notes. Many clients, however, require easy-to-understand graphic images as a means to understanding the schematic presentation. The client must understand the preliminary design to evaluate and approve it, which is necessary for the project to continue successfully.

The preliminary client presentation must communicate the underlying project research and the constraints that have led to the preliminary design. These include preliminary budgetary information, preliminary scheduling information, research of appropriate building codes, and programming information. Generally, at a minimum the preliminary schematic design presentation requires a floor plan as a means of communicating the space plan. When the project involves more than one floor, each floor plan and stacking plan is typically included in the preliminary presentation.

The floor plan should be drawn to scale and include a north arrow and titles. If the

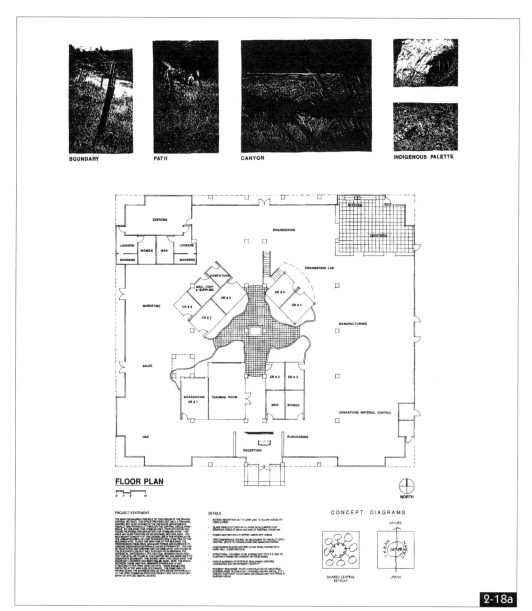

BOUNDARY   PATH   CANYON   INDIGENOUS PALETTE

FLOOR PLAN

NORTH

PROJECT STATEMENT

DETAILS

CONCEPT DIAGRAMS

SHARED CENTRAL RETREAT

2-18a

FIGURES 2-18a AND 2-18b
Professional schematic design presentation.
By Bruck Allen Architects Inc. Project team: Christopher Allen, Mark Bausback, Brian Church, and Randall Rhoads

designers wish to communicate several design schemes, the various floor plans must be labeled clearly with some sort of notation system, such as "Scheme 1" or "Concept 1." Any additional drawings presented, such as elevations and sections, should include appropriate titles and scale information.

Some preliminary presentations include programming information, floor plans, and minimal additional graphics, whereas other projects require preliminary presentations that include additional drawings such as elevations, sections, and preliminary perspective drawings, as well as models and materials samples. The following chapters cover some of these additional forms of preliminary presentation. A successful presentation of the preliminary schematic design communicates information to the client and other interested parties and allows for input, comments, criticism, and approval. Figures

VIEW FROM LOBBY

MAIN AXIS VIEW

VIEW FROM MEZZANINE
CONFERENCE ROOMS

VIEW FROM MANUFACTURING

2-18b

2-17a and 2-17b are examples of a schematic design presentation for the sample project and are based on issues covered to this point. Figures 2-18a and 2-18b are examples of a professional schematic design presentation. Figures C-2a and C-2b on page 53 show steps for preparing a schematic floor plan presented to show departmental grouping rendered in Photoshop.

Most often, designers come away from a preliminary presentation with lists of suggestions from the client. These range from minor corrections or clarifications to major changes in functional, conceptual, or aesthetic aspects of the design.

The information generated by feedback to the first schematic presentation allows the designers to move forward in the refinement of the design. Depending on project requirements and constraints, and the number of changes requested by the client, more schematic presentations may be required. It is common for smaller, less complicated projects to receive quick general approval, allowing the designers to move forward in the design process. Larger projects can require many additional meetings and presentations before the client grants approval of the schematic design.

In interviewing designers, I have found great variety in the formality, visual quality, and quantity of information included in preliminary design presentations. Clearly, there is a range of styles of presentation, and firms have varying standards. Even with this great variety, there seem to be elements of consistency. Most designers describe a need to communicate very clearly in early presentations and to make sure that the client understands the elements of the design presented. Most also describe the importance of making clear the very preliminary nature of the design. Many designers find that clients need time to settle into ideas; thus, pinning things down too early can be frightening and frustrating for them.

DESIGN DEVELOPMENT

The design development of a project involves finalizing the space plan and fully developing all the components of the design. All aspects of the design must come together and be resolved in this phase of the project. It is useful for students to know that the goal is to have the design of a project completed in the design development phase. It is important to keep in mind that the phase following design development is construction documentation, which involves preparation of the project for construction. In large firms the project is often handed from the design team to the production team upon completion of design development.

In a perfect world, every detail would be considered and resolved in the design development phase of a project. For the most part, design development drawings are drafted accurately and to scale. Some designers create design development drawings that are somewhat sketchy, and others create extremely precise, highly detailed drawings. In either case, the entire volume of a space must be explored and refined to ensure a successful design project and to allow for a smooth transition into the construction documentation phase of the project.

The presentation made upon the completion of the design development phase is often seen as the comprehensive final design presentation of a project. This presentation must include every possible element of the design to ensure clear communication of the final design. Orthographic drawings—including detailed floor plans, ceiling plans, detailed elevations, sections, and design details—are generally part of the presentation. In addition, technical drawings, millwork drawings and samples, materials samples, and furnishings and fixtures samples and images are often included in the final design development presentation.

Smaller projects often move quickly from schematic to design development and involve minimal presentations. More complex projects require many interim presentations and meetings. Weekly or biweekly design meetings are not uncommon on large or complex projects. Final design presentations vary enormously because of the variety of projects and working styles of designers. Clearly, there is no existing industry standard for the preparation of design development presentations. It is with pride and sometimes secrecy that firms and designers create successful presentations.

Although design presentations reflect the concerns, aesthetics, and tastes of designer(s) and client, communication is the one constant in their preparation. The final design presentation must clearly communicate all elements of the design. For the project to move forward, the design must be understood and approved by the client. In addition to the client or end user, a wide range of individuals may have to review and approve the design.

Projects dependent on public funding, such as libraries and municipal buildings, often require public review of the design. Many require design approval of municipal agencies or local community groups. Investors and consultants must often review design presentations before a project can move forward. All of these individuals form the eventual audience for the design presentation, and understanding this audience is key to the successful communication of the design.

The following chapters offer information on additional visual devices employed in the design and presentation of projects. These are discussed separately for purposes of clarity, but all are used throughout the design process as a means of exploring and communicating the design.

REFERENCES

(Contains both works cited and recommended reading. Annotations where appropriate.)

The Association for Qualitative Research. *Glossary: Mood Boards*. http://www.aqr.org.uk/

Ballast, David. *Interior Design Reference Manual*. Belmont, CA: Professional Publications, 2006.

Ching, Francis. *Interior Design Illustrated*,3rd edition. Hoboken, NJ: John Wiley & Sons, 2004

———. *A Visual Dictionary of Architecture*. New York: John Wiley & Sons, 1995. *A beautiful and inspiring book.*

Crowe, Norman, and Paul Laseau. *Visual Notes for Architects and Designers*. New York: John Wiley & Sons, 1995. *A great guide to various types of notational drawing.*

Guthrie, Pat. *Interior Designers' Portable Handbook*, 2nd edition. New York: McGraw-Hill, 2004.

Harwood, Bouie. "An Interior Design Experience Program, Part II: Developing the Experiences." *Journal of Interior Design* 22(1), 15–31.

Henley, Pamela. *Interior Design Practicum Exam Workbook*, 2nd edition. Belmont, CA: Professional Publications, 2002.

Karlen, Mark. *Space Planning Basics*, 2nd edition. Hoboken, NJ: John Wiley & Sons, 2003.

Koberg, Don, and Jim Bagnall. *The Universal Traveler*, 3rd edition. Menlo Park, CA: Crisp Publications, 2003. *A wonderful primer on creative thinking; it continues to be helpful after all these years.*

Laseau, Paul. *Graphic Thinking for Architects and Designers*. New York: John Wiley & Sons, 2001. *Another great book on graphic thinking and design graphics from Mr. Laseau. Graphic thinking is described in detail in the volume's first chapter.*

Peña, William, Steven Parshall, and Kevin Kelly. *Problem Seeking*. Washington, DC: AIA Press, 1987.

C-1a

C-1b

FIGURES C-1a AND C-1b

This concept or mood board set an aesthetic direction for a library interior that is evident in a later presentation of materials (Figure C-1b) and were used to create a mural in the library entry area. Note the palette at the left of Figure C-1a, created by Photoshop's color sampler.

By Meyer, Scherer & Rockcastle, Ltd.

FIGURES C-2a AND C-2b

Using Photoshop to color a plan (Figure C-2b) to clarify departments and programming information for the sample project featured in Chapter 2. Refer to Figure 5-9a (Steps 1 and 1a) for information about importing CAD files into Photoshop. Directions are as follows:

1. ICON TOOL: Polygonal Lasso Tool. Make a new layer for each programming space or similar function spaces. Take Polygonal Lasso Tool and select an area of the bubble diagram (or of more developed floor plan) that is to be a particular programming space (in this case it's the conference room).

2. ICON TOOL: Paint Bucket (or Brush Tool). Take Paint Bucket Tool and select color desired to represent a particular program space. Paint Bucket the room a solid color. Change the layer to be on "multiply" option (this allows the background line work to read through color put on floor plan).

3. Continue Steps 1 and 2 for the rest of the programming exercise. This is helpful for both designers and client to visualize adjacencies and program elements in a color or graphic diagram. Different colors should be used for each programming space; however, similar tones can be used for smaller departments within each adjacency.

STEP 1:   STEP 2:   C-2a

LEGEND

A	ACCOUNTING	E	ENGINEERING
B	BREAK	F	FLEX SPACE
C	CONFERENCE	M	MARKETING
CM	COPY / MAIL	MG	MARKETING GROUP
D	DESIGN	R	RECEPTION
DM	DESIGN / MODEL	S	STORAGE
DG	DESIGN GROUP	T	TESTING

STEP 3:   C-2b

C-3

FIGURE C-3

Rendering media, materials, and tools.

1. Spray fixative
2. Transfer paper
3. Glue stick
4. Gouache and brush
5. Removable tape
6. Rubber cement
7. Acrylic gesso
8. Rubber cement thinner
9. Cotton pad (for use with thinner and pastels)
10. Marker blender
11. Vellum
12. Marker paper
13. Illustration board
14. Black mounting board
15. Canson paper
16. Museum board
17. Handmade paper
18. Kraft paper
19. Watercolor paper (hot press)
20. Watercolor paper (cold press)
21. Ink pens
22. Snap-off cutter
23. Colored pencils (wax-based)
24. Dry pastels
25. Pastels scraped into powder
26. Baby powder (for use with pastel powder)
27. Studio markers
28. Marker refill
29. Watercolor brushes
30. Watercolor paint

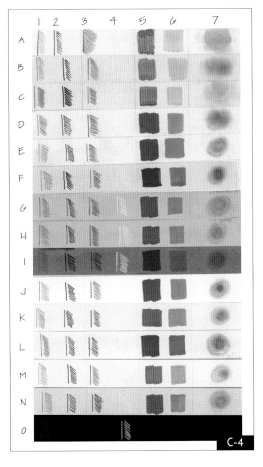

FIGURE C-4

Matrix showing examples of various rendering surfaces and media.

1. Graphite
2. Ink
3. Wax-based colored pencil (color)
4. Wax-based colored pencil (white)
5. Studio marker (colored)
6. Studio marker (gray)
7. Dry pastel (powder)
A. Vellum
B. Trace paper
C. Drafting film
D. Marker paper
E. Bristol paper
F. Blueline diazo print paper
G. Canson paper (textured side)
H. Canson paper (smooth side)
I. Kraft paper
J. Bristol board
K. Museum board
L. Watercolor paper (cold press)
M. Illustration board (hot press)
N. Mat board
O. Black mounting board

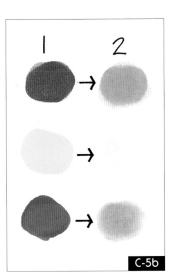

FIGURE C-5b

Special blender markers can be used to pick up an intense color (1) and apply it to the drawing surface (2).

FIGURES C-5a

1. Nothing applied to alter pencil
2. Marker blender applied over pencil
3. Gesso applied under pencil
4. Warm gray marker under pencil
5. Cool gray marker under pencil
6. Red marker under pencil
7. Yellow marker under pencil
8. Blue marker under pencil
A. Red-orange colored pencil (wax-based)
B. Yellow colored pencil (wax-based)
C. Blue colored pencil (wax-based)

C-6a

FIGURES C-6a AND C-6b

Perspective rough-out using prepared grid. Notice that boxes are used as guides for drawing furnishings, fixtures, and architectural elements (Figure C-6a). Final perspective rendering by a professional design illustrator (Figure C-6b). Marker on bond paper. This rendering is treated with minimal marker application, with excellent results.

Project: University Church of Hope, Minneapolis, Minnesota. Design by CNH Architects, Inc. Illustration by Janet Lawson Architectural Illustration

FIGURES C-7a AND C-7b

Pastels make fast work of large flat areas of color—they streak far less than markers. Using powder scraped from a chalk-stick pastel mixed with baby powder the pastel can be applied using a cotton pad or swab.

C-6b

C-7a

C-7b

C-8a

C-8b

C-8c

FIGURES C-8a, C-8b, AND C-8c
The first step in rendering floor plans on bond paper is the application of gray markers to shadow locations (Figure C-8a). The second step in rendering floor plans on bond paper is the application of colored markers (using a straightedge). It is best to use subdued marker color to give mere indications of color and texture (Figure C-8b). The final step in rendering floor plans on bond paper is "tuning up" color by adding multiple layers of colored marker and colored pencil. When tuning up color, markers may be applied freely without the use of a straightedge. Shadows are enhanced with washes of colored pencil (Figure C-8c).

FIGURES C-9a AND C-9b

The first steps in rendering this floor plan on bond paper involved laying in shadows and general material hues using a straightedge for marker application in the direction shown (Figure C-9a). The final steps in rendering this floor plan on bond paper involved tuning up hues and adding variety to the limestone floor tiles so that they illustrate the variety inherent in the material (Figure C-9b). Colored pencil was added to floor, tabletop, and chairs. A rendered perspective drawing of this kitchen can be found in Figures C-24a and C-24b.

Design and line drawing by Courtney Nystuen

C-9a

C-9b

GREAT ROOM FLOOR PLAN
600 SQ. FT. (+) STAIR / FOYER
SCALE: 1/4" = 1'-0"

C-10a

GREAT ROOM FLOOR PLAN
600 SQ. FT. (+) STAIR / FOYER
SCALE: 1/4" = 1'-0"

C-10b

FIGURES C-10a, C-10b, AND C-10c

The first steps in rendering this floor plan on bond paper involve layering a coat of Sand Prismacolor marker on the entire drawing surface; stairs, counter-tops, window seat, and fire-place were also coated with Eggshell Prismacolor marker; layers of Cool Gray 10% marker were added to the sinks, appliances, and inside fireplace (Figure C-10a). Figure C-10b shows the tile floors coated with Terracotta Prismacolor marker in a linear fashion so that differences in tile shades would be visible. Shadows were added with Cinnamon Toast Prismacolor markers except for gray areas, which were layered with additional Cool Gray 10%. The final tune-up was done with white, cream, and green chalk pastel (in powder form), and with additional shadows laid in with Walnut and Gray Prismacolor markers. Sharp white Prismacolor pencil was used for tile grout lines. Additional Prismacolor pencils were used to add detail and to aid in color movement through-out the plan (Figure C-10c).

By Nicole Banaszewski

C-10c

FIGURE C-11
Spot rendering is a time-saving technique allowing for a small descriptive area to be fully rendered (bond paper, marker, colored pencil).

FIGURE C-12
Time is also saved by washing large areas with the appropriate colors and detailing only portions of each material (bond paper, marker, colored pencil).

PROPOSED FLOOR PLAN - 1ST FLR.
1/4" = 1'-0"

BATH

UP

A

KITCHEN

B

ENTRY

FIRE ESCAPE

C-13a

PROPOSED FLOOR PLAN - 2ND FLR.
1/4" = 1'-0"

BATH

WALK-IN CLOSET

BEDROOM

DW

OPEN TO BELOW

C-13b

FIGURES C-13a AND C-13b

Student design-development presentation rendering
on bond paper with marker and colored pencil.
Design and rendering by Ardella Pieper

C-15a

C-14

FIGURE C-14
Rendered plan for use in a preliminary student presentation. Colored pencil on bond paper copy.
Design and rendering by Martina Lehmann

C-15b

FIGURES C-15a, C-15b, AND C-15c
A first step in rendering elevations on bond paper is the application of gray markers to shadow locations (Figure C-15a). The second step in rendering elevations on bond paper is the application of colored marker (using a straightedge). It is best to use subdued marker color, to give mere indications of color and texture, and to avoid overly dark or intense marker color (Figure C-15b). The final step in rendering elevations on bond paper is tuning up color by adding multiple layers of colored marker and colored pencil. When tuning up color, markers may be applied freely without the use of a straightedge. Shadows are enhanced with washes of colored pencil (Figure C-15c).

C-15c

ELEVATION (A)

0' 1' 2' 4'

C-16a

FIGURES C-16a AND C-16b
A first step in rendering this elevation on bond paper involved laying in general material hues in values lighter than the final will depict. A straightedge was used for marker application in the direction shown.

ELEVATION (A)

0' 1' 2' 4'

C-16b

C-17a

C-17b

FIGURES C-17a AND C-17b
Rendered elevation and section for use in a preliminary presentation. Pastel, marker, and ink on printed bond paper copy.
Design and rendering by Smart and Associates

STEP 11:

C-18a

STEP 13:

C-18c

STEP 12:

C-18b

STEP 12A:

FIGURES C-18a, C-18b, AND C-18c
These are color details taken from the
instructions for rendering elevations
using Photoshop (Figures 5-9f, 5-9g,
and 5-9h).

STEP 9:

STEP 10:

STEP 11:

C-19a

STEP 13:

STEP 13A:

C-19b

FIGURES C-19a AND C-19b
These are color details taken from the instructions for rendering using Photoshop (Figures 5-10e and 5-10g on pages 163 and 164).

C-20a

C-20b

FIGURES C-20a AND C-20b

An elevation and plan drawn
using AutoCAD and rendered
in Photoshop (following the
steps discussed in Chapter 5).
By Ciarah Coenen

BAR ELEVATION SOUTH

C-21

FIGURE C-21
This elevation was rendered by hand and then imported into Photoshop.
By Cuningham Group Architecture, P.A.

FIGURE C-22
Rendering by a professional design illustrator for a design-development presentation. Marker and colored pencil on bond paper. Notice the movement of color throughout the composition.
Project: Ward House at Winchester Gardens, Maplewood, NJ. Design: Arthur Shuster, Inc.
Illustration: Janet Lawson Architectural Illustration

C-22

C-23

FIGURE C-23
Rendered perspective
included in a student design-
development presentation,
created primarily with colored
pencils.
Design and rendering by Jessica Tebbe

FIGURES C-24a AND C-24b
The first steps in rendering this two-point
perspective on bond paper involved laying
in general background material hues in values
lighter than the final will depict. A straightedge
was used for marker application in the directions
shown. Large areas of white space were left in
the countertop areas to indicate a highly reflective
surface. Simple shadows were laid in with warm
gray marker (Figure C-24a). The next steps involved
using additional marker layers for the wood, with
contrast between light and dark surfaces given
special attention. Additional blue and green
marker was applied to plants, decorative elements,
and books. Additional buff-colored marker was
applied in various directions on the floor to
depict reflections. White correction pen was
used for reflections at the leading edges of
countertops and faucets. Black ink and white
Prismacolor pencils were used to depict
leading and receding edges (Figure C-24b).
Designed by Courtney Nystuen

C-24a

C-24b

FIGURES C-25a AND C-25b
The first layers of color for architectural elements in this rendering are laid in with a straightedge in a vertical orientation, whereas the scale figures and other items are applied in a more painterly manner (Figure C-25a). The final drawing (Figure C-25b) has good levels of light to dark contrast and is fresh, not overworked.
By Mary Wawra

C-25a

C-25b

C-26a

FIGURES C-26a AND C-26b
A color and value study on bond paper with marker is a helpful step in successful rendering (Figure C-26a). The final rendering on bond paper with markers and colored pencil (Figure C-26b). Project: Period interior, Royal Pavilion at Brighton, England.
By Leanne Larson

C-26b

FIGURE C-27a

The first steps in rendering this two-point perspective on bond paper involved laying in general background material hues in values lighter than the final will depict. A straightedge was used for marker application in the directions shown. The top surfaces of the sofa and floor were left blank to prepare for the use of dry (chalk) pastels. Simple shadows were laid in with warm gray marker on the floor, while the wall surfaces received cool gray markers.

C-27a

FIGURE C-27b

The next steps involved using dry (chalk) pastels for the orange flooring and top areas of the couch (lighter blue areas) as well as the pillows. The orange pastel was applied freely and then erased as required for the floor; the same was done with the blue on the window. Blue and orange pastels were also washed into the bookcase, small vertical areas of the lamp, and the white rug. Black pens in varying widths were used for leading and receding edges.

C-27b

FIGURE C-27c

The previous drawing further "rendered" in Photoshop by following the instructions in Figures 5-23a through 5-23f.

FIGURE C-27d

Designers can also use Photoshop for quick color studies by following steps similar to the following: For quick color studies of walls, floors, furniture, and other items: select the item and trace around the image using the polygonal or magnetic lasso tool (example shown tracing sofa). Go to "Image," then choose "Adjustments," then select "Hue/Saturation." Use the hue sliders to change the color (examples show hue function). For additional color manipulations go to "Image," then choose "Adjustments," then choose "Color Balance."

C-27c

C-27d

FIGURE C-28
A CAD generated line drawing, traced over by hand and imported into Photoshop and rendered using Photoshop's airbrush tool.
By Cuningham Group Architecture, P.A.

FIGURE C-29
Rendered perspective included in a student schematic-design presentation. Marker, colored pencil, and ink on Canson paper with bond-paper insert. Note that a small icon of the floor plan is included to indicate direction of view (cone of vision).

FIGURE C-30

Rendered perspective and design details included in a student design-development presentation. Note that the floor plan is used as a project graphic in the title area. Marker, ink, and colored pencil on bond paper.
Design and rendering by Kelly Urevig

ROLLING PIN RACK DETAIL

C-30

FIGURE C-31

Drawing rendered on marker paper using markers only. The use of bold, strongly directional marker strokes enhances the drawing, which was completed in two hours (including the two-point perspective drawing).
Design and rendering by Jack Zellner

C-31

FIGURE C-32
Rendered perspective included in a student design-development presentation. Marker and pencil on bond paper. Notice the vertical application of marker and portions of paper left blank to serve as highlights.
Design and rendering by Susan Reische

FIGURE C-33
This is a hand-drawn sketch rendered with markers on tracing paper.
By Cuningham Group Architecture, P.A.

FIGURES C-34a AND C-34b
Computer generated images for
a senior thesis project presenta-
tion. Images created using
Rhinoceros modeling software.
Design, model, and rendering by
Ciarah Coenen

C-35a

FIGURE C-35a AND C-35b
Professional computer-
generated image.
Project: Wilsons, the Leather
Experts. Software: Form-Z
(modeling) and Electric Image
Animation System (rendering).
Designed, computer-modeled, and
rendered by Craig Beddow,
Beddow Design • Digital Architecture

C-35b

FIGURE C-36
Professional computer-generated image. Software: Autodesk VI24 and Architectural Desktop 2.
Designed, computer-modeled, and rendered by Robert Lownes, Design Visualizations.

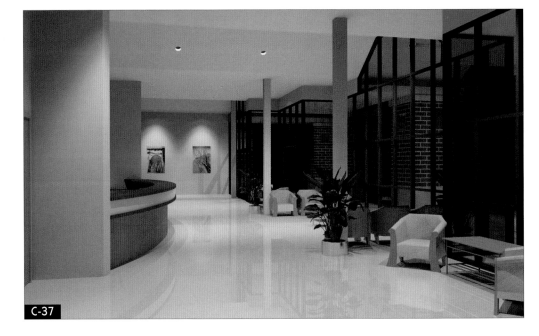

FIGURE C-37
Professional computer-generated image. Software: Autodesk VI24 and Architectural Desktop 2.
Designed, computer-modeled, and rendered by Robert Lownes, Design Visualizations

C-38a

FIGURES C-38a, C-38b, AND C-38c

A detail of a model drawn and rendered in SketchUp (Figure C-38a). The presentation was composed in Photoshop and the elevations were rendered in Photoshop (Figure C-38b) as was the floor plan (Figure C-38c). Materials were scanned and imported into Photoshop as were some of the conceptual images.
By Ellie Feenstra

C-38b

C-38c

FIGURES C-39a AND C-39b
Presentation boards with marker renderings done on bond paper (CAD plots) mounted on mat board. Presentation includes material samples, a key plan, and related elevations. Figure C-39b is a detail of the rendering.
By Vicky Salzieder and Laura Eysnogle

FIGURES C-40a, C-40b, AND C-40c

Boards presented with marker renderings done on bond paper (CAD plots) set on an intermediate board surface creating shadow lines on mat board surface (Figures C-40a and C-40b). Material samples (Figure C-40c) are also placed on an intermediate board surface or neatly wrapped creating an attractive and visually consistent presentation (especially given the range in board shapes).

By Ellie Feenstra and Stephanie Holmblad

FIGURES C-41a ANDC-41b

Presentation boards with marker renderings done on bond paper (CAD plots) set behind window mats. Presentation includes material samples mounted on the board surface.

By Sunny Reed

FIGURES C-42a AND C-42b

Boards presented with marker renderings done on bond paper (CAD plots) mounted on mat board.

By Amber Liestman

C-43a

FIGURES C-43a AND C-43b
Rendered perspective and
floor plan drawings done
on bond paper with markers
set behind window mats
for presentation.
By Megan Gruner

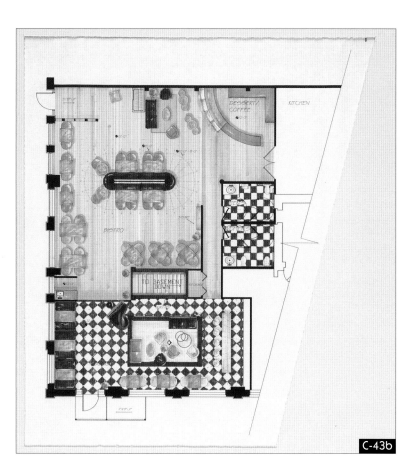

C-43b

FIGURES C-44a AND C-44b
Portions of a presentation communicating various conceptual directions for a project, composed in Photoshop. Perspective sketches at right within each "board" were modeled using SketchUp and then "drawn over" with marker on tracing paper.
By Cuningham Group Architecture, P.A.

● Clinic Floor Plan

● Dining Room

C-45a

C-45b

FIGURES C-45a AND C-45b
Portions of a thesis presentation composed in Photoshop. The nonrendered floor plan is keyed to detailed floor plans rendered in Photoshop.
By Amber Liestman

FIGURES C-46a AND C-46b
Portions of a presentation
composed in Photoshop.
Line drawing were imported
and rendered in Photoshop.
By Matt Saunders

Laughin' & Relaxin' Lagoon
C-46a

Escape the outside world,

relax inside a desert tent,

and take in a whole new

experience at the Oasis.

Theater entrance and Interior
C-46b

FIGURES C-47a AND C-47b
Portions of a presentation composed in Photoshop. Hand-rendered items were imported and set "on top" of light versions of early project graphics.
By Matthew Saunders

FIGURES C-48a, C-48b, AND C-48c

Portions of a thesis project composed in Photoshop and InDesign. Note the documentation of the project process through the many drawings and sketches included in Figure C-48a. Information about the plan is conveyed via keyed elements in Figure C-48b. Hand-rendered sketches as well as elevations rendered in Photoshop are shown in Figure C-48c.

By Laura Sudbrock

C-49a

C-49b

C-49c

FIGURES C-49a, C-49b, C-49c, C-49d, C-49e, C-49f, AND C-49g

A range of design drawings and presentation elements for a professional project. This project began with some preliminary project concept sketches (Figures C-49a and C-49b) called "droodles" by their designer, Thom Lasley. Lasley then worked with a professional design illustrator to clarify and communicate the design with colored preliminary conceptual sketches. Harris Birkeland's sketches were used as a means of communicating the spirit of the design to the client early in the design process (Figures C-49c, C-49d, and C-49e). Interior Designer Jane Rademacher researched and selected a wide range of materials, which were presented on large, dynamic boards (Gatorfoam board) with logos by the Ellerbe Becket graphic design staff (Figures C-49f and C-49g).

C-49d

C-49f

C-49e

C-49g

12 IDEAS FOR ARCHITECTURE OF AUTHENTICITY AND CREATIVITY

CULTURE

PEOPLE, PEOPLE, PEOPLE
Lots of individual choices.

"BETTER A GREAT PAIR OF JEANS THAN A CHEAP SUIT"
Make the ordinary extraordinary.

GRACEFUL CHANGE
Daily, by client, next generation.

CREATIVITY

A MESSY PROCESS
Embrace the complexity of the creative process.

BACKGROUND AND FOREGROUND
A foil for your creativity and an expression of it.

MATERIALITY
Sight, sound, touch, smell, taste.

THE WALL
Provide a vehicle for your work and is where "openness" and "closedness" gets played out.

A GREAT TOOL
Offer excellent functionality.

COMMUNITY

THE NEIGHBORHOOD
The site and surrounding context influence design.

BASIC BUILDING
Reveal the best characteristics of the building.

STREET PRESENCE
It is your tradition.

DO THE RIGHT THING
Sustainable design.

C-50a

C-50b

C-50c

FIGURES C-50a, C-50b, C-50c, C-50d, C-50e, C-50f, C-50g, C-50h, AND C-50i

Design drawings, graphics, samples, models and presentation elements for a professional project. The "Project Design Principles" were arrived at after many visioning sessions and discussions with the client about their culture, values, goals and expectations; these were condensed and communicated in the "Design Principles" board (Figure C-50a) and used as a touchstone throughout the project. Budgetary, planning and other design decisions were consistently tied to these principles and are reflected in later presentation tools.

Many hand sketches were generated (one is illustrated in Figure C-50b) in order to study the relationship between the "solids" of rooms versus the "voids" of circulation areas and paths including stairways that would best foster connectivity between departments. Use of daylight and the creation of simple, clearly articulated pathways were fundamental concerns and were studied in many varying plans. These studies reflect many of the issues and concerns expressed in the previously discussed Design Principles and led to design decisions reflected in later floor plans (Figure

C-50c) and sections (Figure C-50d) that illustrate stair design and floor-to-floor relationships.

Scale models were used to study design elements and custom furniture (Figures C-50e and C-50f), followed by full-scale furniture mock-ups (Figure C-50g). Figure C-50h depicts a working session and client review of large samples including actual furniture, large fabric samples, paint samples and design drawings; inclusion of these elements allowed clients to touch and test them. Perspective views conveyed the final design to the clients and end users (Figure C-50i).

By Meyer, Scherer & Rockcastle, Ltd. All images courtesy of Meyer, Scherer & Rockcastle, Ltd.

C-50d

C-50e

C-50f

C-50g

10th FLOOR MAIN ENTRY LOBBY

C-50i

C-50h

3

PARALINE AND PERSPECTIVE DRAWINGS

Drawings depicting three-dimensional views differ greatly from orthographic drawings in that they offer a more natural view of space. It is important to note that these three-dimensional views (also known as pictorial drawings) are useful at every phase of the design process. Pictorial drawings work well in the various phases of the design process as a method of examining and refining ideas, and should not be reserved merely as a means of final project presentation.

The purpose of this chapter is to present a wide range of three-dimensional drawing methods and procedures. These methods range from freehand sketches to measured, hard-lined perspective illustrations. Students of design should seek a method or methods that work well for them as individuals. The goal, then, is to find drawing methods that are useful as tools throughout the design process and to realize that pictorial drawing is a way of seeing that is useful for all designers.

Unlike orthographic projections, three-dimensional views allow for a single depiction of a large portion of an interior space. This type of drawing can also help clients to clearly understand the design of a project. In addition, three-dimensional views of a space allow the designer to see and explore the entire volume of space and make design decisions accordingly.

Designers can create these drawings by hand and through the use of computers. Some designers state that they can explore the total volume of a space in the preliminary design phases only when drawing it in perspective by hand. Many designers have mentioned that they use a combination of hand sketching and computer-generated perspective imagery.

Increasingly, design graduates are expected to have the ability to create three-dimensional views both by hand and with the use of computers. This is because understanding the basics of creating hand-drawn three-dimensional views allows a designer to work more effectively by computer and also grants the ability to create quick sketches in client meetings (and elsewhere).

Some designers use computer-generated three-dimensional imagery from the inception of a project and create no hand drawings at any point in the design process. Software used by those working this way includes Ashlar-Vellum® and form-Z® from Auto-DesSys. Others generate two-dimensional design drawings on AutoCAD (various releases) and then use these to generate three-dimensional views on AutoCAD.

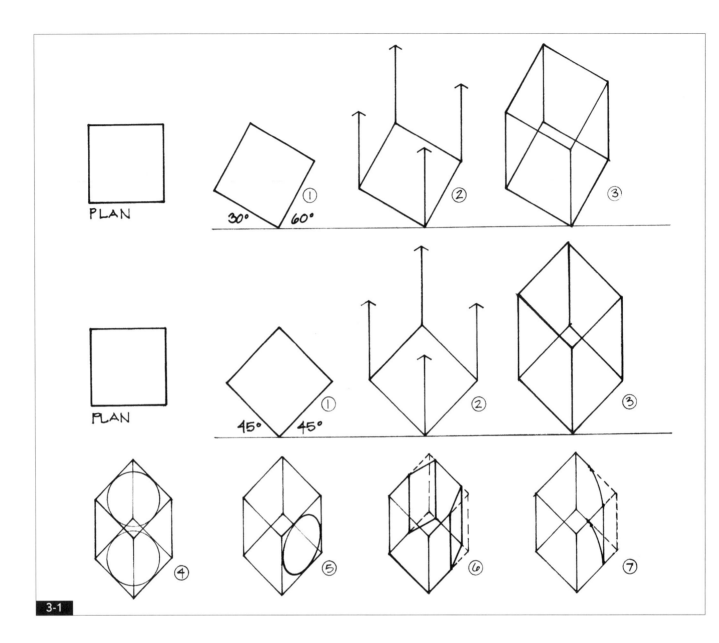

PLAN

30° 60° ①

②

③

PLAN

45° 45° ①

②

③

④

⑤

⑥

⑦

This chapter provides step-by-step instructions on a range of hand-drawn perspective methods. However, given the range of software available, there are no explicit directions provided for creating computer generated perspective drawings because each software product has very distinct properties. It is also worth noting that hand drawing works effectively early in the schematic design phase as a means of generating many varied ideas about a given space. Using the quick sketching techniques covered in this chapter will help a designer generate a wide range of ideas rapidly without first creating plans and elevations.

Pictorial drawings are created as line drawings (or wire frames) and used as such in presentations or are rendered upon completion. Some perspective and paraline line drawings work very well in communicating a design to an audience without the addition of value or color rendering. This is especially true if additional descriptive items such as materials and finishes samples are also used in the presentation. Therefore, it is worthwhile to attempt to generate descriptive line drawings that communicate a design successfully and to see rendering as a secondary step in the drawing process.

The tools and materials used in pictorial drawings are similar to those used in orthographic projection drawings and the other forms of graphic communication mentioned previously. An abundance of tracing paper is probably the most important material in the production of perspective drawings. The transparency and low cost of tracing paper make it highly useful as a visualization tool. As soon as a drawing becomes confusing to sort out, a new sheet of tracing paper can be overlaid. When tracing paper is used as an overlay, a variety of colored pencils can be used as a visual aid in the construction of three-dimensional drawings.

Both pencils and pens can work well in the construction of three-dimensional views when working by hand. Although the choice of implements is highly personal, quick-sketching methods are best accomplished with marking pens that provide quick visual impact. Marking pens also eliminate the use of erasers, which actually helps with visualization. This approach is tough at first but worth the effort.

Hand-drawn refined measured paraline and perspective drawings are most often constructed in pencil on tracing paper, with many layers of paper and a variety of colored pencils used. These drawings often require the use of drafting tools but are also drawn freehand by some individuals. The final hard-lined measured paraline or perspective line drawing is often done on high-quality vellum or drafting film with drafting pencils or ink pens. This allows for the line drawing to be reproduced by a variety of reprographic methods on a variety of papers. Once reproduced, the drawing may be incorporated into a presentation with or without rendering. Information on rendering and reprographics is available in Chapter 5.

PARALINE DRAWINGS

PARALINE DRAWINGS are quick, accurate, and useful in the communication of interior form. The method of construction of these drawings is based on the relationship of three principal axes (x, y, and z). Although there are several types of paraline drawing, all share common characteristics: (1) paraline drawings have parallel lines drawn as parallel, and lines do not converge to vanishing points; (2) vertical lines are drawn as true verticals in paraline drawings; and (3) paraline drawings are drawn using some method of proportional scale.

Plan Oblique Drawings

One type of paraline drawing commonly used in the communication of interior environments is known as a PLAN OBLIQUE. Figure 3-1 provides a quick reference of plan oblique construction. Plan obliques can be constructed quickly because they are drawn by projecting directly off the floor plan. Drawing a plan oblique requires the rotation of the floor plan to appropriate angles as measured against a horizontal baseline. The most common angles of plan rotation or orientation are 30 degrees–60 degrees and 45 degrees–45 degrees, although plan obliques may be drawn at any two angles that together equal 90 degrees. Vertical elements are drawn by projecting locations vertically from the plan to the appropriate height. Horizontal elements are drawn using the same angles as those used in the orientation of the plan.

Because they are generally projected from existing plans, these drawings are created quickly and can be used throughout the design process as an aid in seeing and understanding the environment. The angle

FIGURE 3-1

Quick reference: plan oblique construction.

1. Rotate scaled plan to appropriate angles (shown here, 30 degrees–60 degrees and 45 degrees–45degrees).
2. Draw vertical lines upward to appropriate height in scale.
3. Lines parallel to the base plane (the floor plan) are drawn at the same angles as plan.
4. Circles found on the plan and its parallel planes are drawn as circles.
5. Circles found on vertical planes are drawn as ellipses.
6. Create an enclosing box to measure and locate nonaxonometric lines.
7. Create an enclosing box to measure and plot irregular and curvilinear lines and planes.

FIGURE 3-2
A plan oblique drawing of a residential storage area.

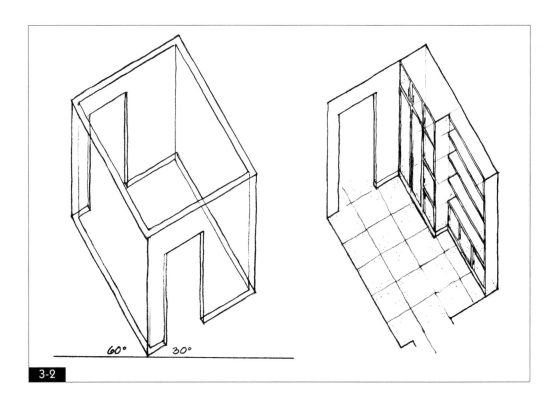

3-2

FIGURE 3-3
A plan oblique drawing of a residential basement remodeling project.

3-3

FIGURE 3-4
A plan oblique drawing of an office environment (from the Eco Toys project discussed in Chapter 2).

3-4

of rotation changes the orientation of the drawing and must be considered in the construction of these drawings. The angle of rotation used allows for varying views and emphasis on particular portions of the space. Often plan obliques employ some method of visual elimination of portions of walls to depict the space successfully. This is often done by cutaway views or by ghosting in portions of walls.

Circles and curvilinear forms can be drawn in plan obliques using a number of methods. Circles found in the true-size planes on plan oblique drawings retain their true size and form. This means that a true circle found in a plan (and on surfaces parallel to the plan) remains a true circle in a plan oblique. Circles or curvilinear lines found on the vertical nonfrontal planes (those drawn at angles extending from the plan) appear as ellipses. (For additional information on ellipse construction, see Figures 3-14 and 3-15.)

The location of free-form curvilinear lines can be approximated by plotting locations on the plan and extending them vertically to the appropriate height. Curvilinear forms found on nonfrontal planes can be approximated using a grid to plot locations and transferring them to the appropriate location of a gridded area on the oblique drawing.

Objects or lines that are not parallel to any of the three primary axes are not measurable in scale and can be tricky to draw. To draw nonaxonometric lines and objects, an enclosing box can be created within the axonometric framework. The enclosing box can provide measuring lines with which to locate the end points of the object lines. Nonaxonometric lines that are parallel to one another remain parallel in plan oblique drawings.

Plan oblique drawings are quick to create and are useful as an aid in the design process. However, although they are a simple and effective means of visualization for the designer, they can be confusing for clients who are not accustomed to viewing this type of drawing. Figures 3-2, 3-3, and 3-4 are examples of plan oblique drawings.

Isometric Drawings

An ISOMETRIC is a paraline drawing based on the use of 30-degree angles. Unlike plan obliques, isometrics cannot be constructed by simple rotation and projection of the plan. Instead, the drawing of an isometric requires the reconstruction of the plan in scale with the two ground-plane axes (x and y axes) at 30 degrees. All elements that are parallel to the ground plane are drawn at 30 degrees. As in other types of paraline drawings, vertical elements remain vertical in

isometric drawings. Scale measurements can be made along any of the three principal axes (x, y, and z). Figure 3-5 provides a quick reference of isometric construction.

All circles and circular lines in isometric drawings are drawn as ellipses. Readily available isometric ellipse templates can be used in isometric drawing. For additional information on ellipse construction, see Figures 3-14 and 3-15. Lines not parallel to the three principal axes are created by using an enclosing box method to locate the object(s). Isometric drawings offer a balanced view and the least distortion of any paraline drawing. They are also rather easy to create in most CAD programs. Figures 3-6a and 3-6b illustrate a method of drawing isometrics using AutoCAD.

Isometric drawings can be used at any phase of the design process as a means of communicating form and spatial relationships. Isometrics are also used in technical and construction documents. Although isometrics offer some advantages, they are somewhat inflexible and do not emphasize any particular portion of the space.

FIGURE 3-5

Quick reference: isometric construction.

1. Redraw plan, in scale, with x and y axes at 30 degrees.

2. Draw vertical lines upward to appropriate height in scale.

3. Lines parallel to the x and y axes are drawn at the same angles as plan.

4. All circles are drawn as ellipses in an isometric drawing.

5. Create an enclosing box to measure and locate non-axonometric lines.

6. Create an enclosing box to measure and plot irregular and curvilinear lines and planes.

STEP 1 STEP 2 STEP 3
STEP 4 STEP 5 STEP 6

3-6a

FIGURE 3-6a
Quick reference: creating isometric drawing using AutoCAD
(two-dimensional environment).
The drawing setup requires
starting a new drawing in
AutoCAD, and right clicking on
the bottom of tool bar on polar
tracking and choosing "Settings"
option and changing polar
angle increment settings to "30
degrees." With that complete,
complete the following steps:

1. Draw a vertical line that is
the desired height of the object
using the desired feet and inches
(in this case, 2'6").

2. At the base of the object
draw the first angled (30
degrees) line length using the
desired feet and inches (in this
case, 5'0"); copy this line above
at parallel location to create the
top of the object.

3. Draw the depth of the
object by creating an angled
line (30 degrees) in the desired
dimension (in this case 1'10") at
the bottom of the object and
repeat for the top parallel line
of the object.

4. Using the same angles consistently (30 degrees), complete
the object by drawing the
required lines (dashed lines
show the hidden isometric
lines).

5 and 6. Add details as follows. For the drawers: Draw line
from the top of the unit to the
bottom. Type "Divide" command to divide the line into
three equal parts (make sure
OSNAP "Nodes" are turned on).
Continue this method for additional cabinets and drawers.
Note: In Isometrics use copy
lines rather than off-setting lines
(off-setting does not follow the
30-degree angles).
Note: This instructionn is continued in Figure 3-6b (on the
following page).

PERSPECTIVE DRAWINGS

PERSPECTIVE DRAWING offers a natural view of interior space and for this reason is commonly used in design presentations. Many design students (and some design professionals) have difficulty creating clear, natural-looking perspective draw-ings. This is unfortunate because perspec-tive sketching and drawing is an excellent design tool that can—and should—be used throughout the design process to generate and refine ideas. Using perspective draw-ing only in finalized design presentations can result in weak design projects and lost opportunities for discovery.

An understanding of basic perspective principles allows designers to draw quickly and fairly accurately. Quick perspective drawings are helpful as visualization tools for designers. In addition, an understand-ing of basic principles and estimated sketching techniques allows for the cre-ation of fresh, attractive drawings that can be used in design presentations.

The ability to draw simply measured or estimated freehand perspectives allows for the rapid expression of ideas, which helps in the generation of ideas and solutions. Certainly the capacity to produce labori-ously created mechanical perspective drawings is important in design practice, but equally important is the ability to express ideas rapidly. It is worth stating that some CAD programs require that the design be complete and fully expressed in plan or elevation drawings prior to the gen-eration of a three-dimensional view, which also points to the need for skills with quickly hand-drawn perspectives.

Perspective Basics

Creating successful pictorial drawings requires a working knowledge of basic principles of perspective. Many of these

FIGURE 3-6b

Quick reference *continued*: creating isometric drawing using AutoCAD (two-dimensional environment). Upon completion of the previous steps, do the following:

1. At starting point, draw line for height of room using correct feet and inches (8'0").

2. At starting point, draw lines for base of walls using correct feet and inches. Copy the same lines up 8'0" to create top of walls.

3. Copy each top and base line over 3½" to show wall thickness; add door in desired location.

4. Add detail to door frame. Add wall fixtures in desired locations.

5. Place vanity in room.

6. Copy base lines over for floor tile pattern.

Note: Remember to use "Aligned Dimension" command for dimensioning items since drawing is in Isometric Mode.

STEP 1   STEP 2   STEP 3

STEP 4   STEP 5   STEP 6

3-6b

principles remain constant regardless of the method of drawing employed. Therefore, it is worthwhile for students to become well acquainted with the fundamental terms and principles of perspective drawing.

Understanding the concept of the picture plane is fundamental to understanding perspective drawing. The PICTURE PLANE is an imaginary transparent plane through which the area to be drawn is viewed. It can be visualized as a giant sheet of glass standing between the viewer and the area to be drawn. Once the drawing is begun, the surface of the drawing paper represents this picture plane. We cannot create successful perspective drawings without first visualizing the picture plane and its relationship to the items to be drawn on the surface of the paper. Understanding that the paper surface can be seen as a reproduction of the picture plane is fundamental to good perspective drawing.

It is the relationship of an object to the picture plane (and to the location of the viewer) that creates a given perspective view of the object. For example, a box that has its front face (plane) parallel to the picture plane is in a position that creates a one-point perspective drawing (see Figure 3-7).

Turning the box so that the entire front corner is on edge in relation to the picture plane creates a two-point perspective view of the box (see Figure 3-8).

Tweaking the box so that only the top (or bottom) corner touches the picture plane creates a three-point perspective view of the box (see Figure 3-9).

All three types of perspective employ a HORIZON LINE representing the viewer's eye level. A box held high above the viewer's eye level (horizon line) allows a view of the

FIGURE 3-7

A box drawn in one-point perspective has its front plane parallel to the picture plane.

FIGURE 3-8

A box drawn in two-point perspective has its front corner viewed on edge in relation to the picture plane.

FIGURE 3-9

All planes of the box are oblique to the picture plane when viewed in three-point perspective.

Drawings for Figures 3-7 through 3-9 by Justin Thomson

bottom of the box. As the box is moved below the eye level of the viewer (the horizon line), a view of the top of the box is possible. In all types of perspective drawing, perspective lines converge to a VANISHING POINT (or points, in two- and three-point perspectives).

The general location of the viewer is often called the STATION POINT. It is from this point in space that the item is seen by the viewer. Another important perspective principle, shared by all three types of perspective, is the CONE OF VISION. The cone of vision represents the angle of view, or sight range of the viewer. This concept is based on the reality that humans cannot view all of a space at a given time. As we approach a given space, we focus on one

area at a time, owing to the natural limitations of our vision.

The cone of vision, or angle of view, can be seen as representing the natural limits of human sight. Elements that exist within the cone of vision of the viewer can generally be drawn without excessive distortion. Those elements that exist outside of the cone of vision become distorted and cannot be drawn successfully.

Perspective drawings show objects becoming smaller as they recede toward the vanishing point(s); that is, items decrease in size as they move away from the viewer. This perspective principle is referred to as DIMINUTION OF SIZE. As a result, a box drawn correctly will appear larger when closest to the viewer and smaller as it

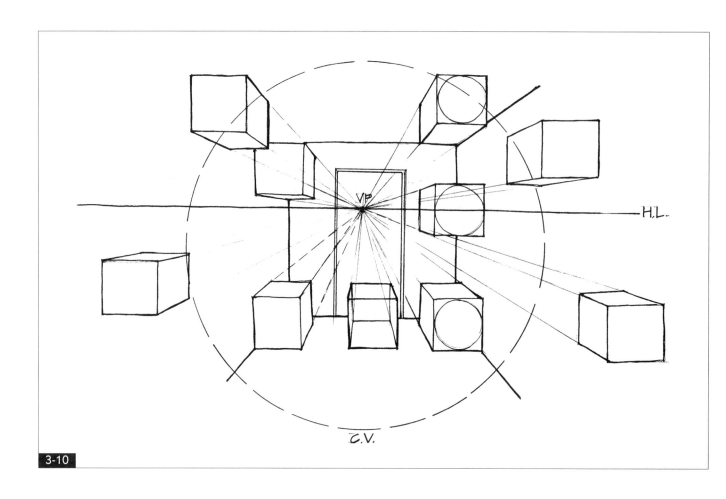

FIGURE 3-10

Quick reference: one-point perspective principles. Perspective lines converge to a single vanishing point (V.P.), located on the horizon line (H.L.). The front faces of the cubes and the back wall of a room are viewed parallel to the picture plane. Those elements with faces touching the picture plane can be drawn in scale. One-point perspective drawings have true vertical, horizontal, and perspective (depth) lines. Items located outside of the cone of vision (C.V.) tend to appear distorted. Items appear to diminish in size as they recede from viewer, which makes boxes of the same size appear smaller when they are located in the rear of the room.

moves farther from the viewer. Because items diminish in size, they cannot be measured consistently in scale; therefore, a variety of methods of measurement have been devised.

Although there are a number of nuances that create more complicated relationships of object to picture plane and horizon line, those mentioned here are fundamental perspective relationships. An effective way to become skilled at drawing in perspective is to practice drawing simple boxes in various relationships to the picture plane and to the horizon line. The ability to sketch a box in perspective in such various relationships allows for the eventual capability to draw more complex objects constructed from boxlike forms. To sketch boxes in perspective successfully, additional information about perspective drawing is required.

One-Point Perspective

One-point perspective views portray an object or environment with one plane parallel to the picture plane. In addition to this parallel orientation to the picture plane, one-point perspective views make use of one vanishing point, located along the horizon line, to which all perspective lines converge. The horizon line is a horizontal line that represents the viewer's eye level, usually between five and six feet from the floor. One-point perspective is considered the easiest type of perspective to draw because the entire plane that is parallel to the picture plane can be measured in scale. Figure 3-10 illustrates one-point perspective principles.

Ease of construction of one-point perspective is also based on the fact that lines that are vertical in reality remain vertical,

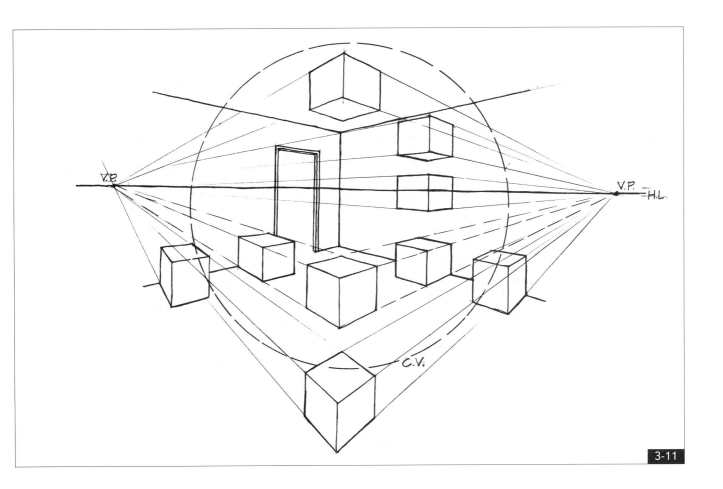

horizontal lines remain horizontal, and only lines indicating perspective depth are drawn converging to the vanishing point. Although they are easy to draw, one-point perspective views can be unnatural-looking and can become distorted. Despite their drawbacks, one-point perspective drawings are highly useful during the early stages of design and are often used by designers for ideation (idea generation).

Two-Point Perspective

Two-point perspective drawings portray objects and volumes on edge in relationship to the picture plane. Another way of stating this is that two-point perspective depicts the primary faces of a volume oblique to the picture plane. This means that two-point perspectives offer a view of the front corner of objects or the rear cor-

ners of rooms and environments. In two-point perspective, an object's edge (or the corner of a room) is drawn first and can be used as a vertical measuring line from which perspective lines recede toward two vanishing points. The two vanishing points lie on the horizon line, one to the left and one to the right. As with one-point perspective drawings, the horizon line is always horizontal and represents the viewer's eye level. Figure 3-11 illustrates the principles of two-point perspective.

Apart from the horizon line and elements that lie along the horizon line, there are no horizontal lines found in accurate two-point perspective drawings. Instead, lines that are not true verticals converge to one of the two vanishing points. Only one vertical measuring line can be drawn in scale owing to the fact that perspective lines converge to two

FIGURE 3-11
Quick reference: two-point perspective principles. Perspective lines converge to two vanishing points (V.P.s), located on the horizon line (H.L.). Boxes are viewed from the front corner, and rooms generally from the back corner in relation to the picture plane. Two-point perspective drawings have true vertical lines as well as perspective (depth) lines. In two-point perspective, the front edge (or back edge) touching the picture plane can be measured in scale. Items located outside of the cone of vision (C.V.) tend to appear distorted. As with all forms of perspective, items appear to diminish in size as they recede from viewer, which makes boxes of the same size appear smaller when they are located in the rear of the room.

FIGURE 3-12

Quick reference: three-point
perspective principles.
Perspective lines converge to
three vanishing points (V.P.s),
two located on the horizon line
(H.L.) and one usually above or
below the horizon line. All
planes of a box are oblique to
the picture plane. All lines
drawn in three-point perspective drawings converge to a
vanishing point. No portion of a
three-point perspective drawing can be measured in scale.
Items located outside the cone
of vision (C.V.) tend to appear
distorted. As with all forms of
perspective, items appear to
diminish in size as they recede
from viewer.

FIGURE 3-13
Quick reference: sketching in
two-point perspective.

1. Practice drawing boxes
that look square.

2. Boxes look distorted when
the front corner equals less than
90 degrees—this means V.P.s
are too close.

3. Boxes look distorted when
the front corner equals greater
than 140 degrees—this means
V.P.s are too far apart.

4. The front corner can be
divided equally to serve as a
measuring line.

5. Bisecting diagonals divide
a square drawn in perspective.

6. Diagonals also divide
rectangles.

7. Boxes can be extended
using diagonals. Extend a diagonal from bottom corner
through midpoint of a square.
Where the diagonal meets the
perspective line (line to V.P.), a
new box is formed.

8. Diagonals can also extend
a box vertically.

9. Slanting parallel lines converge at a common point. This
point is called a vanishing trace
(after Ching, 1975), or V.T.,
and is directly below or above
the V.P.

3-12

vanishing points, causing objects to look
smaller as they recede away from the viewer
toward the vanishing points. Two-point perspective drawings can be tricky to measure
and confusing to create. However, two-
point perspective drawings appear more
natural and suffer from less distortion than
other types of perspective.

Three-Point Perspective

Three-point perspective is not commonly
used in traditional illustration of interior
space. Three-point perspective portrays an
object or volume with all principal faces
oblique to the picture plane. All lines in this
type of perspective converge to vanishing
points. Generally, three-point perspectives
are constructed with two vanishing points
on the horizon line, one to the left and one
to the right, with an additional vanishing
point above or below the horizon line. It is
best to center the third vanishing point
above or below the left and right vanishing
points. Figure 3-12 is a quick reference to
three-point perspective principles.

The use of three vanishing points creates
highly dynamic drawings that may easily
become distorted. Because all lines converge to vanishing points, no true-scale
measuring line can be employed. This

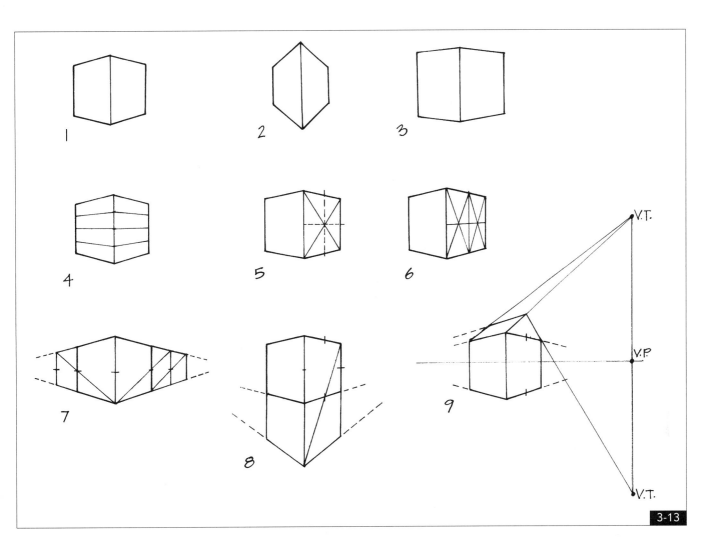

means that drawing three-point perspectives requires good visulization skills. Three-point perspective is most useful for portraying single objects, such as furniture or products, that by design should be dynamic, unusual, or attention-grabbing. Three-point perspective creates an "ant's-eye view" or "bird's-eye view" and is also used in some types of animation.

DEVELOPING VISUAL SKILLS

To develop visual skills and learn to "see" in perspective, students should practice drawing simple square-looking boxes in one-, two-, and three-point perspectives. I believe that the ability to draw accurate-looking boxes lies at the heart of successful perspective drawing. Figure 3-13 illustrates important principles of perspective sketching.

Boxes drawn in two-point perspective will appear distorted when the two vanishing points are located too close to each other on the horizon line. The vanishing points should be kept far enough apart to create an angle of 90 degrees or greater at the front edge of the cube. At the same time, the front edge of the cube should be less than 140 degrees (see Figure 3-13).

In two-point perspective the front corner (also known as the *vertical leading edge*) of an object is often used as a VERTICAL MEASURING LINE. This line can be scaled and then used to measure portions of the object

FIGURE 3-14

Sketching stairs in two-point perspective.

1. By measurement or estimation, plot the width and depth of the stairs on the floor plan. Locate a height plane by extending vertical lines to the appropriate height (the top of the stair run). Divide the height plane to create the appropriate number of risers.

2. Draw a line from the vanishing point through the height plane at the first riser measurement; this creates the first riser. Draw a diagonal line from the forward height of the first riser through the top of the height plane and continue this diagonal until it is directly above the V.P.; this is the vanishing trace (V.T.). Draw a second diagonal from the vanishing trace to the location opposite the forward riser.

3. Draw lines from the V.P. through each riser measurement on the height plane. Continue these lines until they intersect with diagonals; these are the forward riser locations.

4. Tread locations are found by extending vertical lines down to the next riser measurement; lines indicating treads converge to the appropriate vanishing point.

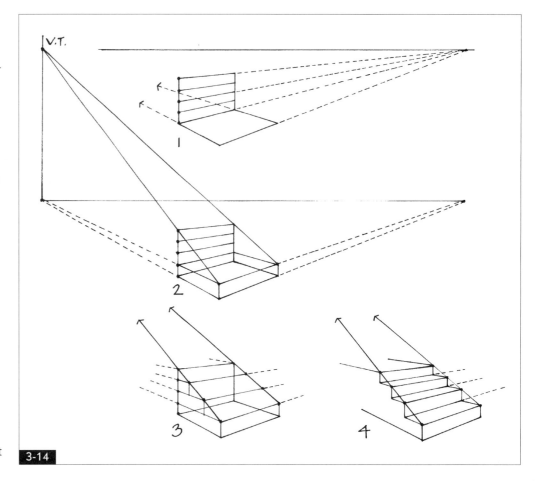

that recede toward the vanishing points. Vertical measuring lines allow for fairly accurate measurement of vertical elements of drawings. In principle, this line is the only element of a drawing that can be accurately scaled because the front corner that serves as a measuring line is touching the picture plane—or is very close to it (see Figure 3-13).

For dimensions that cannot be measured on vertical surfaces, a number of very simple proportional devices can be employed. One such method of proportional perspective measurement involves the use of diagonal lines as a means of subdividing squares and rectangular planes in perspective. Each face of a square can be subdivided into visually equal portions at the intersection of two diagonals. The intersection of diagonals drawn from corner to corner of a square

locates the midpoint of that square. Rectangular planes are also divided in this manner. Diagonal subdivision of rectangular planes is a significant perspective principle and is useful in all methods of perspective drawing (see Figure 3-13).

The use of diagonals can also aid in adding, extending, and duplicating boxes drawn in perspective. One method of doing this requires locating the midpoint of a single box or cube, then drawing a diagonal from the bottom corner of the cube through the midpoint of the far side of the cube. The diagonal is then extended from the midpoint to the top perspective line (that which recedes to the vanishing point). Where the diagonal meets the perspective line of the original cube, a new vertical is drawn, creating a second square that is visually equal in perspective (see Figure 3-13).

It is useful to learn to draw boxes with elements that have slanted surfaces, such as gabled roofs. These slanted surfaces do not fall on the primary horizon line. Instead the lines that form the slanting surfaces converge at a point directly above or below the vanishing point for the box. This point, known as a VANISHING TRACE (after Ching), is a line to which all parallel lines in the same plane will converge. A vanishing trace is employed because lines that are parallel always converge at a common point (see Figure 3-13).

A vanishing trace is also useful in relation to drawing stairs. Stairs can be drawn by first plotting the base of the stair (the width and depth as found on the floor plane). The height of the stair must then be located on a height plane. The height plane must be divided equally (use the forward vertical as a measuring line) in increments that equal the required number of risers. The first riser can be found by drawing a line from the appropriate vanishing point forward through the noted riser height and onward to the riser location as noted on the floor plan.

The next step involves drawing the vanishing trace. A vanishing trace is found by drawing a diagonal line from the forward location of the height of the riser to the top of the stair run (as measured on the height plane) and onward to a location directly above the vanishing point.

With this vanishing trace located, a second diagonal is drawn to the opposite side of the stair. Risers and treads are then located where measuring increments brought forward from vanishing points intersect with diagonals. Figure 3-14 gives instructions for stair construction.

Ellipses

Circles and curves are drawn as ELLIPSES in perspective. An understanding of ellipses and how they are drawn can help create natural looking perspective drawings (see Figures 3-15 and 3-16). Understanding the relationship of the major and minor axes of an ellipse is essential to successful perspective drawing. The MAJOR AXIS is an imaginary line that is found at the widest part of an ellipse, and the MINOR AXIS is found at the narrow diameter of the ellipse. An ellipse's major axis is greater than its minor axis. The major and minor axes always appear at right angles (90 degrees) to each other regardless of the position of the object. When found on horizontal planes, such as floors and ceilings, an ellipse's major axis is horizontal.

The centerline of a cylinder or cylindrical object is drawn as an extension of the minor axis. Because it is an extension of the minor axis, this centerline always appears at a right angle to the major axis. This means that the centerline of a complicated object, such as the axle of a wheel or the cylindrical base of a piece of furniture, can be drawn as an extension of the minor axis.

Understanding the relationship of the minor and major axes and the location of the centerline can eliminate distortion in the drawing of circular forms in perspective, and allows for freehand sketching of ellipses as well as construction of complex linear perspectives.

One method of ellipse construction involves using planes as an approximation guide for the ellipse (see Figure 3-16). This is done by first drawing a plane, which resembles a square in perspective, then dividing the square using a diagonal. On each diagonal, approximately two-thirds of the distance from the center point of the square, a dot (or mark) is drawn. The ellipse is then approximated by drawing curved lines from the dots on the diagonals to the midpoints of each side of the plane. With the rough approximation complete, the major and minor axes can be approximated to aid in refinement. The minor and major axes should not be

Ellipses.
1. Circle.
2. Ellipse. In perspective drawings, circles are drawn as ellipses.
3. The major axis is found at the widest diameter of an ellipse.
4. The minor axis is found at the narrow diameter and is always at 90 degrees to the major axis.
5. The centerline of a cylinder is drawn as an extension of the minor axis (also at 90 degrees to major axis).
6. When found on a horizontal plane such as a floor, the major axis is horizontal. Our view of the ellipse varies according to the location of our eye level (horizon line); elliptical templates are used to easily approximate the various views.

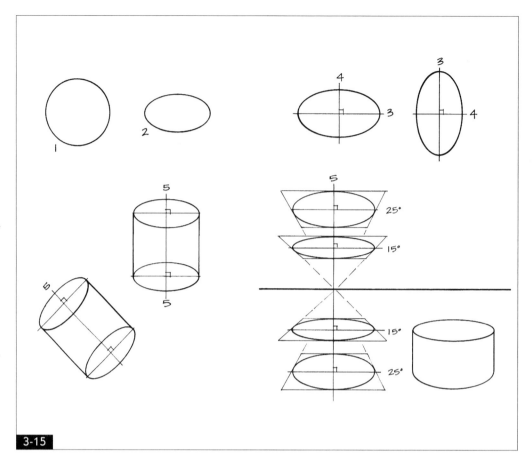

3-15

confused with the diagonal divisions of the plane, as these are separate items.

Many designers use elliptical templates to create accurate ellipses and curvilinear forms. The use of elliptical templates is based on the locations of the major axis, the minor axis, and the centerline of the form. When templates are used, the two-thirds estimating method is not employed.

Clearly, methods mentioned for drawing ellipses underscore the need to be able to draw a square-looking box accurately. This skill is perhaps the single most effective tool in freehand perspective drawing. It is worthwhile for students to practice by filling pages with boxes drawn to look square in two-point perspective. Once this skill has been developed, the box is drawn as an enclosing form, like a packing crate,

then portions of the box are subtracted to reveal the object within (see Figure 3-17). Starting with a simple box, and adding boxes using diagonal division, allows us to sketch items in boxes that are not square but may be elongated in a number of directions. Figure 3-18 depicts the steps involved in creating drawings in which an enclosing cube is employed to construct items that are quite different in form from the original enclosing cube.

The ability to visually assess freehand perspective drawings that have been constructed from simple boxes lets us understand and see form and spatial relationships. Employing the principles of perspective mentioned thus far allows for better drawing and for the use of perspective drawing as a design tool.

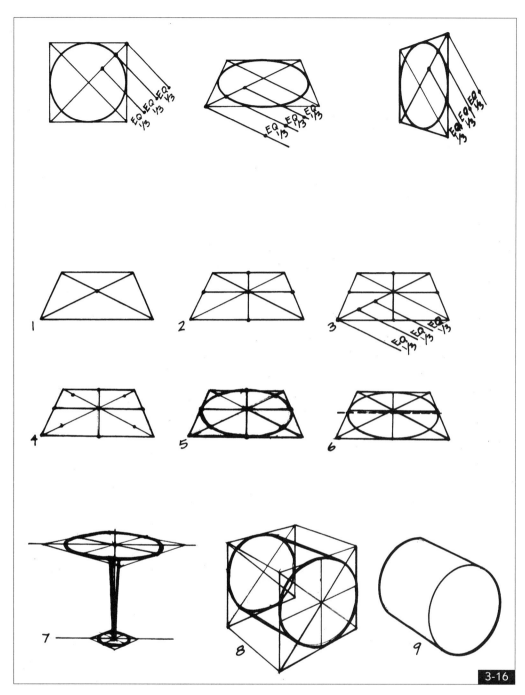

FIGURE 3-16

Quick reference: estimated ellipse construction. Based on their geometry, as shown at the top of the figure, ellipses can be estimated by creating an enclosing plane and plotting locations on diagonals.

1. Create an enclosing plane that appears square in perspective and divide the plane with diagonals (as in diagonal division). Mark the center as located by the diagonals.

2. From the center mark, extend lines vertically and horizontally; these lines will define midpoints of the enclosing plane. Mark the locations where these lines are tangent to (touching) the enclosing plane.

3. Divide each half of the diagonal into thirds and make marks at these locations.

4 and 5. Sketch the ellipse by locating the mark two-thirds from center and drawing connecting curvilinear lines from the two-thirds mark to the adjacent midpoint mark. Refine the ellipse by visual assessment.

6. Note: quarter divisions of the square are not the major and minor axes. These divisions are for estimation purposes only. The major axis is actually slightly forward of center (dashed line).

7. The central leg of this table is formed by a center line extending from the top minor axis to the lower minor axis.

8. A full cylinder can be sketched using an enclosing cube to create the forward and rear planes; these are then used to form the required ellipses.

9. Refine the final drawing by visual assessment.

FIGURE 3-17

Quick reference: two-point sketching using estimated boxes.

1. Sketch a box that approximates the dimensions of the object. Make sure the vanishing points are generously spaced. Create a measuring line at the front corner of the box. Mark equal divisions of the measuring line (these can be eyeballed or estimated with diagonal division).

2. Use the measuring line and diagonal division to rough out details and proportions.

3. Overlay with clean tracing paper and refine details.

4. Use a clean overlay for a final drawing; a combination of freehand and drafted lines often look best.

Drawing by Leanne Larson

3-17

REFERENCES

(Contains both works cited and recommended reading. Annotations where appropriate.)

Ching, Francis. *Architectural Graphics*. New York: John Wiley & Sons, 1996.

———. *A Visual Dictionary of Architecture*. New York: John Wiley & Sons, 1995.

Drpic, Ivo. *Sketching and Rendering Interior Space*. New York: Whitney Library of Design, 1988.

Forseth, Kevin, and David Vaughn. *Graphics for Architecture*. New York: John Wiley & Sons, 1980.

Hanks, Kurt, and Larry Belliston. *Rapid Viz*. Los Altos, CA: William Kaufman, 1980.

McGarry, Richard, and Greg Madsen. *Marker Magic: The Rendering Problem Solver for Designers*. New York: Van Nostrand Reinhold, 1993.

FIGURE 3-18
Quick reference: two-point sketching using estimated boxes.

1. A single square looking box can be extended, this case doubled (see Figure 3-13) with additional boxes added to contain additional design elements such as the curved arms on this sofa.

2. Additional details can be roughed out using the enclosing forms (boxes). Lines going to the appropriate vanishing point can serve as visual aids used to sketch items such as the beginning of the curves shown dashed (note that dashed lines originate from consistent points in perspective). Items such as the legs can be sketched into boxes as visual aids in the drawing process.

3. A clean overlay is drawn using the drawing roughed out in Step 2.

3-18

Olofsson, Erik, and Klara Sjölén. *Design Sketching*. Klippan, Sweden: Keeos Design Books, 2005.
   A beautiful and helpful book focused on product design sketching.

Pile, John. *Perspective for Interior Designers*. New York: Whitney Library of Design, 1985.

Porter, Tom. *Architectural Drawing*. New York: Van Nostrand Reinhold, 1990.

4 DRAWING AND SKETCHING INTERIOR ENVIRONMENTS

The same concepts that allow us to sketch objects using enclosing boxes can be employed in sketching interior environments. There are many methods of measured linear perspective drawing that work well in the creation of accurate, beautiful drawings. However, it is important to note that all of the most accurate and refined methods of manual perspective drawing require a great deal of time, ranging from one hour to eight hours or more. These may be appropriate for final design development presentations, but time constraints require designers to develop quick sketching techniques in order to use drawings throughout the design process. Quick sketching is beneficial as a design tool, a presentation tool, and a way of seeing the world and recording details successfully.

ESTIMATED ONE-POINT INTERIOR PERSPECTIVE DRAWINGS

The easiest method of quick sketching interior environments has as its foundation the box-sketching techniques discussed previously. This estimated method allows us to create a perspective of a 10-foot-square room by drawing a giant 10-foot-square box in one-point perspective. Figure 4-1 is a quick reference to this esti-mated one-point perspective method. It is important to note that this method is unusual in that it requires that a square-looking room is estimated, necessitating visual accuracy developed by practice.

The estimated sketch method is started by drawing a horizontal line to serve as the horizon line; this is the viewer's eye level. A square (that serves as the back wall of the room) can then be drawn that is 10 feet by 10 feet (in any appropriate scale or eye-balled). The horizon line should bisect the square at its vertical midpoint. Next, a single vanishing point is located on the horizon line slightly left or right of center. Perspective lines indicating depth are created by drawing lines from the vanishing point through all four corners of the square. The overall depth of the room is simply estimated.

The key to this method is the ability to estimate the forward depth of the square room. The depth must be estimated in a way that makes the room look square. This is the tricky part—which takes some practice. Once this is accomplished, architectural elements can be drawn by using measurements found on the back wall (the original square) and estimating depth. Diagonal bisection of planes can be used to find depths of walls and corresponding objects.

FIGURE 4-1

Quick reference: estimated one-point interior sketching.

1. Draw a 10' x 10' square in a workable scale (½" or 1").

2. Divide the square using diagonals. Draw a horizontal line through the center. This is the horizon line (H.L.); it is at roughly 5' high. Place a vanishing point on the horizon line slightly left or right of center.

3. Draw perspective lines from the V.P. through the corners of the original square, creating wall and ceiling lines. Now estimate the depth of the room—make it look square.

4. Use diagonals to divide the original square (see Figure 3-13), which is now the back wall. By dividing the back equally in four, you will create 30' height increments.

5. If necessary, a grid can be estimated through diagonal division. On side walls, verticals are located where height lines intersect diagonals.

6. Use measuring increments (created in Step 4) or a grid to locate objects and architectural elements.

7. Use a clean overlay to create a line drawing.

8. To raise or lower the ceiling, simply draw lines from the V.P. to the appropriate height on the back wall and extend these lines forward. Diagonal extensions can be used to enlarge the room (see Figure 3-13). Curves are found by plotting and sketching in appropriate locations.

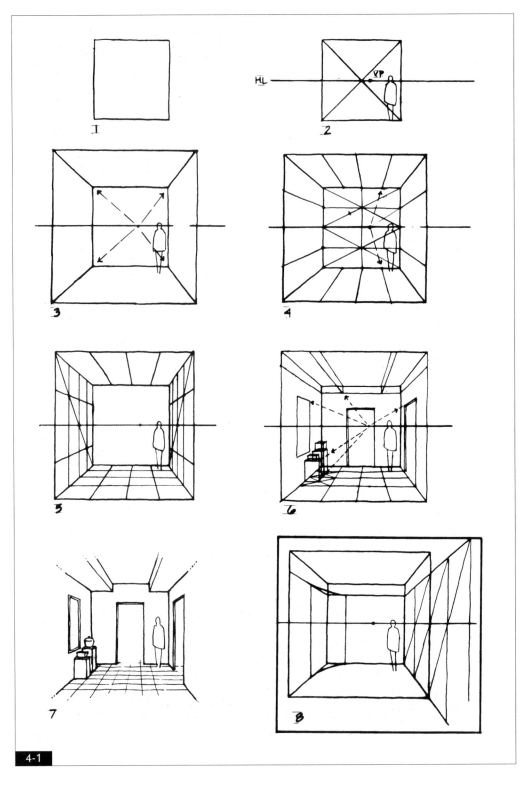

4-1

Because many rooms do not have 10-foot ceilings, it is often necessary to "lower" the ceiling by redrawing it at 8 to 9 feet. This is accomplished by locating the desired height on the back wall (the original measured square) and cutting the wall off at the desired height. Similarly, ceilings can be raised by adding the appropriate dimension to the back wall (the original square) and extending the walls to the desired height.

Most rooms are not perfectly square, and this method allows for the original 10-feet-by-10-feet square to serve as the starting point for a room of another shape. Dividing and adding to the room using diagonal bisection allows for the creation of a variety of room sizes. Once again, the ability to see and to create the original square room and use it as a guide for drawing a more complicated enviroment is the key to the success of this method.

In drawing estimated one-point interior perspectives, complicated items or architectural elements are easiest to draw when placed on the wall(s) parallel to the picture plane. The location of the single vanishing point is important because walls and objects located very close to their vanishing points can become quite distorted. It is useful to draw a few quick thumbnail sketches of the space, using the estimation method, to locate the vanishing point and visualize the space being drawn. Thumbnail sketches aid in the location of an appropriate view of the space and the location of the vanishing point.

4-2a

4-2b

4-2c

FIGURE 4-2a
This first step in constructing this drawing requires drawing the square-looking room shown in Figure 4-1 and modifying it. The bold lines in this drawing indicate the back wall of the original 10' x 10' room; dashed lines indicate the areas in which the room was elongated to set up the structure of the larger environment (in this case a hotel lobby and hallway). With the basic proportions of the environment complete, furnishings and additional elements can be roughed in.

FIGURE 4-2b
The drawing can be continued by adding necessary details and refining design elements.

FIGURE 4-2c
A final clean copy of the drawing can be traced and readied for rendering if necessary. Note: Perspective drawings benefit from the inclusion of scaled human figures; they have been omitted from this drawing in order to clearly show details to the reader.

4-3a

4-3b

Nook Area

FIGURE 4-3a

This first step in constructing this drawing requires drawing the square-looking room shown in Figure 4-1 and modifying it. The bold lines in this drawing indicate the back wall of the original 10' x 10' room; dashed lines indicate the areas in which the ceiling was altered, in this case to indicate a shed roof in a small New Mexico cabin. With the basic proportions of the environment complete, furnishings and additional elements can be roughed in.

FIGURE 4-3b

The drawing can be continued by adding necessary details and refining design elements and a final clean copy of the drawing can be traced and readied for rendering if necessary.

Note: Perspective drawings benefit from the inclusion of scaled human figures; they have been omitted from this drawing in order to clearly show details to the reader.

This estimated method is an approximation method. Measurements are based on rough approximations. For example, the horizon line is placed at roughly five feet in height, providing a view of the space from a five-foot eye level. We can imagine that most pieces of furniture fit into a 3o-inch-high packing crate. Therefore, much of the furniture is roughed in as 3o-inch-high boxes. Human figures drawn to scale should be included in interior perspectives and are best placed with eye levels at (or near) the horizon line. More information regarding scale figures can be found in Appendix 5.

This method of quick sketching, using rough approximations, allows designers to draw space as they design it. It also allows perspective drawing to be integrated into the design process during the schematic design and design development phases of a project prior to the completion of a full set of orthographic drawings (see Figures 4-2a through 4-2c, 4-3a, 4-3b, and 4-4a through 4-4c). Practice generating these types of drawing can provide the skills necessary for drawing quickly and directly in client meetings with simple pens and no tools (see Figures 4-5a and 4-5b). Most of the more refined methods of linear perspective require complete scaled plans and elevations, thus necessitat-

ing that the design be complete prior to the creation of the perspective drawings. The more refined perspectives are useful as a means of presentation but are not as helpful as a quick means of exploring design options or brainstorming.

ESTIMATED TWO-POINT INTERIOR PERSPECTIVE DRAWINGS

One-point interiors are helpful and easy to create but are limited in use because of problems with distortion, particularly in drawing furniture and freestanding objects. Because of the limitations of one point perspective, it is important to learn to draw two-point interior perspectives quickly using the estimation method.

The same concepts used in drawing boxes and estimated one point interiors are employed in estimated two-point perspective sketching. In the two-point method a 10-feet-by-10-feet square room is drawn first as a guideline for further development. Figure 4-6 is a quick reference for the estimated two-point perspective method.

The 10-feet-by-10-feet room is created by first drawing a single vertical measuring line with four equal segments noted (in any appropriate scale or eyeballed). This verti-

4-4a

4-4b

4-4c

FIGURE 4-4a

The first step in constructing this drawing requires drawing the square-looking room shown in Figure 4-1 and modifying it. The bold lines in this drawing indicate the back wall of the original 10' x 10' room; dashed lines indicate the areas in which the room was altered, in this case to create a much larger exhibition space.

FIGURE 4-4b

With the basic proportions of the environment complete, the basic design elements can be roughed in.

FIGURE 4-4c

Given the complexity of this environment, some extra steps are required to refine the design. Signage can be generated, photocopied, and pasted onto the drawing. Additional elements can be copied onto the drawing surface as the drawing is completed. Or the drawing can be scanned into Photoshop and have additional details such as signage or art added digitally as shown C-27a through C-27d on page 72.

cal measuring line serves two important functions: first, it is the only true measuring device in the drawing; second, it can become the back corner of the room(s) being drawn. A horizontal line is then drawn through the middle of the vertical line (bisecting it at the five-foot mark). This is the horizon line or viewer's eye level.

Two vanishing points must be placed on the horizon line. One should be located fairly close to the vertical measuring line; this is referred to as the *near vanishing point*. The second should be located far from the vertical measuring line; this is referred to as the *far vanishing point*.

Next, draw a line from the near vanishing point to the very bottom of the vertical measuring line and extend it forward, creating the floor line. Repeat the process with the far vanishing point. Lines are then

4-5a

kiosk   LOWER   HIGHER.

4-5b

FIGURE 4-5a and 4-5b
Practicing estimated one-point sketching leads to the ability to do quick sketches in client and team meetings. These drawings were done in less than ten minutes using simple ink pens.

drawn from each vanishing point to the top (the tenth increment) of the vertical measuring line and extended forward, creating the ceiling line.

At this point in the drawing we have created the floor, two walls, and the ceiling location of the room. The depth of the room must now be estimated. The overall room depth is approximated by visually assessing the room and creating a square-looking box of a room. As with one-point estimation, this is the tricky part. The key is the ability to estimate the depth of a 10-feet-by-10-feet square room, which takes some practice.

With the use of this method, architectural elements and freestanding objects are located by measurement and estimation. The vertical measuring line can be used to find vertical measurements; these are taken from the vanishing point through the vertical measuring line and plotted on the appropriate wall. In cases where objects are freestanding, heights can be determined by extending a line from the vanishing point through the appropriate height on the wall to the location of the object. Depths are estimated using diagonal division and extension—dividing the walls with diagonals and finding the midpoint of the room

at the intersection of the two diagonals.

The originally estimated square room can be modified to create a lower or higher ceiling by simply extending or reducing the dimensions of the original vertical measuring line and extending lines to the vanishing points. The walls of the room can be reconfigured easily by diagonal subdivision and extension. The ability to see and to create the original square-looking room and use it as a guide for drawing a more complicated environment is the key to the success of this method.

In drawing two-point interior perspectives, complicated items and architectural elements are easiest to draw when placed on the wall created by the far vanishing point. This is because the wall generated by the near vanishing point tends to become distorted. A common distortion problem in two-point perspective drawing is caused by locating the two vanishing points too close to each other. This creates a distorted, unnatural-looking view of the space. If in the process of using this method your drawing becomes distorted, it is best to start over with the vanishing points located farther from each other.

As with one-point sketches, it is useful to do a few thumbnail sketches of the space

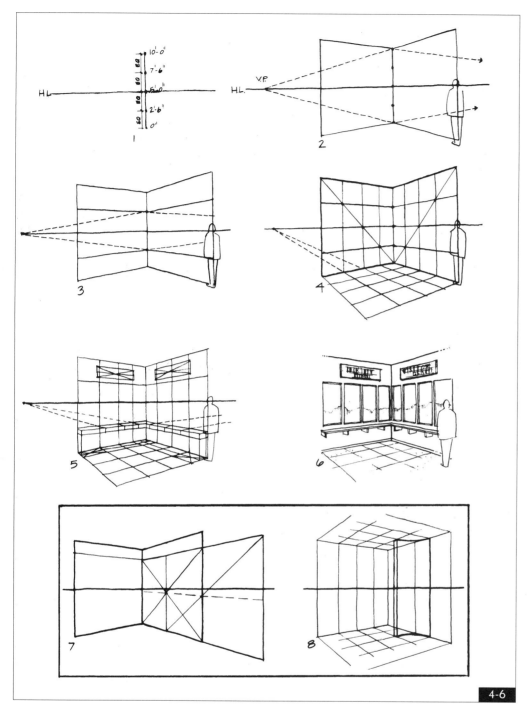

FIGURE 4-6

FIGURE 4-6
Quick reference: estimated two-point interior sketching.

1. Draw a single vertical line to serve as a measuring line. Divide the line into four equal segments. At the midpoint, draw a horizontal line; this is the horizon line (H.L.).

2. Place two vanishing points on the H.L., one near to the near vanishing point (N.V.P.) and one far from the far vanishing point (F.V.P.) the measuring line. Draw lines from each V.P. through the top and bottom of the measuring line. This creates floor and ceiling lines. Now estimate the depth of room—make it look square.

3. Draw lines from each V.P. through all increments on the measuring line; these will serve as height measurement lines.

4. To create a grid, draw diagonals on each wall. Then, at the intersection of the diagonal and each height line, draw a vertical.

5. Use the grid to estimate architectural elements and objects. Note: Grids are not always necessary; for simple spaces it is best to simply estimate measurements.

6. Use a clean overlay for tracing and refining the drawing.

7. Raise or lower the ceiling by estimating the desired height. Extend the room using diagonal division (see Figure 3-13 on page 105).

8. Curved surfaces are estimated by using a grid.

to locate the vanishing points and visualize the space being drawn. Thumbnail sketches allow for the location of an appropriate view of the space and the proper positioning of the vanishing points.

This estimated two-point perspective method is an approximation method. Measurements are based on rough approximations. For example, the horizon line is placed at roughly 5 feet in height. This gives the drawing the overall view at eye level of the viewer. We can imagine that most pieces of furniture fit into a 3o-inch-high packing crate. Therefore, much of the

4-7b

4-7c

FIGURE 4-7a

This first step in constructing this drawing requires drawing the square-looking room shown in Figure 4-6 and modifying it. The bold lines in this drawing indicate the back wall of the original 10' x 10' room; dashed lines indicate the areas in which the room was elongated (to the left) and the ceiling was lowered to roughly 8' above the floor.

FIGURE 4-7b

With the basic proportions of the environment complete, furnishings and additional elements can be "roughed in."

FIGURE 4-7c

The drawing is then continued by adding necessary details and refining design elements. A final clean copy of the drawing can be traced and readied for rendering if necessary. In preparing this more refined drawing, templates were used for hanging lamps and tools were used for edges of furniture. Figures C-27a through C-27d on page 72 show the process of color-rendering this drawing and using Photoshop for finishing touches. Note: Perspective drawings benefit from the inclusion of scaled human figures; they have been omitted from this drawing in order to clearly show details to the reader.

furniture can be sketched into the space as 3o-inch-high boxes. Human figures drawn to scale should be included in interior perspectives and are best placed with eye levels located at or near the horizon line. This method of estimating two-point perspective drawings perspective allows drawing to be integrated into the design process during the schematic design and design development phases of a project (see Figures 4-7a through 4-7c, and 4-8a through 4-8c, which show the various steps in constructing "estimated" two-point perspective drawings for a range of projects).

Methods of estimated sketching, using rough approximation as described here (also known as *eyeballing* drawings), permit designers to draw a space as they design it. This type of sketching allows perspective drawing to be integrated into the design process. Sketching in perspective lets us visualize spaces three-dimensionally rather than merely view space in plan,

4-8a

4-8b

4-8c

FIGURE 4-8a

This first step in constructing this drawing requires drawing the square-looking room shown in Figure 4-6 and modifying it. The bold lines in this drawing indicate the back wall of the original 10' x 10' room; dashed lines indicate the areas in which the room was elongated (to the rear of the original square).

FIGURE 4-8b

With the basic proportions of the environment complete, the basic design elements can be roughed in. This particular drawing was done very early in the design process and was used to consider the entire volume of the retail design. Type was printed and pasted into the signage area as a means of understanding scale issues.

FIGURE 4-8c

A final clean copy of the drawing can be traced and readied for rendering if necessary. In preparing this more refined drawing, some elements were drawn freehand while tools were used for others. The type (the word *sushi*) shown in the previous figure was modified (by hand) to relate directly to the right vanishing point.

where a sense of volume is often missing. Visualization skills are fundamental to the design of interior environments.

Most of the more refined methods of linear perspective require complete scaled plans and elevations, thus necessitating the design to be complete prior to the creation of the perspective drawings. The more refined perspectives often appear highly realistic in contrast to the estimated methods. Refined, measured linear perspectives are most useful as a means of presentation for clients, end users, real estate professionals, investors, and the general public.

FIGURE 4-9a
Quick reference: two-point plan projection.

1. Draw a horizontal line; this is the picture plane (P.P.). Select the desired angle of view and orient the plan so that the rear corner touches the picture plane. Locate the station point (S.P.); make sure all desired elements fit within a 60-degree cone of vision projecting from the S.P. to the desired areas in plan. Locate the station point one to three times the height of the interior space from the focal point of the drawing.

2. Draw lines from the S.P. to the P.P. that are parallel to the walls of the floor plan; the locations of the intersections of these lines and the P.P. are the setup vanishing points, vanishing point right (V.P.R.) and vanishing point left (V.P.L.).

3. Draw a horizontal line below the plan setup; this is the horizon line (H.L.). Project the location of V.P.L. and V.P.R. vertically to the H.L.; this relocates the vanishing points. Project a line from the rear corner of plan vertically to the H.L.; this will be the measuring line (M.L.). It can be measured in scale (to match plan); it will also be the back corner of the room. The horizon line must be located at 5' to 6' in scale on the M.L. (normal eye level).

4. Draw lines from the V.P.L. through the top and bottom of the M.L. These are the wall and floor lines. Repeat this step with V.P.R. Next, draw lines from the S.P. through the ends of walls (in plan) to the P.P. Project these locations vertically onto the drawing.

5. Draw lines from the S.P. through window locations, or any other elements (in plan), to the P.P. Project these locations vertically onto the drawing. Heights are determined by measuring from M.L. or from an available elevation.

REFINED LINEAR PERSPECTIVE METHODS

The perspective drawing concepts and skills covered thus far can help us gain valuable visualization skills. These skills are easily transferred to the more refined, measured methods of linear perspective. Therefore, the ability to draw well in estimated perspective allows us to draw well in refined, precisely measured perspectives.

The ability to create refined perspective presentation drawings is useful for all environmental designers. Most firms have at least one employee (and often several) who is considered to be a perspective drawing or rendering specialist. Such individuals are often called upon to do much of the detailed perspective drawing and rendering for the firm. It is also quite common for firms to hire professional design illustrators and renderers to create highly detailed drawings as required for particular project presentations. Firms often select a particular professional illustrator's style to enhance a project. Increasingly, digital modeling software is used to create perspective "drawings" used in presentations; some of these programs are discussed in later in this chapter.

A wide variety of methods of measured perspective drawing are used in practice. I have found that certain methods work best for certain people. People who draw well in measured perspective employ the particular method that works best for them. For this reason a variety of methods are discussed briefly and illustrated in the following sections. Students should experiment with the described methods to discover a personal method of measured perspective drawing.

TWO-POINT PLAN PROJECTION METHOD

Two-point plan projection, is also known as the *common method* or the *office method*. A comparable method is used commonly for exterior perspectives, and a similar one-point method is used as well. The plan projection method requires a completed scaled floor plan and scaled elevations, which means the project must be well resolved for this method of drawing to take place. Figures 4-9a and 4-9b illustrate step-by-step plan projection instructions.

This method is completely different from any perspective methods discussed previously. Although it is useful and highly accurate, it can be confusing at first because it requires going back and forth from plan view to perspective view. To minimize confusion, one must understand that the floor plan is used to set up the final perspective elements and measurements. In this method the floor plan is manipulated to provide information that is projected onto the perspective drawing.

To begin this method, decisions must be made as to what view of the space is desired, the location of the viewer, and the cone of vision. Key elements of the space must be included within a 60-degree cone of vision. With decisions made regarding the areas to be shown and the orientation of the viewer, the plan is set up against the picture plane (also drawn in plan).

The plan setup must also include the location of the viewer in plan; this is known as the station point, but I like my students to think of it as the head of the viewer in plan. The station point, or location of the viewer, is extremely important to the success of this method. The location of the station point dictates the view of the space, as well as the cone of vision and other key elements, such as the location of the vanishing points.

With the plan set up against the picture plane and the station point located, the

FIGURE 4-9b

Quick reference: locating free-standing objects using plan projection.

1. Draw lines from the S.P. through the edges of the object and extend them to the P.P. Project these locations vertically onto the drawing.

2. To find a floor location, first transfer the furniture location onto walls in plan setup (a). Then draw lines from the S.P. to locations on walls; extend the S.P. to locations on walls; extend the lines to P.P. Next project locations on the P.P. vertically to the appropriate wall in the drawing (b). Draw a line from the V.P. to the location where the wall projection meets the floor (c); extend these lines forward onto the object to find the floor location.

3. Find the height of objects by drawing a line from V.P. (in this case, V.P.R.) through the appropriate height on the M.L. to the wall location (c).

4. The object is completed with lines drawn to the appropriate vanishing points.
Note: Often when a drawing looks wrong or "off," it is because a location was not projected from the P.P.

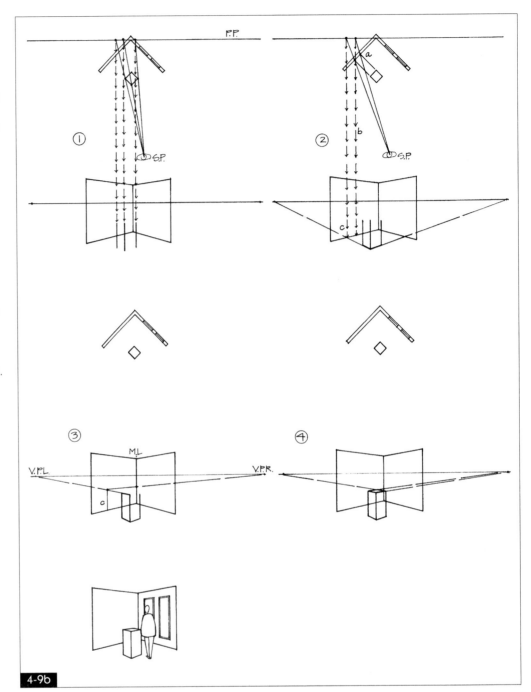

4-9b

vanishing points can be located on the picture plane in plan. This is done by drawing lines from the station point parallel to the walls of the room (or building) that terminate at the picture plane. This method requires that lines be drawn from the station point to the location on the plan, to the picture plane, and then projected onto the perspective drawing.

Most students find it helpful to recognize two separate types of activity within this method: (1) those set up in plan and related to the picture plane and (2) those then projected from the picture plane to the perspective drawing. Measurements of width and depth are projected from the picture plane onto the perspective drawings. Heights are taken from the measuring line or elevation(s) and tranferred to the appropriate location.

The plan projection method is generally accurate and provides an excellent perspective framework. But it can be time-consuming and sometimes leads to unexpected distortion, requiring the entire process to be completed a second time. I find that the method works best for environments based on simple geometric forms rather than those based on complex or organic forms. Figures 4-10a through 4-10j delineate the various steps in a plan projection method drawing for a residential project.

Increasingly, my students are using this method to draw perspective views in Auto-CAD (in the 2-D AutoCAD environment), they do this in order to create drawings with crisp consistent lines weights and in order to have line weights and types that are consistent with drawings drafted on AutoCAD used within the same presentation.

FIGURE 4-10a

1. In beginning the drawing, the desired view must be selected. In this case the plan is oriented to provide a view of the rear corner of the kitchen to include the kitchen cabinets.

2. The picture plane should pass through the rear corner of the plan with the walls you wish to include in the drawing on the left and right.

3. Create a station point directly below the rear corner of the plan (there are other ways to do this, but this is the easiest). The station point indicates the location of the viewer. This point should be located roughly 2 to 3 times the height of the room (in the same scale as the plan).

4. Draw a line (dashed here) from the station point to the picture plane; this line must be parallel to the back walls of the room in plan.

5. The actual perspective drawing is begun by projecting the location of the back corner down vertically through the station point and well below (or above) the plan.

6. The line projected in Step 5 now becomes the measuring line. This line is drawn to the desired height of the room (in this case 9'), in the same scale as the original plan was created. It is helpful to draw "tic marks" that indicate 1' increments on the measuring line.

7. A horizontal line is now drawn to serve as the horizon line for the perspective drawing. In most drawings it should be located at eyeball height, in this case 5'5". The vanishing points should be projected vertically directly from the picture plane onto this new horizon line.

8. If desired, an elevation can be placed alongside the perspective drawing to aid in establishing height measurements.

9. Wall and ceiling lines can now be drawn from opposite vanishing point to the appropriate heights on the measuring line.

4-10a

FIGURE 4-10b

1. Wall and object locations are found by locating the item on the plan and projecting a line from the station point to the location on the plan, onward to the picture plane, and down onto the drawing.

2. In this case a line is drawn from the station point to the cabinet, onward to the picture plane, and then projected vertically from the picture plane to the drawing. Note: If your drawing looks weird, you are not projecting consistently down from the picture plane.

3. The height of the lower cabinets is found by counting off the measuring line, in this case 3'. Some people prefer to obtain the height dimensions by transferring them from the adjacent elevations.

4-10b

FIGURE 4-10c

1. The sink location is found by drawing a line from the station point to the front corners of the sink, onward to the picture plane, and then onto the drawing.

2. The dishwasher is found by drawing a line from the station point to the front corners of the dishwasher, onward to the picture plane, and then onto the drawing.

3. To find the heights of the wall cabinets it is necessary to first locate the height on the original measuring line (in this case the height information is transferred from the adjacent elevation).

4. Because the cabinets are recessed into the wall (see plan), it is necessary to draw a line from the station point to the rear edge of the cabinet, onto the picture plane, and project this location onto the drawing.

5. The lower cabinets are completed when lines are drawn from the edges of the cabinets to the appropriate vanishing points.

4-10c

4-10d

FIGURE 4-10d

1. The angled portion of the lower cabinets is created by drawing a line from the station point to the edges of the angled portion onward to the picture plane, and then the lines are projected onto cabinets in the drawing.

2. The location of the stove is found by drawing a line from the station point to the front corners of the stove, onward to the picture plane, and then down onto the drawing.

3. This piece of furniture is located by drawing lines from the station point to the three visible edges of the object, onward to the picture plane, and then onto the drawing. The height of the object is determined by locating it on the measuring line and then transferring, by use of the vanishing point (dashed lines).

4. The upper cabinets can be completed by working from the measuring line and the vanishing points, similarly to Step 3 above.

4-10e

FIGURE 4-10e

1. The island, which is freestanding, is drawn using a combination of projected lines. Lines are drawn from the station point to the three visible edges of the island, onward to the picture plane, and then down to the drawing, creating the island's corner locations.

2. Because the item is freestanding, its height and actual floor location must be determined by transferring the object location onto walls in plan setup (dashed lines in plan).

3. Lines are then drawn from the station point to the plan wall locations found in Step 2 above, onward to the picture plane, and then onto the corresponding walls in the perspective drawing. Now, working on the perspective drawing, lines are drawn from the left vanishing point to the location where the wall projection (done in Step 2) meets the floor, and these lines are extended forward to the corners of the island. The height of the island is taken from the measuring line and extended using the vanishing points.

FIGURE 4-10f

At this stage, a quick overlay sketch can be created to determine the quality of the perspective drawing and locate any problem areas.

FIGURE 4-10g

1. With the significant features completed, the plan is no longer necessary because most height and spatial relationships can be determined through use of the measuring line and vanishing points.

2. The location of the hood and cabinets above the stove is found by drawing lines upward from the back corners of the stove to the upper cabinets (dashed line with arrows). These locations are brought forward through use of the left vanishing point and then drawn on the front face of the upper cabinets.

3. To finalize the details of the freestanding buffet, dimensions are found on the measuring line, brought "behind" the buffet, and extended using the left vanishing point.

4-10f

4-10g

V. P.

4-10h

4-10i

FIGURE 4-10h
Using diagonal division, various details can be considered and drawn in place.

FIGURE 4-10i
Additional design elements can be estimated or measured.

FIGURE 4-10j
The final clean version of the drawing. Steps involved in rendering this drawing can be found in Figures C-24a and C-24b on page 69.

4-10j

PREPARED PERSPECTIVE GRID CHARTS

Prepared perspective charts are used by designers and design illustrators. Charts are popular owing to their ease of use and speed of drawing construction. Many designers and illustrators use only prepared charts in the construction of perspective drawings.

The charts provide a perspective framework including horizon line, location of viewer, cone of vision, vanishing points, and measuring devices. This framework allows items to be located, measured, and drawn to appropriate vanishing points. Visual accuracy and the ability to draw ellipses and square-looking boxes are required in the use of prepared charts, just as they are in quick sketching. These skills are necessary because grids merely provide a perspective framework and measuring system—they do not do the drawing for you.

Perspective charts are based on a set of given conditions. The location and height of viewer (and corresponding horizon line), vanishing points, cone of vision, measuring increments, and the overall visual emphasis of the space are all given within a particular chart. For this reason it is helpful to keep a set of charts with varying views and spatial relationships for use in various projects. Generally perspective charts cover a huge area and must be manipulated and measured to define the space required in a drawing.

Because the charts contain hundreds of lines, they can be confusing and difficult to read. It is a good idea to use a variety of colored pencils on tracing paper overlays to define the space and record important elements. Elements that establish the space—such as the horizon line, vanishing points, vertical measuring lines, and wall, floor, and ceiling grid lines—can be transferred to tracing paper using various colors. With these elements and other useful notes recorded, the original grid can be removed and a customized grid created. The customized grid should be overlaid with tracing paper and kept for future reference.

Grid charts are useful, relatively quick, accurate, and adaptable. Because one chart

FIGURE 4-11

A prepared perspective grid chart.

4-11

4-12a

4-12b

4-12c

4-12d

FIGURE 4-12a
The prepared chart customized for a particular project, the Royal Pavilion, Brighton, England.

FIGURES 4-12b through 4-12e
The sequence of drawings prepared with the use of a grid, leading to a final line drawing of the Royal Pavilion, Brighton, England.

Drawings for Figures 4-12a through 4-12e by Leanne Larson

4-12e

will not work for all projects, a series of charts is worth having. And, as discussed, all projects require that the grid be manipulated or customized to some degree, which can be confusing, especially for beginners. Figure 4-11 is an example of a prepared grid. Figures 4-12a through 4-12e are a sequence of drawings using a prepared grid drawing. (See Figures C-6a and C-6 b on page 56 for drawings based on a grid used by a professional illustrator.) An additional simplified grid that can be copied and used for constructing drawings can be found in Appendix 6.

USING PHOTOGRAPHS

Photographs can be traced to form a perspective framework. This method is especially useful in renovating existing space where a photograph of existing conditions is used. This method requires that a photograph be taken from the desired vantage point. In this situation it is necessary to be careful that the photograph is clearly taken from a one-point or two-point perspective vantage point. Once the photograph is processed or downloaded, it can be enlarged, and can be printed as necessary. The enlarged photograph is then overlaid with tracing paper, and the drawing can be constructed. Figure 4-13 is a quick reference of this method.

If the photograph is taken with the primary wall parallel to the camera lens (picture plane), a one-point perspective view is generated. The drawing in this case is constructed with one vanishing point located on the horizon line. This is done by tracing over the lines that form the floor and ceiling lines (or any series of major perspective lines). The location where these lines converge is the vanishing point.

A horizontal line is drawn through the vanishing point, and this serves as the horizon line. It is useful to check this location by tracing perspective lines from an additional object in the space and making sure they converge at the same vanishing point. With the vanishing point and horizon line noted, new or proposed design elements can be sketched into the space. Items to be retained in the proposed design can simply be traced from the photograph. Figure 4-13 illustrates this process.

Two-point perspectives can be drawn from photographs that show the two main walls or elements as oblique to the camera lens (picture plane). The system is similar to that used in one-point tracing, except for the fact that two vanishing points must be located and placed on the horizon line. Most often, the correct vanishing point can be

4-13

located by tracing the left floor and ceiling lines (or the corresponding lines of some significant object) to a point of convergence. The left vanishing point is estimated by tracing the right floor and ceiling lines (or the corresponding lines of some significant object) to a point of convergence.

A horizon line is created by drawing a horizontal line connecting the right and left vanishing points. It is imperative that the horizon line link the two vanishing points with a single horizontal line. With the two vanishing points and horizon line located, proposed changes can be sketched into the drawing. All elements to be retained in the proposed design may be traced into the drawing.

Generally photographs taken of existing spaces include a number of interesting background and foreground elements. Human figures, plants, and details of daily life are often captured in photographs. These elements can be traced into the drawing to add interest and liveliness. Students often remove these items, creating lifeless drawings.

Students are sometimes reluctant to trace perspective drawings from photographic images because it could be considered plagiarism. If, however, the photographs provide *only a perspective framework* for new and original design ideas, plagiarism is not an issue. Clearly, plagiarism is involved when a drawing done by another individual is traced without credit given or if a design is lifted in totality and traced. Many professional illustrators and renderers keep a huge file of photographs of human figures, furnishings, and other elements to be traced into drawings as well as files of digital imagery for use in computer-generated drawings.

Digital photographs can be taken and drawn over by hand, creating a sketch of the new design or design elements. These can then be combined, using Photoshop, to create a combination of hand and digital drawing. This is done by hand tracing over the original image using pencil or pen on tracing paper. The traced drawing is then scanned and imported into a Photoshop file containing the orginal photograph. The underlying photograph can be adjusted in terms of brightness and contrast. New layers can be added on top of the original photograph layer—but under the line drawing—to add color and detail to the presentation.

DIGITAL MODELS AND DRAWINGS

Currently, architectural and interior designers are using a range of software programs to create three-dimensional models and perspective "drawings." MicroStation, ArchiCAD, AutoCAD, Revit, and other programs allow for three-dimensional models to be created. These models can be viewed digitally as well as printed. Printed versions can be used as underlays for hand sketching or can be imported into a secondary rendering program for use in design presentations, Examples of such images can be found in Figures 4-14a through 4-14c, 4-15, 4-16a, and 4-16b.

There are also modeling and animation programs such as Autodesk 3ds Max® and VIZ®, Rhinoceros®, and form-Z, which allow for modeling and rendering of architectural environments. Additional information about rendering models and related software can be found in Figures in Chapter 5.

Computer-generated three-dimensional images are highly accurate and provide great flexibility because changes can be made quickly and consistently. Many of the most elegant and complex three-dimensional modeling programs can be rather time-consuming to master, with most design students learning how to use one of the programs while in school. However, advances in technology are leading to three-dimensional

FIGURES 4-14a, 4-14b, AND 4-14c

This is a CAD three-dimensional view generated using AutoCAD (3-D). Figure 4-14a shows the wire-frame version, 4-14b shows a cleaned-up AutoCAD version, and 4-14c shows a version drawn by hand (using 4-15b as an underlay). The fresh line work creates a pleasing approachable drawing. Figure C-28 on page 73 is a final version rendered using Photoshop ("primarily the airbrush tool").

By Cuningham Group Architecture, P.A.

FIGURE 4-15
The background portion of this drawing was originally created in AutoCAD, and the foreground elements were drawn by hand because they were not included in the original AutoCAD view. The drawing was then photocopied.
Design and drawing by Jack Zellner

4-15

FIGURES 4-16a AND 16-b
Preliminary sketches of details for a retail project were created by hand, illustrating the importance of hand drawing skills in design ideation and development. The final design presentation was created in 3D Studio VIZ.
Design and drawings by Dirk Olbrich

4-16a

4-16b

FIGURE 4-17a
Using SketchUp's pencil/line tool is a way to create the base of a solid that can be manipulated to create a model from scratch.

FIGURE 4-17b
Using SketchUp's rectangle tool is another way to create the base of a solid that can be manipulated to create a model from scratch. Once an enclosed surface is formed the surface can be "pulled up" to create a three-dimensional form.

FIGURE 4-17c
Other shapes tools such as the circle shown here create surfaces in a range of shapes, all of which can be "pulled up" using the push-pull tool.

FIGURE 4-17d
Shadows are easily added by selecting "View"—"shadows." A range of views from isometric (shown at left) to plan and elevations (shown at right) are available for viewing by clicking the icon for the desired view.

4-17a

4-17b

4-17c

4-17d

FIGURES 4-18a AND 4-18b
This SketchUp model was built from scratch using the tools shown in the previous figure. SketchUp allows for the easy creation of different views and selection of line styles that give the drawings an appealing sketch quality.

modeling programs with easier learning curves than earlier programs.

One such program is Google's SketchUp, which is a very easy-to-navigate, three-dimensional modeling program that is currently being used by many interior designers, architects, and students. I find it an excellent tool to use in conjunction with hand-drawn images, it is also somewhat inexpensive and is available in a trial version online. Owing to its quick learning curve and quickly generated three-dimensional models, SketchUp is an excellent aid in the design process because it allows for speedy ideation studies as well as more elaborate modeling. SketchUp models can be built directly using the various tools to extrude or "pull up" forms and to add additional details and elements, as shown in Figures 4-17a through 4-17d. While SketchUp's rendering capacity is somewhat limited, it allows for a selection of line weights and styles so that the models it creates serve well as line drawings or as a framework with which to develop hand-drawn overlays, as shown in Figures 4-18a and 4-18b.

In addition to building models from scratch, two-dimensional drawings done by hand or using CAD programs can be imported into SketchUp; walls and other elements can then be "pulled up" or extruded using the two-dimensional drawing as a base, as shown in Figures 4-19a through 4-19g.

4-19a

4-19b

4-19c

4-19d

4-19e

4-19f

4-19g

FIGURE 4-19a
SketchUp also allows for two- and three-dimensional drawings to be imported into files. This is done by selecting "File"—"import" and choosing the desired file.

FIGURE 4-19b
With the file imported the pencil/line tool must be used to trace over all of the necessary lines to create surfaces.

FIGURE 4-19c
With the lines traced to created individual surfaces for walls and objects, the push-pull tool can pull selected surfaces to appropriate heights.

FIGURES 4-19d AND 4-19e
Architectural components, scale figures, furnishings, and other elements can be selected and dragged and dropped (inserted) into the drawing or model. To do this; go to "Window"—"components"—libraries of these elements must first be downloaded into the components files.

FIGURE 4-19f
Textures, colors, and patterns can be used for simple renderings. Go to "Window"—"materials," and then select desired material or color and select the appropriate face in the model. New samples or materials can be imported into this library for use.

FIGURE 4-19g
Printing or exporting into different files is done by selecting "File"—"export." Figures C-38a and C-38b on page 79 show another project presented using a SketchUp model.

DRAWING COMPOSITION AND CROPPING

Care must be taken with drawing composition, regardless of the method used to create a drawing. Generally, a decision must be made regarding what portion or portions of a space should be shown. Most of the drawing methods discussed to this point, whether manual or digital, allow for creation of a drawing that includes large portions of a room, some of which may be unnecessary to include in the final composition. In addition, certain artistic liberties may be taken with cropping or elimination of the elements of a drawing that are awkward or that may create an awkward composition.

In considering drawing composition, it is important to determine if any particular element should serve as a focal point. For example, if a drawing is to serve a tool that communicates the design of a reception desk, the reception desk should be included as completely as possible in the final composition. While this may seem obvious to some, the process of drawing occasionally leads one to forget what he point of the drawing is in the first place. Taking the example of the reception desk further, it is worth noting that including the desk does

not mean it must sit in the center of the composition; centering important items is not necessary—simply including them as fully as possible is most important.

Often when portions of a drawing are edited out or cropped it is helpful to employ some graphic device to make the drawing read well visually. This means that thought should be given as to how the drawing will "begin" and "end" on the the page. Common methods for doing this include using an element of the foreground to serve as an ending or beginning of the drawing as shown in Figure 4-20; in addition, using an architectural element to end the drawing is also useful (see Figure 4-21). Creating a continuous line that forms a frame around the drawing is another useful compositional device (see Figures 4-22 and 4-23). Another method calls for the use of broken lines on elements of the drawing that move past the cone of vision of the drawing (as shown in previous Figures 4-2c and 4-3b). While there are additional graphic devices that may be employed in drawing composition, those mentioned above are perhaps the most common.

With the drawing composition considered and complete, another decision must

FIGURE 4-20

A foreground element (stylized sofa arm) is used as a framing element in this composition along with a range of line weights creating a successful composition.

Design and drawing by Jack Zellner

4-20

FIGURE 4-21

Architectural elements are used to frame this drawing and create a successful composition.

By Matt Saunders

4-21

stair study

4-22

FIGURE 4-22
An outline is used to frame this drawing in conjunction with a foreground element, creating a dynamic composition.
By Matt Saunders

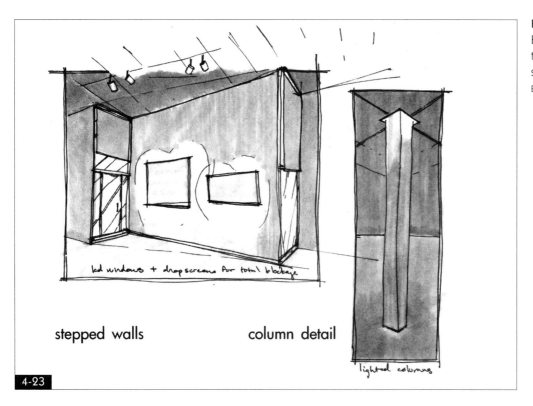

stepped walls

column detail

4-23

FIGURE 4-23
Boxed frames help to make these quick sketches part of a successful composition.
By Matt Saunders

be made as to whether the drawing will remain as a simple, clean, line drawing or further enhanced through rendering. Rendering is covered in detail in the following chapter. Additional information about composing the complete design presentation may be found in Chapter 8, beginning on page 225.

REFERENCES

(Contains both works cited and recommended reading. Annotations where appropriate.)

Ching, Frank. *A Visual Dictionary of Architecture*. New York: John Wiley & Sons, 1995.

———. *Architectural Graphics*. New York: John Wiley & Sons, 1996.

Drpic, Ivo. *Sketching and Rendering Interior Space*. New York: Whitney Library of Design, 1988.

Forseth, Kevin, and David Vaughn. *Graphics for Architecture*. New York: John Wiley & Sons, 1980.

Hanks, Kurt, and Larry Belliston. *Rapid Viz*. Los Altos, CA.: William Kaufman, 1980.

Leggit, Jim. *Drawing Shortcuts*. New York: John Wiley & Sons, 2002.

McGarry, Richard, and Greg Madsen. *Marker Magic: The Rendering Problem Solver for Designers*. New York: John Wiley & Sons, 1993.

Pile, John. *Perspective for Interior Designers*. New York: Whitney Library of Design, 1985.

Porter, Tom. *Architectural Drawing*. New York: John Wiley & Sons, 1990.

5

RENDERING

In the world of architecture and design the term RENDERING is used to describe the visual enhancement of drawings through the use of value or color. Rendering visually enhances drawings, making them more easily understood and allowing for greater visual communication in design presentations. Rendering is often done to convey depth and to allow a two-dimensional drawing surface to appear more three-dimensional, thus revealing the material qualities of forms.

Because rendering can help clients understand a project, it is useful as a means of communication. However, some project budgets and schedules do not allow time for highly detailed renderings, whereas other projects require extensive detailed rendering. This means that projects have different presentation parameters, requiring a range of rendering skills—from quick and loose to accurate and refined.

The level of rendering is also influenced by the phase of the design process in which the presentation takes place. For example, during the preliminary stages of design, it is wise to keep renderings loose and sketchy to avoid having the project pinned down prematurely. It is best to consider carefully the audience and purpose before beginning the actual rendering.

Many students approach rendering with fear and lack of self-confidence. However, an understanding of basic rendering concepts and techniques can allow designers and students to enhance a visual presentation significantly. There are dozens of rendering techniques, materials, and tools available. Practice, study, and the use of reference material can help designers to develop a personal system of rendering.

This chapter is an overview of rendering covering some basic concepts, materials, and techniques. Orthographic drawings are rendered differently than perspective drawings and, for that reason, are covered separately in this chapter. Paraline drawings are rendered in a manner similar to perspective drawings and are discussed with them. Increasingly students are using Photoshop software to render all sorts of presentation drawings; information about that can be found as it relates to each drawing type within this chapter. As mentioned previously, many three-dimensional modeling programs include rendering capabilities. There are also additional specific rendering programs that are used in conjunction with some modeling programs; however, these are not described here as they are all rather complex and require considerable, specific instructions that fall beyond the scope of this book.

RENDERING AS ILLUMINATION

The most important thing to understand about rendering is that, regardless of style, it introduces qualities of illumination to a drawing. This means that good rendering introduces light into a drawing, making it appear more natural and creating the illusion of three dimensions. Rendering requires consideration of the light source, or sources, found in the environment and the resulting value relationships. This is true for quick sketches and elaborate illustrations, for colored and noncolored renderings. The illumination in a rendering is perhaps its single most important aspect.

Simply stated, light falls on an object and illuminates its surfaces to varying degrees. The type of lighting, the location of the light source(s), and the object's material qualities all affect the manner in which the object is illuminated. Without consideration of the light source(s) and the related value relationships, renderings always look like something out of a child's coloring book.

As a light source illuminates an object, it creates varying degrees of light on the object's surfaces. Those areas that receive direct light become the light areas of the object. Shade occurs in those areas not receiving light directly. Shadows are created on the surfaces blocked from receiving light. These varying degrees of light and shade are referred to as VALUE. All good rendering is based on value relationships. Figure 5-1 illustrates light, shade, and shadow falling on an object. Figure 5-2 is a sketch showing similar relationships in the built environment.

MATERIALS, MEDIA, AND TOOLS

The list of materials and tools used in rendering is long and continues to grow. Professional illustrators and renderers employ many methods, use a range of supplies, and generally have distinct personal preferences. An understanding of materials and techniques allows a designer to make wise decisions and work quickly. This means that a basic understanding of mate-

Figure 5-1

This cube is rendered to illustrate value. The top of the cube is light because it is receiving direct light from the light source. Shade (found on the sides of the cube) occurs in those areas not receiving light directly. Shadows are created on the surfaces blocked from receiving light. These varying degrees of light and shade are referred to as *value*. All good rendering is based on value relationships. The front edge of the cube is called the *leading edge* and is drawn in white in this example.

5-1

elevator to gallery level

5-2

rials and media is important. In rendering there are no hard-and-fast rules—anything goes. Great rendering requires exploration and curiosity about how materials will work in a given situation. On page 54, Figure C-3 depicts a range of rendering media, materials, and tools, while Figure C-4 gives examples of various rendering surfaces (papers) and media.

Because there are no absolute rules in rendering, it is wise to do a good deal of casual research. Looking at good rendering, fine art, and illustration is essential. To this end books, periodicals, exhibitions, and visits to design firms are useful. Looking at what works in a successful painting or pastel drawing can teach a great deal about how to work with color markers. Discussions with art supply store personnel can be valuable in acquiring information about paper, drawing surfaces, and other supplies.

Paper and Drawing Surfaces

The type of paper or rendering surface used has a significant influence on the quality of the final product. Many designers limit themselves to working on tracing paper or vellum because these papers are commonly used throughout the design process and are available in design offices.

Tracing paper and vellum have slick surfaces and are transparent, allowing them to be overlaid and easily traced. Graphite pencils, ink pens, and colored pencils and markers are often used with success on tracing paper and vellum. Markers are not absorbed into the surface of these papers, so the color stays rather weak and tends to pool. This creates softer color renderings that often have a watercolor effect, which can be attractive. Colored pencil can be layered on top of marker on these transparent papers to enrich the color and define edges. Using a combination of white, beige or cream, and darker pencils for highlights and refinement can work particularly well.

MARKER, also called VISUALIZING PAPER, is commonly used in advertising and industrial design and is excellent for rich marker renderings. Marker paper is less transparent than tracing paper or vellum but absorbs markers well. Graphite, ink pens, colored pencils, and small amounts of paint (including gouache) can all work well on marker paper. Some heavier types of marker paper may be difficult to see through and require the use of a light table or taping onto a sunny window for tracing. Some types of marker paper can be photocopied and rendered. Pretesting of paper, photocopier toner, and marker compatibility is required.

Plain BOND PAPER, used in standard office copying machines, is highly absorbent and can be used for rendering. Bond paper can be very messy because it soaks up marker dye, but when used with care it can create rich marker renderings. This paper also allows colored pencils to be layered over marker for clarity, crispness, and highlights. Rendering directly on bond photocopies is a fast, popular rendering technique that is becoming the standard in design offices. A word of caution: Some marker base components can smear and dissolve copy toner, resulting in disaster. Pretesting of all materials to be used on bond paper copies is highly advised. Bond paper is also used in plotting of standard CAD drawings and can work to good effect when CAD files are printed or plotted and then will be rendered with markers and pastels.

Marker paper and bond paper allow for mistakes to be carefully cut out and reworked; problem areas can be replaced with new portions—this means that mistakes can be cut out and new portions can be pasted in. In addition, objects with ragged, poorly rendered edges can be cleanly cut and placed on a new sheet of paper. This technique works particularly well with photocopies and is used a great deal in product rendering.

There are many types of nontransparent paper that are used in rendering. These papers require some method of image transfer. TRANSFER PAPER, available from art supply stores, is placed between the original image and the rendering surface; the image is then redrawn and, thus, transferred. A cheap alternative method involves drawing on the back of the original with a soft pencil. The original is then placed face up on the rendering surface, and the image is redrawn, causing it to transfer. With some types of paper, commercial photocopying machines are also effective in reproducing images.

A variety of nontransparent colored papers can work well for stylized, minimally rendered presentations. Canson paper and other types of pastel paper accept graphite, ink, marker, colored pencil, pastel, and small amounts of gouache. This type of colored paper works best when the color selected is used in great amounts in the final rendering. For example, an interior with green slate used abundantly as a finish material can be rendered nicely on similarly green-colored Canson paper. With the appropriate paper color selected, only the highlights, darkest values, and shadows are rendered in, leaving the paper color to serve as the middle value of the rendering.

Many colored papers are highly textured on one side only. Colored pencils used on the highly textured side create a grainy look. Sometimes this is not desirable, so care must be taken in selecting the best side for rendering. Some types of colored paper can be photocopied, allowing for speed in the rendering process. However, tests should be run prior to rendering because copy toner does not adhere well to many types of colored paper.

Print paper used in diazo machines is also used for rendering. Because prints can be run quickly from an original, this method is highly efficient. Presentation BLUELINE, BLACKLINE, and sepia-toned prints are available at commercial blueprint shops and are easily rendered with marker and colored pencil. The choice of print paper is based on the colors used in the rendering. For example, a very warm rendering with a predominance of red, brown, or yellow is best rendered on brown- or black-toned print paper but is difficult to render on blue-toned paper. Large-format photocopying machines are increasingly replacing blueprint machines in popularity. Bond copies are highly absorbent, can offer rich renderings, and are commonly used in design offices for presentations.

Cheap brown KRAFT PAPER like the kind used for paper bags can also be used in rendering. Given the particular qualities of this paper, it should be used only in presentations where its earthy qualities are deemed appropriate. When used for the right project this paper can work effectively. Kraft paper is highly absorbent and practically empties the dye out of a marker, which can be messy. Ink pen, colored pencil, and pastel work well on Kraft paper to define edges and create highlights. Generally this type of paper can be used in photocopying machines.

A variety of specialized art papers and handmade papers can be used for rendering as well. These papers sometimes work in photocopying machines and are then rendered minimally for inclusion in a non-traditional presentation.

BRISTOL PAPER, BRISTOL BOARD, and ILLUSTRATION and MOUNTING BOARDS are, for the most part, highly absorbent and take marker very well. Many professional illustrators prefer illustration board for rendering. Bristol paper comes in a variety of weights, the thinnest of which work in photocopying machines. Illustration and some mounting boards are available in hot press (smoother, less tooth) and cold press (more textured, more tooth). Both hot and cold press boards absorb marker dye well. However, the texture of cold press products can create problems in detailed renderings. Colored pencils and ink pens can look unduly grainy on highly textured surfaces. MUSEUM BOARD is a beautiful, expensive, buttery soft board that comes in white, beige, gray, and black, is highly absorbent, and works well with colored pencil (see more details about museum board in Chapter 6, page 186).

DRAFTING FILMS are sometimes used in rendering. Generally these films are non-absorbent and tend to pool marker dye and ink. Graphite and colored pencils are sometimes used on drafting film. Paint works well on plastic film but requires hours of practice to master.

WATERCOLOR PAPER is used in working with wet media such as watercolor paint. Watercolor paper is available in hot or cold press, in finishes that range from smooth to very rough, and in various weights. Heavier-weight paper is required in working without premounting the paper to a frame. Lighter-weight paper should be presoaked with water, stretched, and taped or stapled to a sturdy frame. Watercolor paper absorbs marker dye readily and can be worked with graphite, ink, colored pencil, acrylic and gouache paint, and just about anything else available commercially for mark making. I find heavily textured watercolor papers very difficult to use for detailed design renderings.

The previous discussion of paper types has primarily involved items rendered manually. When presentations are digitally rendered—or hand rendered, scanned, and printed—the quality of printing or plotting paper should be considered. In some cases high quality PHOTOGRAPHIC PAPER is used.

Rendering Media

A trip to an art supply store makes evident the huge selection of rendering media, from colored pencils to markers and paint. The available rendering media range in price and have advantages and disadvantages. This means that no one item does everything well. For this reason, most renderings require the use of more than one medium, and many renderings require a little bit of everything.

Graphite pencils, lead holders, and mechanical pencils can be used in noncolored renderings. Pencils can be used for contour lines as well as texture, pattern, and material indication. Although pencil can be used to create subtle and beautiful original drawings and renderings, it does not reproduce as well as ink. This means that blueprints and photocopies of pencil renderings depicting variations of value and texture are often less clear than the originals. Deliberate individual pencil strokes reproduce far better than do those portions where the side of the pencil has been used to cover large areas. In cases where a rendering will be heavily reproduced, pencil may be a poor choice.

Ink used in refillable or disposable pens creates excellent line work that reproduces beautifully in both photocopying and diazo machines. Thus ink can be used successfully to create line drawings for reproduction and over-rendering with colored media.

Unfortunately, using ink can be messy and time-consuming. Before ink dries, it can smear and ruin an original. Therefore, it is wise to take care with ink drawings and use ink only as the final step in drawings that have been fully drawn with guidelines in graphite, nonphoto, or nonprint pencil. Inking triangles with raised edges are also helpful.

Refillable technical pens in varying widths are available, as are disposable ink pens. Refillable pens produce the finest quality of line, but they require cleaning and proper maintenance. Disposable ink pens are less consistent in terms of line quality, yet are preferred by some because they do not require cleaning or maintenance. Fine-point markers and various forms of felt-tip pens can be used to create excellent ink renderings. Disposable technical pens are useful in creating line drawings, whereas felt-tip ink markers work well on colored renderings to define edges.

There are three types of COLORED PENCILS: wax-based, oil-based, and water-soluble. I find the wax-based the most useful in rendering. In my experience, Berol Prismacolor wax-based pencils are the easiest to render with. Colored pencils can work well alone, although for rich color buildup they must be layered or manipulated. See Figure C-5a Color Section for examples of colored pencil color manipulation. Without layering, colored pencils can look grainy because the pencil often works only on the top surface of the paper, allowing little valleys to stay uncolored. Underlayering warm colors with deep red pencil and cool colors with indigo blue pencil can diminish the grainy look.

A variety of solvents can be used to decrease the grainy quality of pencil renderings. One of the best is rubber-cement thinner, which is toxic and emits vapors that can cause serious health problems. Use rubber-cement thinner in an appropriate manner, and follow the warning instructions carefully. In using this solvent, a small amount is placed on a cotton swab and applied on top of colored pencil—in a well-ventilated space.

An alcohol-based colorless blender marker is an alternative pencil solvent that poses fewer health hazards. The colorless blender can be applied over the surface of the colored pencil area and worked back and forth, loosening up the pencil.

Often when used alone and overworked, wax-based pencils can produce a buildup of wax. This makes the area look shiny, overdone, and amateurish. The solution to this shiny buildup is to apply a layer of color or gray marker before any pencil touches the paper. The marker functions like a paint primer and allows the surface to accept pencil better. This works well when done with subtle shades of the object color or light values of gray. Coating paper with acrylic gesso also adds a primer coat for pencil renderings.

The appearance of colored pencil rendering varies greatly according to the type and texture of paper used, thus creating a need for experimentation. In addition, the way the pencil is held and the stroke used produce different effects. When used to cover large areas, colored pencils are best applied with angled strokes. Using strokes of roughly 45 degrees is less tiring and produces an attractive rendering. Sharp pencils have a greater surface area and cover large areas rapidly. Pencils also must be kept very sharp when used to define edges and outline objects. In creating outlines or definition, the use of a metal or plastic straightedge is required.

Pencils can be used over marker renderings to enhance color and define shape and value. A sharp white or light-colored pencil works well to clean up messy edges of marker rendering. To create subtle color variations, colored pencil pigment can be chipped away from the pencil using a blade and applied by rubbing onto the drawing surface with a tissue.

ART MARKERS, also called STUDIO MARKERS, and are filled with transparent dye in an alcohol or xylene base solution. Xylene-based markers last longer and are considered by some to have better color rendition. Unfortunately, xylene-based markers produce fumes that can cause health problems. For this reason, some schools, institutions, and design firms have policies prohibiting the use of xylene-based art supplies.

Alcohol-based markers have recently improved greatly and are now widely used. Unfortunately, alcohol-based markers tend to dry up quickly and do not last long. Denatured alcohol or 91 percent alcohol solution can be used to revive markers. Marker tips can be removed and an alcohol solution placed in the marker body, or the marker can be placed (open) with the tip in an alcohol solution. Because they dry up quickly, alcohol-based markers should be tested prior to application on a final rendering; this prevents unwanted streaks and poor color matches.

There are numerous brands of high quality art markers currently available. Many designers and illustrators have distinct personal favorites. Others tend to mix and match brands, based on availability, price, and color selection. Many of my students prefer Pantone Tria markers by Letraset because they have three tip sizes, produce good color rendition, and are refillable. Tria markers also have a chisel point for the marking tip, which works well in rendering nonorganic forms and in using a straightedge for marker application. Prismacolor brand markers have a true range of warm and cool grays and come with a rendering tip that is a modified chisel point, which works well for rendering organic forms and working freehand.

Markers are a popular rendering medium because they are quick to use, do not require extensive setup or cleaning time, and come in an enormous range of colors. However, markers can be difficult to master because they are difficult for beginners to control. Moreover, marker color must be manipulated to portray value, texture, and material qualities successfully.

When possible, marker strokes should be applied against a straightedge. Do not use metal or plastic edges for applying marker color because it smears and causes problems. The best straightedge for marker application is a strip of mat or illustration board.

Marker color is usually layered or touched up with additional media to properly render value and color. A single marker color can be applied in layers to create value contrast. Gray marker as well can be layered under the appropriate color to create value or enrich color. Colored pencil, pastel, and small quantities of paint can be layered over marker color to create value contrast or tune up color.

Regardless of the method used, marker color must be manipulated to reveal form. The most common mistake in marker rendering is neglecting to manipulate marker color and, in so doing, creating "coloring book" images that appear amateurish. Often marker color is too intense for use in interior perspectives. One method for softening marker intensity is to use colorless blender to pick up the marker dye and then apply it to the drawing surface. To do this, apply the marker to slick paper, "pick it up" with the colorless blender, and apply it to the rendering surface (see Figure C-5b on page 55).

DRY PASTELS (sometimes called *chalk*) work well as a complement to marker and colored pencil renderings. These pastels are dry and chalky in contrast to oil pastels. Dry pastels can be used to color an area quickly and can create light washes for highlights. One useful dry pastel technique involves using the edge of a blade to shave off portions of pastel, creating a pastel pigment dust. The pastel dust can be mixed with baby powder, making it easy to work.

The dry pastel and baby powder mixture is then smoothed onto the rendering surface with tissue, cotton pads, or swabs over marker, or used alone to create washes of color. Pastels are also blended into a drawing with a finger, which works far better than simply drawing with a pastel stick. Pastels are available in pencil form; however, these lack the speed of application found with stick pastels.

Many of those involved in rendering find pastels to be a quick and easy product to use. Dry pastels work well on colored paper as a primary rendering medium but are best used in less detailed renderings. Large areas of pastel can be applied neatly when worked against removable tape or sticky back as a masking agent. It is easy to erase or brush pastels from a drawing surface. This makes pastels a far more forgiving medium than markers. I find pastel particularly useful in rendering painted walls and carpeting as it does not streak as markers sometimes do (demonstrated in Figures C-7a, C-7b, On page 56). Finished pastel drawings require the application of fixative spray to keep them in place. This can cause problems in renderings done with markers because fixative can remove marker dye. However, special marker fixative is available.

WATERCOLORS, transparent water-based paints used by many professional illustrators and artists, can be used to create beautiful renderings. However, they are difficult and extremely time-consuming to use. A good deal of practice and experimentation is required in developing watercolor painting skills. Students interested in watercolor rendering are well advised to enroll in a watercolor painting course; information gained there can be used in rendering.

Watercolor rendering requires special tools such as brushes, high-quality paper, and mounting boards. Because it is time-consuming, watercolor rendering is not often used for preliminary or schematic presentations but is instead used in final design presentations.

GOUACHE is an opaque water-based paint. When used straight from the tube, gouache appears opaque; when mixed with water, it can become somewhat transparent. Professional illustrators and renderers use gouache to create rich, realistic renderings. However, like watercolors, gouache painting is time-consuming and requires special skills and equipment. Because it is water-based and is often mixed with water, gouache should be applied only to heavier papers. White or light-colored gouache can be used to create highlights and glints on marker, ink, and pencil renderings. This is best done by mixing white gouache with a small amount of water and applying it to the drawing surface with a fine paintbrush. The gouache should be applied with great care in extremely small quantities only.

An AIRBRUSH is a system that actually propels paint or dye onto a drawing surface. In standard airbrush systems a compressor, hose, and spray gun combine to propel the pigment. Airbrushes produce dazzling, sophisticated images with an amazing range of hue and value. Standard airbrush systems are expensive and require lots of practice. A great deal of setup and cleanup time is required for airbrush use.

Many renderings combine various forms of media. It is not uncommon to see renderings created with marker, colored pencil, a bit of pastel, ink, and tiny areas of paint. The combining of media limits weaknesses and takes advantage of strengths. Some designers create renderings that are collages of a variety of materials and media and come from a range of sources. Some collages make use of computer-generated images combined with hand drawn images and others are created completely digitally as shown in previous Figures 2-16a and 2-16b in Chapter 2, page 46.

RENDERING ORTHOGRAPHIC PROJECTION DRAWINGS

Rendering orthographic projections helps to reveal the material qualities of the design and indicate relative depth. Because orthographic views are by nature flattened views, or use in presentations, they often require rendering as a means of graphic enhancement. With the appropriate enhancement, orthographic views can be used successfully in design presentations. This is fortunate, because orthographic views are created on most projects and are therefore readily available for use in design presentations. For this reason, rendered orthographic views are commonly used for presentations made throughout the design process. Orthographic projections are faster and easier to render than perspective drawings.

The best way to begin a rendered plan, section, or elevation is to create a clean original drawing. For the final rendering to have clarity, complex dimensions and confusing notes should be omitted. Items such as ceramic tile and certain simple textures may exist on the original drawing or can be drawn in as part of the rendering process.

The key to rendering is to consider light, and this is most easily accomplished in orthographic projections by adding shadows. If time allows, additional value contrast, materials, and color rendition can be included in the rendering. Including shadows helps to reveal height and can provide the contrast necessary to enhance the drawing. There are a number of methods for determining shadow location and length; most of these are overcomplicated. Quite often, shadows can be simplified and estimated with few ill effects.

Simplified Shadows

There are two simple systems for estimating shadows in plan drawings. One system employs a consistent shadow orientation

5-3

FIGURE 5-3
A floor plan with simplified shadows, all cast at a consistent 45 degrees.

for the entire plan. Typically this simplified system employs a 45-degree diagonal direction for the light source. Each element and object in the entire plan receives a shadow cast by the same 45-degree light source. Shadows are drawn adjacent to each form in plan at a 45-degree angle, using a standard 45-degree triangle. The length of each shadow is estimated based on the relative height of each form. This method is simple and creates an easy-to-read plan (see Figure 5-3).

Another shadow estimation system involves creating shadows that are cast by the variety of light sources found in the environment. The locations of windows, skylights, and electric light sources are used to cast 45-degree shadows. This system creates shadows that vary from room to room, relative to the natural and electric light sources. Shadows are cast at 45-degree angles (using a 45-degree triangle), based on the location of the light source.

Shadow length is estimated relative to height. This variable shadow system creates dramatic effects that help to indicate window locations (see Figure 5-4). However, plans employing this system require more time, and complex plans can be visually confusing.

Shadows enhance elevations and sections. In these drawings they can be used to indicate the relative depths and the forms of design elements. A simple technique is for shadows to be drawn in section and elevation as cast from top right to bottom left, following a 45-degree diagonal, allowing for the use of a standard 45-degree triangle.

In elevation, shadows are cast at 45 degrees with lengths determined by the relative depth of the object casting the shadow (see Figure 5-5). Shadows drawn in elevation enhance a drawing but should generally be kept minimal in terms of length for purposes of graphic clarity. Where a dramatic rendering is required, shadows can

5-4

be drawn with great lengths to create interest. It is important to note that exterior elevations, unlike interiors, are often drawn with dramatic shadows because they are outdoors and receive large quantities of natural light.

Section drawings have shadows cast by cut elements such as the roof, floors, and walls. Generally the length of these shadows is varied, based on the distance from the cutline to the plane receiving the shadow.

Texture, Pattern, and Material Qualities

It is often useful to render the material properties of design elements in orthographic projection drawings. This is done by delineating the size and location, texture, and finish of both building elements and furnishings. Rendering these elements in plan and elevation drawings is easier and less time-consuming than rendering in perspectives and paraline drawings. For this reason, it is not unusual to see professional design presentations that consist of rendered plans and elevations and nonrendered perspective drawings. When such ele-

5-5

ments are drawn successfully, many clients can distinguish material qualities quite well in rendered orthographic projections.

Rendering materials and finishes can be done quite simply, with—for instance—minimal line work and stippling used to indicate wood and ceramic tile. When necessary, great detail can be added to plans and elevations. There are some fairly

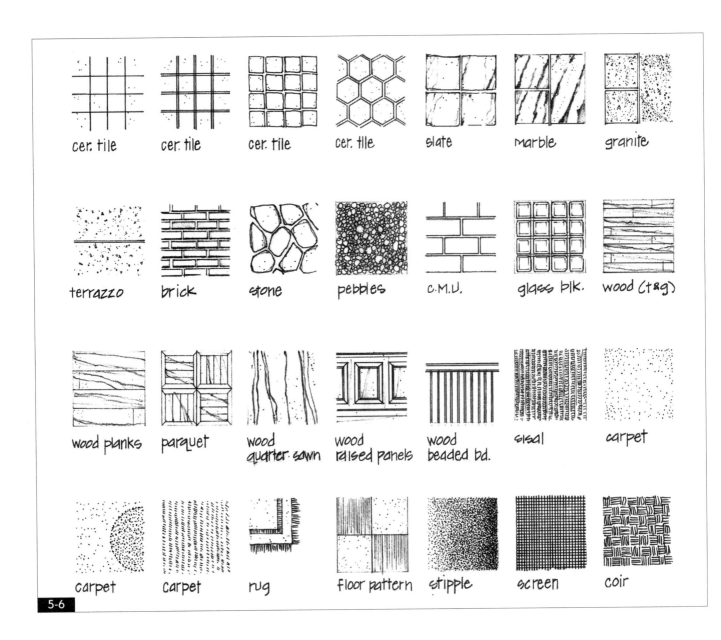

cer. tile	cer. tile	cer. tile	cer. tile	slate	marble	granite
terrazzo	brick	stone	pebbles	c.M.U.	glass blk.	wood (t&g)
wood planks	parquet	wood quarter·sawn	wood raised panels	wood beaded bd.	sisal	carpet
carpet	carpet	rug	floor pattern	stipple	screen	coir

5-6

FIGURE 5-6

Examples of manually rendered finish materials (using lines, and stipples only) for use in orthographic projections. Note: These are not the standard symbols for use in construction documents.

standard conventions for rendering common finish materials in orthographic projection. See Figure 5-6 for examples of orthographic finish materials.

Regardless of the level of detail required for a given project, materials must be rendered in scale and with some indication of texture or surface finish. For example, the most minimally rendered plan should show properly scaled tile locations, wood floors in scale with a slight graining pattern, and minimal stippling for carpet locations. The indication of surface finishes in proper scale allows the plan to indicate accurately the finish material sizes and locations.

When in doubt about the rendering of a particular material, it is best to carefully examine the actual material and render an abstraction of what is visible. For example, no convention exists for rendering a speckled rubber floor tile. This particular tile can be rendered only through examination of its visual qualities. Are the speckles large or small? Are the speckles in a contrasting color? Are they random or in a particular pattern?

Some designers prefer spare, minimally rendered orthographic projections; whereas others prefer a detailed, rather busy style of rendering. This is certainly a matter of taste or personal style. Regardless of personal style, however, renderings of orthographic projections must be drawn in scale and should accurately reflect proportion and true material qualities. Figures 5-7 and 5-8 are orthographic projections rendered with line work, stippling, and shadows.

Generally, accurate visual assessment of materials is a key to successful rendering. In some cases, certain materials simply cannot be rendered in the time allowed, so a legend system can be used to delineate material locations.

Color-Rendering

Prior to beginning any color rendering, a designer should consider the amount of time available and the nature of the project. Project phase, type of project, and the presentation audience are important factors in the selection of a color rendering style. All factors must be considered and the most appropriate media chosen. Color rendering requires a working knowledge of color theory; some basic color information can be found in Appendix 4.

FIGURE 5-7
Floor plan manually rendered using lines, stipples, and shadows (tone) with pencil.

5-7

FIGURE 5-8

Floor plan manually rendered using lines, stipples, and shadows (tone) with pencil.

Color rendering can greatly enhance plan, elevation, and section drawings. The quickest method calls for creating a photocopy or print of an original line drawing and rendering on the copy with pencil, marker, pastel, or a combination of these media (see Figures C-8a through C-17b on pages 57 to 63). Another quick method involves the use of white or colored tracing paper laid over drawings and washed with colored pencil, ink, or washes of marker.

In working on bond copies and print paper, shadows can be rendered into the print with gray markers before the application of any colored marker or pencils.

Areas that are to appear much darker in value should also be laid in gray marker prior to the application of color media. With shadows and darker values applied, marker color, pencil color, or pastels may then be used to create the desired hue.

As stated previously, chalk pastels work well when chipped off the stick to create a colored powder and then applied with cotton balls in areas such as carpeted portions of floor plans or large washes of painted areas in wall elevations. Because rendering on bond and print papers is quick and relatively easy, they are often used for design presentations. Figures C-8a through C-10b on pages 57 to 59 show the steps in rendering bond paper copies of plans. Figures C-7b, C-17b, and C-17b, show elevations washed with pastels to indicate color and material locations. Some varieties of colored paper can be photocopied and rendered.

In some cases, when little time is available, orthographic drawings can be spot rendered; this means that only a small portion of the drawing needs to be rendered accurately to indicate the materials used throughout the project (see Figure C-11). This technique is effective when the spot that is rendered clearly depicts the range of materials used in the project. Another timesaving method involves using the correct color in a particular area and defining elements accurately in part of that area. For example, a large tile area can be indicated by applying the correct marker to the entire tiled portion, with only a limited number of tiles outlined in pencil, ink, or marker to show the tile size and shape (see Figure C-12).

Techniques and Tips for Manual Rendering

All rendered orthographic projections require shadows. Shadows should be considered prior to rendering, and a shadow plan should be created with each shadow located. Shadows can then be rendered in colored pencil, ink, or marker.

Because they can remove ink and colored pencil, markers should generally be used for a base coat. This means they should be applied before the use of ink or colored pencil. However, when necessary, light markers and colorless blenders can be used to remove areas of pencil that have become too waxy.

Plans, elevations, and sections require that large areas of marker be applied in deliberate strokes with a straightedge. Large areas of carpet or wood flooring should be applied with the lightest marker color possible, applied with a straightedge.

Additional layers of marker can be applied to tune up marker color and to add nuances where required. In rendering natural materials such as wood and stone, marker color should vary slightly; this requires going over particular areas with a second application of marker.

Unsuccessful marker renderings of orthographic projections generally suffer from one or more of the following: strokes not created with a straightedge, marker color that is too intense, lack of value contrast (no highlights or dark values), or a combination of these flaws.

Colored pencil is often applied over gray or colored markers to add highlights, intensify dark areas, and enrich color. Marker color alone is often too intense for use in interior renderings and requires the addition of colored pencil to soften and subdue the color.

Unsuccessful colored pencil renderings often suffer from heavy-handed use of a single color, pencil strokes that are all over the place, unsharpened pencil points, or a combination of all three.

Digital Rendering

Increasingly, designers are using graphics editing software such as Photoshop to render orthographic drawings digitally. This involves importing the drawing into Photoshop and using either scanned imagery from actual material samples, material images from other digital sources such as manufacturers' online resources, or archival materials and books such as those from *Architectural Surfaces* by Judy Juracek (2005). This process requires paying attention to the actual scale of materials images as they are imported into scaled drawings as well as to the quality of resolution of the files for both the materials and the drawing.

FIGURE 5-9a

Instructions for rendering a plan drawn using AutoCAD in Photoshop begin with:

1. In AutoCAD switch to paper space and "plot" the elevation as a PDF in scale desired (such as ½" = 1'0")—this is done in the plot window but instead of plotting saves the file as a PDF (this may require a full version of Adobe Acrobat).

1a. In Photoshop create a new file.
—Make canvas dimensions 8½" x 11" or desired size.
—Resolution 300 -CMYK mode
—Open PDF Plan file (created in AutoCAD, Step 1).
—Drag PDF Plan onto new 8½" x 11" canvas; center on canvas.
—In Layer Palette: Rename the layer "Plan Line Work", lock the layer and then select "Multiply" as shown in Step 4, Figure 5-9b.

1b. Floor plan is now ready to render.

2. Get jpg image of wood planks/flooring. Select wood image with Rectangle Marquee tool. Go to "Edit" and select "Copy." Note that the wood flooring as well as other elements to be "rendered" in, must be visually assessed for appropriate size/scale. On way to adjust scale is to go to "edit" and select "Transform" and select "Scale".

FIGURE 5-9b

3. ICON TOOL: Magic Wand. With Magic Wand Tool select area of floor that is to be rendered as wood flooring. Hold down "Shift" button and continue selecting all floor surfaces that are to be rendered as wood.

4. Go to "Edit" and select "Paste Into." Change wood flooring layer to be on "Multiply" option (this allows the background line work to read through all images put on floor plan).

One way to start this type of rendering is to create a drawing in AutoCAD and switch to "paperspace" and set a viewport to desired scale and go to the plot window and "save as a PDF" (Portable Document Format)—(the PDF should be created at a resolution of 300 dpi, or the final image will be terrible). The PDF can then be imported into a new Photoshop file also set at a resolution of 300 dpi and in CMYK (cyan, magenta, yellow, and black) mode—more information about files and resolution can be found in Chapter 9, page 268. Adding layers of materials and surfaces, shadow, and additional details on to the orthographic drawings completes this type of rendering. Using this method requires that materials are scaled by eye in a manner that is appropriate to the rest of the drawing. Figures 5-9a through 5-9h and 5-10a through 5-10h illustrate doing this type of rendering and the Color Section shows portions of these directions in detail (see Figures C-18a, C-18b, C-18c, C-19a, and C-19b). Figures C-20a and C-20b show CAD drawings rendered in Photoshop and Figure C-21 is rendered by hand and composed in Photoshop.

RENDERING PERSPECTIVE DRAWINGS

Rendering perspective and paraline drawings is often more difficult and time-consuming than rendering orthographic projections. This is due to the complex nature of perspective drawing. Light, shade, and shadow must be rendered in perspective drawings. Moreover, the surfaces of objects recede toward vanishing points, creating complexity in rendering colors and materials. However, rendering adds richness, interest, and reality to perspective drawings, allowing for successful visual communication.

Rendered perspectives can help the proposed design to become real to a client and are thus excellent sales and communications tools. For this reason rendered perspectives are often used in formal final design presentations. There are many perspective rendering techniques, varying from those that can be accomplished quickly to those that require days for completion.

The time and budget constraints of a project influence the rendering method selected. When scheduling and budgets allow, professional illustrators may be hired to create highly detailed or dramatic renderings. Quickly drawn perspectives rendered with value and almost no color may be used on some projects. Sometimes, minimally rendered black-and-white perspective drawings are used in tandem with rendered floor plans because they can be produced quickly. Because projects vary in terms of design fees and schedules, it is useful to be aware of a range of rendering techniques and basic perspective rendering concepts.

All rendering requires that the source of light and its influence on the environment be considered. In perspective rendering, however, light and its relationship to the object(s) rendered must be considered above all else. What is the light source or sources? How do the rendered materials react in relationship to the light source? Every stroke of the marker or pencil is actually determined by the relationship of light to the object.

Understanding the relationship of light, value, and shadow on basic forms in perspective is required for successful perspective rendering. The cube, cylinder, sphere, and cone are basic shapes that are found in combination in more complex objects. Learning to render these basic shapes in a variety of noncolor media is a useful preparation for the eventual rendering of color and materials. The basic shapes are most easily rendered with a light source above

STEP 1:   STEP 1-A: STEP 1-B: STEP 2:

5-9a

STEP 3:   STEP 4:

5-9b

STEP 5:   STEP 6:

5-9c

FIGURE 5-9c

5. Make a copy of the wood floor layer. This will duplicate the wood image on top of the original. Move new image over to fill remainder of floor space (when rendering a lot of the same material in a floor plan, randomly rotate and flip the duplicate images for realistic patterning).

6. Link all duplicate wood layers and select "Merge Linked." Opacity can be lowered to allow wood image to read more realistic in rendering.

STEP 7:   STEP 8:   STEP 9:

5-9d

FIGURE 5-9d

7. Using a granite jpg image.
Select image with Rectangle
Marquee tool. Go to "Edit" and
select "Copy."

8. ICON TOOL: Magic Wand.
With Magic Wand, select countertop areas.

9. Go to "Edit" and select
"Paste Into." Change granite
layer to be on "Multiply" option
(as shown in Step 4, Figure
5-9b).

FIGURE 5-9e

10. Using a rug jpg image.
Select image with Rectangle
Marquee tool. Go to "Edit" and
select "Copy." Magic Wand rug
area in floor plan and select
"Paste Into."

FIGURE 5-9f

11. ICON TOOL: Magic Wand,
Paint Bucket and Brush Magic
Wand appliances and furniture.
Paint Bucket neutral color
(plants: use Brush Tool and various green tones for realistic rendering).
Note: See Figure C-18a for a
color version of this image.

STEP 10:

5-9e

STEP 11:

5-9f

STEP 12:

STEP 12A:

5-9g

STEP 13:

5-9h

FIGURE 5-9g

12. ICON TOOL: Burn Tool. Duplicate wood floor layer-change name to be called "shadows." Turn off original wood floor layer and save in Layer Palette as backup if needed in case of error while making shadows.

Change Burn Tool settings:
—Brush: Size 35+/-
—Range: Shadows
—Exposure: 50%+/- 12a.

ICON TOOL: Burn Tool. Select the "shadow" layer and choose the Burn Tool. For straight shadows (such as counter) click on side of counter (hold "Shift" button down) and click to bottom of counter. Continue making shadows around remainder of items in floor plan. Note: See Figure C-18b on page 64 for a color version of this image.

FIGURE 5-9h

13. FINAL TOUCHES: Opacity of layers can be changed down so the final tone of the rendering feels holistic. Walls can be filled in if desired (use Magic Wand and Paint Bucket). Dodge Tool can be used to add light reflections on floor or furniture just as Burn Tool created shadows). Note: See Figure C-18c on page 64 for a color version of this image.

and slightly to the right or left. The light source in this position creates three distinct values—light (value 1), medium (value 2), and dark (value 3)—and a cast shadow (4). Figure 5-11 illustrates this light source setup in relation to a variety of simple forms. In some cases light bounces from a surface up onto the sides of an object, lightening it slightly close to the bottom even on the darkest value areas, especially when there are multiple light sources.

In this light-source setup, the top surface of a cube receives the most light (value 1), followed by the side closest to the light source (value 2). The side farthest from the light source receives the least light and is darkest (value 3), and typically the cast shadow (4) is adjacent to the darkest side (see Figure 5-11).

A cylinder with this lighting setup has its top surface rendered as the lightest (value 1). Light curves around a curving surface, creating levels of value contrast that also curve around the cylinder. On a simplified nonreflective cylinder, the portion of the cylinder closest to the light is rendered with the medium value (value 2) and the portion farthest from the light source is rendered the

STEP 1:   STEP 1-A: STEP 1-B: STEP 2:

5-10a

FIGURE 5-10a

Instructions for rendering an elevation drawn using AutoCAD in Photoshop begin with:

1. In AutoCAD switch to paper space and plot the elevation as a PDF in scale desired (such as ½" = 1'0", see Figure 5-9a, Step 1).

1a. In Photoshop create a new file.

—Make canvas dimensions 8½" x 11" or desired size.

—Resolution 300 -CMYK mode

—Open PDF Elevation file (created in AutoCAD, Step 1).

—Drag PDF Elevation onto new 8½" x 11" canvas; center on canvas.

—In Layer Palette: Rename the layer "Elevation Line Work," lock the layer and then select "Multiply" as shown in Step 4.

1b. Elevation is now ready to render.

2. Take a digital photo or go online and find a jpg image of a brick wall. Select brick image with rectangle marquee tool. Go to "Edit" and select "Copy." Note: When importing material imagery such as the brick wall one can scale the item by careful examination or "eyeballing" the scale.

STEP 3:   STEP 4:

5-10b

STEP 5:   STEP 6:

5-10c

FIGURE 5-10B

3. ICON TOOL: Magic Wand With Magic Wand. Select first surfaces that are to be brick. Hold down "Shift" button and continue selecting all surfaces in elevation that are to be rendered as brick.

4. Go to "Edit" and select "Paste Into." Change brick layer to be on "Multiply" option (this allows the background line work to read through all images put on elevation).

FIGURE 5-10C

5. Select brick image layer and make a copy of the layer. This will duplicate the brick image. Move new image over to fill remainder of wall with copies of original brick layer. When rendering large areas of the same material in an elevation; randomly rotate and flip the duplicate images for realistic patterning (this eliminates pattern repeats).

6. Link all duplicate brick of layers and select "Merge Linked." Opacity can be lowered to allow brick image to read more realistically in rendering.

STEP 7:   STEP 8:

5-10d

STEP 9:   STEP 10:   STEP 11:

5-10e

STEP 12:

5-10f

FIGURE 5-10d

7. ICON TOOL: Magic Wand. With Magic Wand select first window mullion (hold down "Shift" button and continue magic wand the remainder of the mullions).

8. ICON TOOL: Paint Bucket. Select gray from color palette and pour color into mullions.

FIGURE 5-10e

9. ICON TOOL: Magic Wand. Select first section of glazing then hold down "Shift" button and continue selecting all glazing in elevation that is to be rendered as sky.

10. ICON TOOL: Magic Wand. Take a picture of the sky or go online and get a jpg image of sky. Select sky image with Rectangle Marquee tool. Go to "Edit" and select "Copy."

11. Go to "Edit" and select "Paste Into" (change sky layer setting to read "Multiply" as noted in Step 4).
Note: See Figure C-19a on page 65 for a color version of this image.

FIGURE 5-10f

12. Select the sky layer and change opacity down so the color and intensity of the sky image matches the brick in the elevation.

FIGURE 5-10g

13. ICON TOOL: Burn Tool. Duplicate the brick layer and change the name to "shadows"; move to the top of the Layer Palette.
Change settings to:
—Brush: Size 35+/-
—Range: Shadows
—Exposure: 50% +/-
13a. ICON TOOL: Burn Tool. Select the "Shadow" layer and choose the Burn Tool. Click on top left side of column (hold "Shift" button down) and click to bottom of column. Repeat for realistic shadows on columns. Note: See Figure C-19b on page 65 for a color version of this image.

FIGURE 5-10h

14 (optional). ICON TOOLS: Magnetic Lasso Tool. Use images of people from digital photographs, magazines or Internet. Use the Magnetic Lasso Tool to trace outline of figure. Distort image with "Blur" or "Watercolor" filters. Change down opacity of figure (they provide scale but should not distract from architecture).
15. FINAL TOUCHES: Opacity of layers can be changed or tweaked so the final rendering appears complete.

STEP 13:   STEP 13A:

5-10g

STEP 14 (OPTIONAL):   STEP 15:

5-10h

darkest value (value 3). The shadow (4) is generally located on the surface next to the darkest portion of the cylinder (see Figure 5-11). Cylinders are frequently drawn in a more complex manner because they often pick up reflective light, causing a dark reflection next to the medium value of the cylinder, as well as a light reflection on the dark value. This is the case when rendering highly reflective material such as metal. The portions of the cylinder farthest from the light source, which recede from the viewer, also receive medium to dark values.

A sphere with the described lighting setup has its top portion rendered as lightest (value 1), and as the surface curves away from the light source, values are blended in a range from medium (value 2) to dark (value 3). The shadow (4) is generally found on the surface next to the darkest portion of the sphere. Generally values are rendered into a sphere with curved strokes that follow the form of the sphere. Often a bright highlight can be found toward the top portion of the sphere in the location of the lightest value. The darkest portion, of a sphere is sometimes rendered with a narrow adjacent highlight on reflective surfaces (see Figure 5-11).

A cone is rendered with the portion closest to the light source lightest (value 1), with adjacent areas of the cone rendered darker (value 2 and ranging to almost value 3); the portion of the cone farthest from the

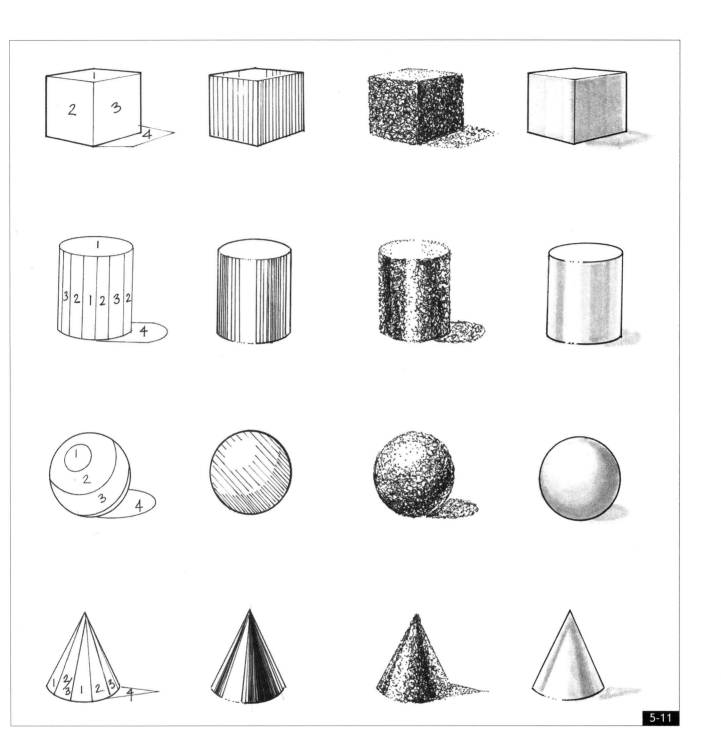

5-11

light receives the least light and is darkest (value 3). A shadow is most often found on the surface next to the darkest value of the cone. A cone with a reflective surface is rendered with the darkest portion, adjacent to a highlight indicating surface reflection (see Figure 5-11).

It is essential to be able to render these basic forms with a minimum of three values plus a shadow. Complex, detailed rendering requires more value contrast to illustrate more complex lighting situations. However, creating a minimum of three values plus a shadow

FIGURE 5-11

The basic shapes are most easily rendered with a light source above and slightly to the right or left. The light source in this position creates three distinct values—(1) light; (2) medium; (3) dark—and a cast shadow (4).

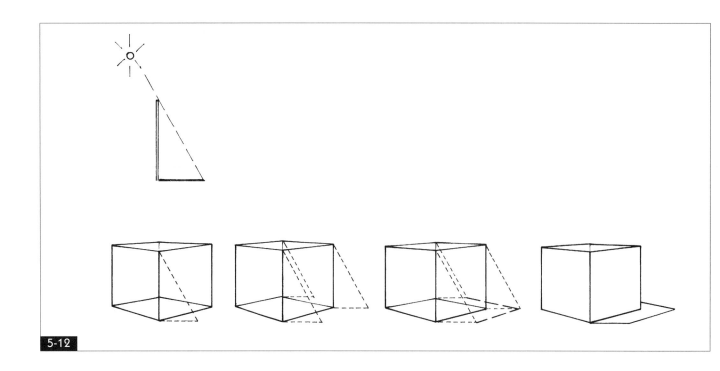

5-12

FIGURE 5-12
Quick reference: simple parallel shadow construction. Construct shadows by selecting an angle formed by the light source and using this angle consistently to create triangles at appropriate corners of the object. The bases of the triangles are then connected to one another to form the shadow.

often allows a rendering to be visually successful.

Shadows in Perspective Drawings

In quick sketch renderings fewer values than the three discussed can be used in combination with rendered shadows. When time is scarce, a drawing can be slightly rendered by the inclusion of shadows only. There are a variety of methods of shadow construction, most of which are rather confusing and over technical. The important things to remember about shadows in perspective renderings are that shadows are absolutely necessary, especially on floor surfaces; shadows should be handled in a consistent fashion throughout the rendering; and shadows need not be absolutely technically accurate to work well. Although shadows are necessary, they can be simplified and minimized for ease of rendering.

The easiest method of shadow construction employs sets of parallel lines that are cast as the bases of triangles. Shadows are constructed by selecting an angle formed by the light source and using this angle consistently to create a triangle from each corner of the object. The bases of the triangles are then connected to each other to form the shadow (see Figure 5-12).

More dramatic shadows can be created by the use of a shadow vanishing point. This method requires that the light source be located somewhere above the horizon line. A shadow vanishing point is then plotted directly below the light source, on the horizon line. Lines are drawn from the light source through the top corners of the object. Lines are then drawn from the shadow vanishing point through the bottom corners of the object. These two sets of lines form the shadow location. The lines determining the length of the shadow are drawn by connecting the two sets of lines, as shown in Figure 5-13.

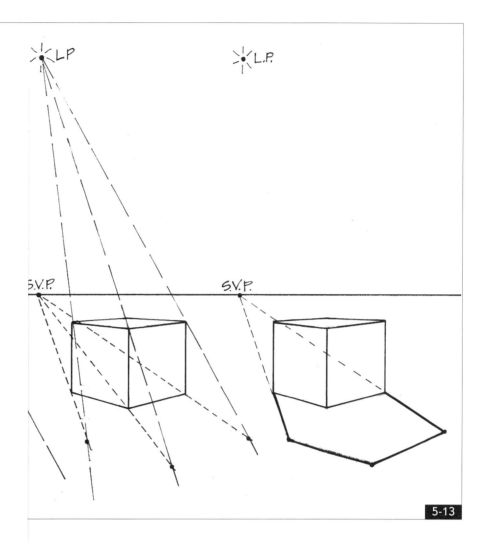

5-13

quick freehand renderings. Detailed, refined renderings require lines drawn with tools. The use of varying line weights can quickly define and enhance a drawing. This is particularly true in outlining and defining the overall form of an object.

The way the edges of an object are outlined can greatly enhance the graphic quality of a quick rendering. The edges of an object that lead toward the viewer are called LEADING EDGES. Leading edges are generally kept very light in line weight and are sometimes drawn in white pencil or gouache. The edges of an object that recede away from the viewer are sometimes called RECEDING EDGES. Receding edges can be

whereas polished metal is best ren   red with gray markers or ink washes. Messy scribbles and hatch marks look best on

FIGURE 5-13

Quick reference: shadow construction with a shadow vanishing point (S.V.P.). Decide on the location of the light source (L.P.). Plot a shadow vanishing point (S.V.P.) directly below the L.P. on the horizon line. Draw lines from the L.P. through the tops of the appropriate corners. Draw lines from the S.V.P. through the bottoms of the appropriate corners of the object. The lines determining the length of the shadows are drawn by connecting the two sets of lines (in this case the two sets of dashed lines where the tic marks are).

FIGURE 5-14

1. The edges of an object that lead toward the viewer are called *leading edges*; these edges are generally kept very light in line weight (a). The edges of an object that recede away from the viewer are called *receding edges* (b); these can be drawn in a very bold line to define the form of the object.

2. As lines recede, they can become bolder (c).

3. The use of leading and receding edges can quickly enhance a drawing.

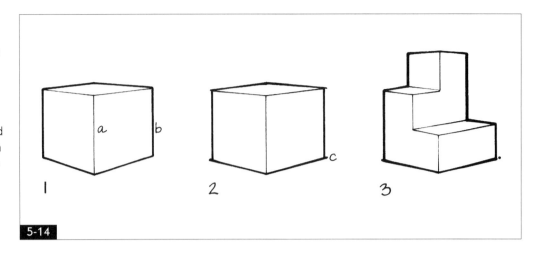

5-14

drawn in a very bold line weight to readily define the form of an object. The use of varying line weights to delineate leading and receding edges can greatly enhance a rendering. Figures 5-14, 5-15, and 5-16 illustrate the use of leading edges and varying line weights. Occasionally the quality of the line work employed creates a focal point in the drawing that serves to enhance the entire composition (see Figure 5-16). Line weights can also be used to aid in creating focal points and define compositional elements as shown in Figures 5-17 and 5-18

The best way to ensure that value and shadow relationships are included in every rendering is to create a value study prior to beginning the actual rendering. To create a value study, take a copy of the perspective line drawing and mark the values that will be rendered in each area. Shadows and highlights should be included (see Figure 5-19a).

The three values and the shadow can be created without the introduction of color by using graphite pencils, ink pens or washes, markers, pastels, gray markers, or gray or white pencils. The values can be created using lines, scribble marks, hatching and cross-hatching, stippling, and shading by using the side of a pencil on edge. Marks made in ink will allow the best reproduction (see Figure 5-19b).

Perspective drawings rendered with gray markers can work well in design presentations when combined with material sample boards or colored orthographic renderings. In addition, creating gray marker renderings can teach design students a great deal about value and marker application. For this reason, students should practice rendering with gray markers.

Gray marker renderings require that markers be applied with accurate and deliberate strokes. In most renderings the tops of horizontal surfaces are rendered in the lightest value, using very small amounts of marker. These lightest areas can have marker applied in circular strokes that are nondirectional. Also on these lightest surfaces, light gray marker (10 to 20 percent gray) can be applied vertically or at an angle representing light reflection. For light surfaces a dusting of gray pastel mixed with powder can be applied.

Floors and walls of interior perspectives require special consideration concerning marker application. It is easiest to render walls by applying marker strokes vertically

5-15

FIGURE 5-15
This clean line drawing of an information desk employs leading and receding edges.

5-16

FIGURE 5-16
This drawing of the proposed renovation of a Victorian residence employs leading and receding edges. In addition, the dramatic use of bold line work in the foreground archway creates an inviting composition. Note: This perspective was sketched from a photograph. The lines on the floor indicate tape that was placed at one-foot increments on the floor during photography; these locations were later used as proportional markers.
Drawing by Jack Zellner

FIGURE 5-17

This drawing employs a range of line weights to create focal points and define areas of interest in the composition. Notice that the heavy lines are used to bring elements in the foreground to the viewer's attention. See Figure C-46a on page 86 for a rendered version of this drawing.

By Matt Saunders

FIGURE 5-18

This drawing employs a range of line weights to create focal points and define areas of interest in the composition.

By Matt Saunders

5-17

5-18

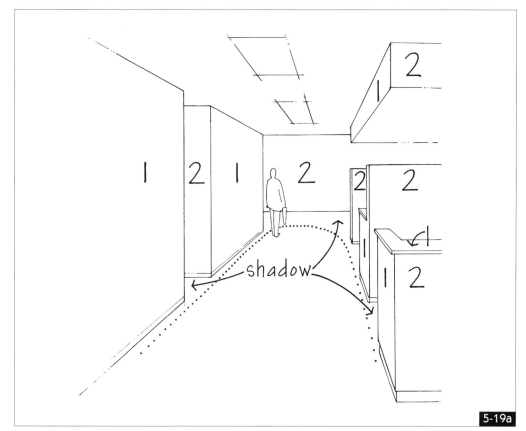

shadow

FIGURE 5-19a
A value study is an important first step in rendering a perspective drawing.

FIGURE 5-19b
Value relationships can be rendered using lines and stipples. In this drawing the back wall was rendered in a value darker than the other walls, which is a slight adjustment in values from those shown in the previous figure.

5-20a

5-20b

FIGURES 5-20a AND 5-20b
It is useful to apply marker with a straightedge. Markers used on wall and floor surfaces are often applied with a vertical stroke for the first layer; secondary layers can be applied freehand or with tools, depending on the desired effect.

with a straightedge (see Figure 5-20a). It is difficult to apply marker strokes horizontally or aiming toward a vanishing point because the lines will overlap and distort the perspective.

A quick look at any floor surface will reveal many shadows, values, and highlights. No floor surface can be rendered by the application of a single marker layer applied consistently—this will look amateurish. Reflective and polished floors must be rendered with a range of lights, darks, and highlights (see Figure 5-20b). Carpet must be rendered with a range of values, or it will appear flat and artificial.

Walls in most environments receive varying amounts of light, so they must vary in value in order to work well in a rendering. Typically in one-point perspective the rear wall can be rendered in a medium value with the two adjacent side walls rendered very light—or not rendered at all (see Figure 5-20b). In two-point perspective, walls should vary in value to indicate light-source locations (see Figures 5-21 and 5-22). Depending on the locations of the

light source(s), a single wall plane may have variations in value. For example, those walls with accent lights or sconces may be very light at the sources of light and become darker as they recede from the light sources.

Gray marker renderings are useful study tools and can be used in design presentations. Special care must be taken in these renderings to create value contrast, to include shadows, and to use a range of values on floor and wall surfaces. Markers should be carefully applied, and strokes should relate to the structure, form, or direction of an object. With these aspects considered, gray marker renderings can serve a valuable purpose.

Color-Rendering Interior Perspectives

Adding color to renderings enhances design communication. It is best to think of color rendering as existing on a continuum, progressing from lightly rendered to fully rendered. Project constraints and the materials used often dictate the level of finish a color rendering will have. As with all aspects of design presentation, the designer must consider the audience, the conceptual issues, the phase of the design process, and the amount of time available. Color rendering requires a working knowledge of color theory; basic color information can be found in Appendix 4.

Colored renderings generated in the schematic phase of a project should reflect the preliminary nature of the presentation. This means that renderings created for schematic design presentations often hint at the color, finish, and design details of a project. Renderings created for a final design development presentation may be far more refined to allow for communication of details and actual material finishes (see Figure C-22 on page 67). Some designers

prefer that renderings retain a sketch like quality so as to reflect the conceptual nature of the project. Others use only highly detailed realistic renderings to fully communicate project design and to eliminate guesswork by the client.

Regardless of the level of finish, most renderings require that a color and value study be completed prior to the final rendering. To create a color and value study, take a copy of the perspective line drawing and mark the values, shadows, and highlights that will be rendered in each area. Colors must be fully tested on the study prior to beginning the final rendering.

Minimally colored perspectives work well when time is limited, when the actual materials have not been finalized, or when one or two hues are predominant. This

This gray marker interior study was completed in 20 minutes using marker paper and gray markers.
Drawing and design by Jack Zellner

FIGURE 5-22

This gray marker rendering was created using gray markers and a small amount of white pen (for the light fixture) on marker paper.

Drawing and design by Kristy Bokelman

method is sometimes referred to as *underrendering*, which allows for the introduction of color, but only hints at actual materials.

Shadows are rendered in color in a variety of ways. Shadows often contain the color of their surface in a very dark value. In addition, the color of the object casting the shadow can be subtly washed into the shadow. Shadows are often created by applying warm gray (for warm colors) or cool gray (for cool colors) marker to the appropriate location prior to the application of colored marker or colored pencil. In very soft colored pencil renderings shadows can be created in pencil in the surface color, in a complementary color, or in gray (see Figure C-23 on page 68, which is a soft colored pencil rendering).

COLOR MOVEMENT is another key aspect of color rendering. Color movement is based on the idea that light and color bounce around in the environment. Capturing the reflection of light and the movement of color makes renderings appear rich and interesting. Objects and surfaces should never be rendered in just one color of marker; instead they should have additional color washed or dotted into them. For example, a red apple sitting on a wood table will bounce a bit of red onto the table surface, and an adjacent wall may also pick up a dot of red from the apple. Because green is the complement of red, a bit of green can be washed into the apple and dotted onto the table as well (see Figures C-22, C-24a, and C-24b on pages 67 and 69).

A simplified method of creating color movement requires that when a color is used on a surface, that same color is washed or stippled into a minimum of two additional surface locations. Incorporating movement of color is a bit strange at first, but it is a useful rendering trick. Objects sitting close to one another actually wash each other with color, and this color movement must also be considered in rendering.

Along with color movement, renderings require COLOR VARIATION. A hue such as green should be rendered with variations of that hue, not with one layer of forest green marker. Of course, creating value contrast does to some extent create value variation. However, hues should be varied to communicate the actual inherent variation of color found in many materials. Wood floors, for example, have variety owing to graining patterns and actual variations in hue from board to board. Plants have leaves with a range of hues and values; new leaves appear bright and fresh, older leaves become yellow or brown. This type of natural variation in hue must be communicated in renderings. This means that it is not advisable to use any single color of marker for any natural surface—it always looks unnatural.

Color variation can be used to create a focal point in a drawing as well. The focal point of a drawing may contain richly rendered colors. As the surfaces recede from the focal point, they can fade away. This technique creates a lively rendering; it also highlights important points and requires less rendering time.

Interior perspective renderings are complex and vary greatly in technique. It is important to note that there is no single way to render any particular material or setting. The way items are rendered must reflect design intent. For this reason rendering requires the use of extensive reference material. A clip file (or reference file) with hundreds of images of figures, surfaces, materials, plants, and entourage elements is fundamental. It is by examining

images that one can render them in a manner appropriate to the project. Professional illustrators keep vast reference archives containing everything from gardening catalogs to plumbing supply catalogs. Sometimes appropriate images can be enlarged and photocopied to reveal value and shadow relationships.

Techniques and Tips for Manual Rendering

The actual marker strokes used in color rendering interior perspectives should follow the form of an object or be applied with diagonal or curved strokes, indicating highlights and shadows. It is often best to apply marker strokes vertically for walls and floors.

Unsuccessful marker renderings most often suffer from inappropriate use of color and poor marker application. Marker color should not be overpowering; for the most part, it should be subdued and enriched by colored pencil and color movement. Many colored markers are far too intense to be used on large areas of renderings without blending, manipulation, or "tuning up" with pencil or pastel.

Colored pencil and ink can be used to create profile lines and define edges on marker renderings. White gouache and dry pastels can tone down marker color and create highlights and glints. These are applied over the desired layers of marker.

Highly detailed colored perspectives are not used in every design project, but they are used when the project and client can benefit from them. Professional illustrators often create highly detailed color renderings. However, the tools and techniques used by illustrators and designers can also be employed by students in the creation of in-process design renderings. These renderings can be used throughout the design process as communication tools. On pages 69 to 72, Figures C-24a through C-27b are

STEP 1:

STEP 1-A:

STEP 1-B:

5-23a

STEP 2:

STEP 3:

STEP 4:

5-23b

STEP 5:

STEP 6:

5-23c

STEP 7:   STEP 8:   5-23d

STEP 9:   STEP 10:   5-23e

FIGURE 5-23a

When rendering perspective drawings in Photoshop, drawings can be imported from scanned unrendered (line only) or partially rendered drawings like this one as well as from modeling programs. Techniques covered in Figures 5-9a through 5-9h and 5-10a through 5-10h can be used in perspectives. However, the nature of perspective requires that the skew/transform tool be used to orient materials/surfaces to the vanishing points as illustrated in the following steps. The method shown here requires that materials are scaled by eye when imported into Photoshop.

1. Begin with a two-dimensional perspective drawing (created by hand, SketchUp, or a CAD program; in this case we are showing a previously rendered version as an example but this could be done with any perspective view).

1a. In Photoshop, create a new file.
—Make paper size as desired (i.e., 8 ½" x 11")
—Resolution 300
—CMYK mode

1b. Perspective is now ready to render in Photoshop.

FIGURE 5-23b

2. Get JPG image of brick wall. Select brick image with Rectangle Marquee tool. Go to "Edit" and select "Copy."

3. ICON TOOL: Polygonal Lasso Tool. With Polygonal Lasso Tool select area of wall to be rendered as brick.

4. On the perspective line work layer. Go to "Edit" and select "Paste Into." Change brick layer to be on "Multiply" option (this allows the perspective line work to read through all images put on the drawing).

FIGURE 5-23c

5. Grab the corner grips on the image (while holding the "Shift" button) scale the image up to fit the size of the room.

6. On the brick layer go to "Edit," choose "Transform," then choose "Skew." Grab the top grip and pull vertically down until the image conforms to the ceiling line work of the perspective. Grab the bottom grip and pull vertically up until the image conforms to the floor line work of the perspective. The image may shrink in this process requiring

scaling the image up a bit once you have it skewed to the correct angles. Change opacity of brick if desired.

FIGURE 5-23d

7. ICON TOOL: Magic Wand Tool or Polygonal Tool. With the Magic Wand Tool or Polygonal Tool, select the items you do not want to be rendered as brick (furniture, lighting, artwork, and bookcase) and delete those portions of the brick layer.

8. Repeat Steps 5 through 7 for opposite brick wall, wood floor, and artwork.

FIGURE 5-23e

9. To render outside windows: Get JPG image of cityscape (or trees, etc.). Optional: Use Watercolor Filter to tone down the sharpness of image). Select cityscape image with Rectangle Marquee tool. Go to "Edit" and select "Copy."

10. Follow steps similar to those described in Steps 3 through 6 and place cityscape image in window and skew. Change opacity if desired.

FIGURE 5-23f

FIGURE 5-23f

11. ICON TOOL: Dodge Tool. The Dodge Tool (with white shown in the color palette) can be used to get "sun glare" streaks on glass.
Change Dodge Tool Settings:
—BRUSH: SIZE 50+/-
—RANGE: Highlights
—EXPOSURE: 75%+/-
12. Final Rendering (Optional—faded edges). ICON TOOL: Eraser Tool. Duplicate Brick Wall, Wood Floor, and Cityscape Layers (turn off original brick wall, wood floor, and cityscape layers and save in layer palette as backup if needed in case of error while adding final touches to rendering). Select Eraser Tool and change settings:
—Mode: Brush
—Brush Size: 300+/-
—Opacity: 75%+/-
—Flow: 50%+/-
Trim the sides of the brick, wood floor, and cityscape so the edges of the rendering fade off the page. Figures C-27c and C-27d on page 72 illustrate the final steps in this process.

STEP 11:

STEP 12: Final Rendering (Optional - faded edges)

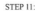

5-23f

perspective renderings with step-by-step instructions. Figures C-28 through C-33 present a range of perspective renderings created by students and professionals.

Digital Rendering Perspective Drawings

Increasingly designers are using graphics editing software such as Photoshop to render perspective drawings digitally. This involves importing the drawings into Photoshop and using digital imagery in a manner similar to that discussed on page XX of this chapter. It should be noted that this can be done with perspective drawings created by hand as well as drawings created digitally.

This process of using Photoshop as a rendering tool requires paying attention to the actual scale of materials images as they are imported into scaled drawings as well as to the quality of resolution of the files for both the materials and the drawing. Much like rendering orthographic by hand, "Photoshopping" perspectives involves importing the drawing and using digital imagery and manipulation of opacity and various tools to create shadows and value rendition. See Figures 5-23a

through 5-23f for tips on using Photoshop for perspective rendering, as well as Figures C-27c, C-27d, and C-28 on pages 72 and 73.

While Photoshop is secondary image manipulation software often used to render quickly by "eyeballing" the imagery, there are also specialized programs such as Autodesk 3ds Max and VIZ, Rhinoceros, and Form-Z (RenderZone), which allow for modeling and highly detailed photorealistic rendering. There are also specialized rendering programs such as Lightscape, RenderCity, and Artlantis that produce amazing results; unfortunately many of these have rather high learning curves. Detailed information about how to use these programs falls outside of the scope of this book however for a quick review of the results that can be expected from this type of program see Figures C-34a through C-37 on pages 76 to 78.

Currently, SketchUp may be the easiest modeling and rendering software to learn quickly; for simple rendering it will certainly suffice as shown in C-38a, C-38b, and C-38c on page 79 . The SketchUp rendering process is described in the previous chapter in Figure 4-19a, page 139.

REFERENCES

(Contains both works cited and recommended reading. Annotations where appropriate.)

Doyle, Michael. *Color Drawing*, 2nd edition. Hoboken, NJ: John Wiley & Sons, 2006.

Drpic, Ivo. *Sketching and Rendering Interior Space*. New York: Whitney Library of Design, 1988.

Forseth, Kevin, and David Vaughn. *Graphics for Architecture*. New York: John Wiley & Sons, 1980.

Green, Gary. *Creating Textures in Colored Pencil*. Cincinnati, OH: North Light Books, 1996.

Hanks, Kurt, and Larry Belliston. *Rapid Viz*. Los Altos, CA: William Kaufman Inc., 1980.

Juracek, Judy. *Architectural Surfaces*. New York: W.W. Norton & Co., 2005. *Full of beautiful images that can be imported into digital renderings via the accompanying CD.*

——. *Natural Surfaces*, New York: W.W. Norton & Co., 2002. *Full of beautiful images that can be imported into digital renderings via the accompanying CD; this volume is particularly helpful for skies and exterior foliage.*

Linn, Mike. *Architectural Rendering Techniques: A Color Reference*. New York: John Wiley & Sons, 1985.

McGarry, Richard, and Greg Madsen. *Marker Magic: The Rendering Problem Solver for Designers*. New York: John Wiley & Sons, 1993.

Porter, Tom. *Architectural Drawing*. New York: John Wiley & Sons, 1990.

6

SCALE MODELS

The use of three-dimensional scale models allows designers to study the volume of a given space. Unlike drawings and graphics, which exist on a two-dimensional surface, these models reveal the three-dimensional qualities of form. Scale models provide designers with the opportunity to comprehensively study and review the elements of a design.

Scale models vary widely in terms of finish, refinement, and time spent in construction. Generally the level of refinement of a model reflects the stage of the design process in which it is constructed. This means that in the preliminary stages of design, models are often quickly constructed and reflect the preliminary nature of the design; these are referred to as STUDY MODELS or WORKING MODELS. As a project proceeds into design development, models often become more refined and detailed. Those models used as a means of presenting a fully developed finalized design are often very refined and painstakingly crafted and are commonly referred to as PRESENTATION MODELS or FINISHED MODELS.

Most study models present simplified or abstracted versions of finishes, materials, and colors, yet all elements must be presented in accurate scale. Presentation models also often depict design elements in a simplified manner, with all elements accurately scaled; however, they are considerably more refined than study models. On some occasions finished models are constructed for design presentations with all materials, colors, and finishes depicted accurately. Professional model makers most often construct these highly accurate models. Many architecture and design firms have full-time model makers on staff; other firms hire model-making consultants as required. These professionals employ a wide variety of materials, techniques, and equipment—ranging from band saws to laser cutters—in the construction of beautiful scale models.

The construction of any model must begin with deciding its purpose. If the purpose is study and eventual refinement of an in-progress design, a study model is constructed. If the model's purpose is to present a fully developed design to a client, a presentation model is constructed. Furthermore, in constructing a presentation model, thought should be given to the nature of the design presented as well as the audience. For example, if the model is meant to communicate the spatial relationships or functional aspects of a space, the model maker may simplify and abstract the finishes so that they are not the focus of the model.

6-1

Figure 6-1
Various paperboards used in model making.
1. Foam board (white)
2. Foam board (black)
3. Foam board (colored)
4. Corrugated board (commonly called cardboard)
5. Ripple wrap
6. Chipboard
7. Mat board (with black core)
8. Museum board (white)
9. Illustration board
10. Mounting board (black)
11. Bristol board

Figure 6-2
Cutting paperboard. When cutting paperboard, three separate cuts should be made. First the top paper surface is cut, then the middle surface, and finally, the bottom paper surface is cut.

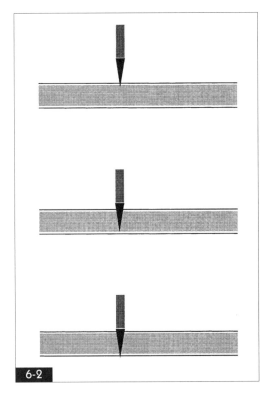

6-2

Projects that are publicly funded often require use of presentation models to gain public approval, and projects funded by investors may also require presentation models. In these cases, the audience must be considered carefully and the model must clearly communicate the design. Models meant for a general audience may require very accurate, realistic depiction of finishes and are often made by professionals.

Models are highly useful as a means of study for students of design. Many design students are more comfortable designing spaces by drawing plans and elevations and avoid constructing scale models. The problem here is that most students have trouble visualizing the totality of a space when they limit their work to two-dimensional drawings.

Often the best way to come to know the totality of a given space is to build a scale model; it is also a wonderful way for design students to improve design visualization skills. Constructing quick study models of in-process designs allows students to "see" a space early in the design process.

MATERIALS AND TOOLS

Study models are often constructed rapidly, using inexpensive, readily available materials. Given the way interior spaces are planned, interior study models are often constructed by attaching vertical elements directly to a drafted floor plan. A basic understanding of materials and construction techniques will allow design students to construct helpful study models. More refined presentation models are often crafted using more refined, and often more expenive materials, these are generally more time consuming to build. An understanding of the materials and techniques used in building refined models is also helpful.

Paperboards

Various types of paperboards available in art supply stores are used in scale model building. For the most part, paper products are inexpensive, lightweight, and easy to cut. Figure 6-1 illustrates a range of paperboards used in model building.

Foam board (also called foam core) is a type of paperboard consisting of polystyrene foam (or Styrofoam) sandwiched between two sheets of paper. Foam core comes in a variety of thicknesses, often $\frac{3}{16}$" or $\frac{1}{8}$", and is readily available in bleached white paper with a white center. Also available are black foam core, consisting of black cover paper and a black foam center, and foam core that is primarily white with one colored top layer.

White foam board is commonly used for study models because its thickness relates well to standard scaled wall thicknesses. Most often foam board is left unpainted to serve as a neutral or abstract presentation of materials. Sometimes, designers cap foam core edges with another paper such as bristol board or museum board to cover the exposed Styrofoam, which gives a more refined appearance.

Foam board is easily cut with snap-off cutters or X-Acto knives. When cutting foam board, it is important to use very sharp blades and to cut in a minimum of three steps. The first cut is made through the top layer of paper, the second cut should go through the middle layer of Styrofoam, and the last cut must cut cleanly through the bottom paper layer (see Figure 6-2).

Do not try to cut through foam board in fewer than these three steps; otherwise the effort will result in jagged edges. Only very sharp blades should be used, because dull ones produce poor results. When required, the paper can be peeled from away from the foam center and the foam can be cut, sanded, or scored. This allows for the creation of angles, curves, and other complex shapes (see Figures 6-3, 6-4, and 6-5).

White glue works well in joining foam board. When required, straight pins are

Figure 6-3

When using foam board, a 45-degree angle is cut by first peeling away a portion of the top surface that matches the thickness of the board. Then the inner material and bottom layer of paper are cut at 45 degrees. Two sheets cut this way can be joined together to form a 90-degree angle.

Figure 6-4

When using foam board, a 90-degree angle can be formed by removing a portion of the top paper surface that is twice the thickness of the foam board. Each side of the foam core is then cut away at a 45-degree angle with the backing paper left in place. The board is then folded to create a 90-degree angle with a continuous paper surface.

Figure 6-5

Create curves with paperboard by first scoring the material (leaving the backing paper intact) and then securing the board in place with glue.

6-6

used to hold joints together while the glue dries. In complex models, angled weights and clamps may be used. Spray adhesive and double-sided tape also work with foam board. As stated, most often foam core is left unpainted, creating attractive, simple study models. If painting is desired, paint must be carefully tested on a scrap of foam core, as some paints dissolve the foam.

Foam board is also used as a mounting surface for materials presentations, drawings, and renderings. Although it works well in this application, foam core can warp, depending on weather conditions, paper surfaces, and adhesives used.

GATORFOAM BOARD is similar to foam core, in that it consists of foam sandwiched between layers of paper. This material is very sturdy and is difficult to cut. Gatorfoam board is best cut on a band saw.

If no saw is available, the material can be scored and carefully snapped off along the scored edge. As with foam board, the outer layers of Gatorfoam board can be peeled away, allowing the inner foam to be cut and sanded. White glue works well in Gatorfoam board scale models, as do spray adhesives and double-sided tape.

Gatorfoam board is available in bleached white as well as black; it also works well in presentation boards, especially for heavy items. Gatorfoam board is used occasionally as a mounting surface for drawings and renderings because it does not warp as easily as foam board.

CORRUGATED BOARD (commonly called *cardboard*) is generally brown in color, inexpensive, and can be used in constructing study models. Corrugated board consists of heavy corrugated paper covered with

FIGURE 6-6

This study model for a workstation is constructed from corrugated board (for vertical partitions), chipboard (for the work surface), and tracing paper (for transparent sliding windows) and is held together with white glue.

FIGURE 6-7
This conceptual study model,
made of bristol board, is a
vehicle for exploring various
thematic issues for a particular
project.
Model by John Urban

6-7

outer layers of heavy brown paper. The outer layers of corrugated board may be peeled away to reveal the corrugated paper center. This corrugated center can then be used to indicate texture. Corrugated board works well in quick study models because it is widely available, inexpensive, and can be cut easily. Although it is easy to cut, this material requires the three-cut method discussed earlier in regard to foam core. White glue works well with corrugated board, as do spray adhesives and double-sided tape. Figure 6-6 shows a study model constructed of corrugated board and chipboard.

Another kind of paper that is currently available looks like the corrugated center portions of corrugated board; this is often referred to as RIPPLE WRAP. Ripple wrap is available in a wide range of colors and is used in the creation of presentation boards, notebook covers, and portfolio covers, as well as in model making.

CHIPBOARD looks like the outer layer of cardboard (corrugated board). It is extremely inexpensive and is used on quick study models. Chipboard cuts easily with a cutter or an X-Acto blade and can be fastened with white glue, spray adhesive, or double-sided tape. Figure 6-6 shows a study model constructed of corrugated board and chipboard. MAT BOARD is paperboard with a colored top surface. It is available with a white or black paper center. Mat board is sometimes used to add color and details to models, and on some occasions models are constructed completely of mat board. MUSEUM BOARD generally has high rag content and is white or off-white throughout. Museum board is used to create pristine study and presentation models because of its attractive appearance.

ILLUSTRATION BOARD most often has a white or buff-colored surface and high rag content, and can be used for model making. Illustration board requires three cuts through the paper surfaces to produce a clean-looking cut area. Black MOUNTING

FIGURE 6-8
Some examples of wood used in constructing presentation models.
1. Balsa wood (strips and blocks)
2. Cherry
3. Walnut
4. Basswood (strips, veneer, and scaled moldings)

BOARD is thin and easy to cut, as is BRISTOL BOARD (or bristol paper), which is often white. Figure 6-7 is a conceptual model made of bristol board.

Chipboard, mat board, museum board, black mounting board, and bristol board are easily cut, lightweight, easy to glue, and often used in model making. Because they are thinner than foam core, they work in smaller-scale models. In large-scale models these thinner paperboards are laminated (layered together using glue or double-sided tape) or used in conjunction with additional paperboard, wood, or plastic.

Wood

Wood is used often in scale model building. Because it is more costly and time-consuming to work with, it is not used as often as paper products in quick study models. It is, however, used widely in models during the design development of a project and for final presentations. Because of wood's warmth and natural beauty, it is often treated very simply and abstractly in models. It may be sanded, stained, or sealed but is rarely painted or heavily embellished. Wood is particularly useful in models where it is to be a major interior finish.

A variety of wood products useful in model building are available in hobby stores. Particular wood species offer certain advantages. Figure 6-8 illustrates wood products used in models.

BALSA WOOD is a light and porous wood that can be cut with a blade or knife (or a saw on larger pieces) and requires no power tools for cutting. Because it is easy to carve, balsa wood is used for toy making, crafts, and scale model building. Balsa wood is readily available in blocks, strips, sheets, and veneers (very thin sheets) in a wide range of sizes. Because of this wood's fibrous nature, it may appear rough even after sanding. Although balsa wood can be cut easily, it can be difficult to cut evenly because of the structure of the wood.

BASSWOOD is an attractive, smooth, light-colored hardwood that is very popular for model building. It has only slight graining patterns, giving it a neutral appearance useful in models. In addition, basswood is relatively easy to cut and work with. Unlike balsa wood, basswood can be sanded smooth if handled carefully. Basswood is sold at many hobby stores, especially those that specialize in railroad models or miniature houses. It is available in blocks, sheets, veneers, strips, dowels, cut with siding patterns, and in scaled ornamental moldings. Thin sheets and strips of basswood can be cut with a sharp X-Acto blade or a utility knife, whereas thicker slabs and blocks require hand saws or power tools.

Other hardwood species such as walnut, mahogany, cherry, and teak—available in sheets, veneers, and blocks—are used in models. Because these woods have distinct patterns of graining and coloration, they are often used to accent basswood models. In constructing highly detailed models, it is helpful to use the actual wood species that is proposed for a particular design. Often hard-to-find wood veneers are available at local specialty woodworking shops.

White glue is often used in the construction of wood models. It is best applied sparingly, which provides better adhesion and a neat appearance. Because white glue requires time to dry, items should be weighted, clamped, or otherwise held in place as the glue dries. In some cases instant glue is used on wood models. Many expert model makers rely on slower versions of instant glue such as Slow Jet or Slo-Zap, especially when gluing small or complex items.

Plastics and Foam

Plastics are used by professional model builders and by industrial designers for scale models, mock-ups, and working prototypes. Styrene, polystyrene, and Balsa-Foam are some of the most popular plastics for use in model and prototype construction. Figure 6-9 illustrates types of plastic used in model building.

STYRENE sheets, strips, rods, and I-beams are available at hobby shops in a range of sizes with a white finish. A variety of grooved and scored sheet styrene is available in patterns that resemble tiles, siding, and other finish materials. Sheet styrene is cut by scoring with a sharp blade and then snapping along the scored area. Sheet styrene is best glued with specialized plastic cement that creates a fast and strong bond that actually fuses the joint.

STYRENE FOAM insulation board is lightweight and readily available at lumberyards and home-improvement stores. This material is most often sold in blue, pink, and gray in a range of thicknesses. Sheets of styrene foam can be glued together (or laminated) to form the desired width and depth. The best means of cutting styrene foam is a hot wire cutter. Nonrepositionable spray adhesive

6-9

works well as a glue in layering foam. Styrene foam presents a problem in terms of toxicity and does not accept paint well. It is best used unpainted in study models or as an abstraction of material form.

BALSA-FOAM is a tan-colored, nontoxic, phenolic polymer resin foam that is easier to work with than standard styrene foam. Balsa-Foam can be readily cut with simple hand tools (knife blades, cutters, and saws) and is easily glued with low-melt hot glue or spray adhesive. If required, Balsa-Foam can be painted with acrylic or enamel paints. It is available through model railroad shops and catalogs geared to industrial designers.

SINTRA is a polyvinyl chloride product used in point-of-purchase displays and signage construction. This material is used increasingly by model makers. Much like sheet styrene, thin sheets of Sintra are cut by scoring and breaking along the score. Sintra is available in varying thicknesses and colors and can sometimes be painted with acrylic paints over appropriate primers (this works only for models; displays require different paints). Paint may be applied by brush, airbrush, or spray can.

Adhesives and Tools

Model making requires tremendous patience in measuring, cutting, gluing, and attaching. Certain tools and adhesive products can make the job of model construction easier. However, the most important tools of all are patience and allowing the proper amount of time. Figure 6-10 illustrates popular modeling tools and adhesives.

FIGURE 6-9
Plastics are often used in study models and for portions of presentation models.
  1. Styrene foam (cut into blocks)
  2. Balsa-Foam[tm] (cut into cylinders)
  3. Sintra[tm] (colored)
  4. Sintra (white)
  5. Styrene (strips, rods, grooved sheets, plain sheets)

FIGURE 6-10

Model-building tools and adhesives.

1. White glue
2. Slow instant glue
3. Glue accelerator
4. Glue stick
5. Rubber cement
6. Double-sided tape
7. Transfer tape
8. Masking tape
9. Painter's tape (removable)
10. Spray adhesive
11. Sandpaper
12. Small file
13. Tack cloth (for removing debris after sanding)
14. Small, heavy angle plate (used as a weight)
15. Large paper clips
16. Small clamps
17. Straight pins
18. Utility knife
19. Snap-off cutter
20. Excel (or X-Acto) knife
21. Metal builders square
22. Cork-backed metal ruler
23. Steel straightedge with knob
24. Cutting pad

6-10

WHITE GLUE, such as Elmer's Glue-All, is used a great deal in model construction. It works well on paper, foam core, Gatorfoam board, and wood. White glue forms an excellent bond; however, it takes some time to dry. This means that the items being glued must be held in place by clamps, weights, or hands. Generally, white glue should be applied in thin layers to create neat, tight joints. White glue applied in thick layers does not hold well and looks terrible.

RUBBER CEMENT is an excellent adhesive for bonding paper and light fabrics to paperboard in models or materials presentations. When using rubber cement, be sure to apply the cement lightly to both surfaces, let it dry a bit and become tacky, and then attach the two surfaces. This type of application allows for repositioning of the cement. Rubber cement is flammable and can produce toxic vapors.

INSTANT GLUES have the advantage of drying quickly and the disadvantage of drying so fast that mistakes are made. Many model builders use slow versions of instant glue, such as Slow Jet or Slo-Zap. These slower quick glues allow for objects to be set in place and repositioned. Once the items are in place, an accelerator such as Zip Kicker or Zap Kicker is sprayed on the joint, and the glue dries instantly.

The use of slow glues and accelerators is necessary in constructing detailed and refined models with complex elements. These instant glues work well on wood but not on styrene. They are highly toxic and flammable, and should be used only according to manufacturer's instructions in extremely well-ventilated work areas.

DOUBLE-SIDED TAPE (including transfer tape), masking tape, and painter's tape all work well in model construction. Double-sided tape is excellent for attaching and layering sheets of paper, foam core, and wood veneers. It works better than spray adhesive, which can cause warping of dis-

similar surfaces. In some instances carpet tape, which is a heavy duty double-sided tape, may be used to attach heavier items.

TRANSFER TAPE is sold in rolls; it is sticky on both sides yet contains no sheet of plastic to hold the adhesive. It can be applied by hand or with a transfer tape gun (sold in some art supply stores). Transfer tape works well for layering paper and thin veneers and causes little telegraphing of the tape through the veneer. This tape is excellent for attaching paper to foam core or mat board and generally causes no warping.

MASKING and PAINTER'S TAPE work for masking off areas and bonding items together. Long-Mask, or painter's tape, looks similar to masking tape but is blue in color. The advantage to painter's tape is that it is easily removable and leaves no residue even after several days. This allows the model maker to leave the tape in place while paints and glues dry, without having to remove the tape too soon.

SPRAY ADHESIVE is used like spray paint. The adhesive is sprayed from a can onto the appropriate surfaces. Some types of spray adhesive adhere permanently, and others allow for repositioning. Spray adhesives are very popular with design students. In model making, spray adhesive is most commonly used in attaching copies of plans and elevations onto foam core for use in study models. This is a fast and effective method of study model construction.

Although spray adhesive is quick, it is important to note that paper applied with spray mount to foam board will eventually wrinkle or bubble if applied to large surface areas. It is wise to use repositionable spray mount in model construction and materials presentations. However, almost all spray adhesives can cause wrinkling and warping of paper and foam board if left for any period of time. One trick to removing a spray adhesive is to use a hair dryer to warm it before attempting removal. The overspray from spray adhesives can be messy. These adhesives also generate fumes and are flammable.

STUDIO TAC is an alternative to spray adhesive. This is a double-sided adhesive sheet sold in a range of sizes. Studio Tac is peeled away from a backing paper and applied to the object for mounting; it is then peeled away from another backing surface and mounted. Studio Tac works best in adhering lightweight items such as paper and paperboard. It produces no overspray or fumes.

HOT GLUE GUNS are electric guns that heat and dispense hot (or very warm) glue. Glue guns hold sticks of glue that melt and are pushed through a nozzle; they are popular with many hobbyists and have some applications for models. However, hot glue is messy, hard to control, and in many cases does not produce a strong bond. Hot glue is used more often in the construction of quick study models than in refined presentation models. Hot glue can cause gaps to form in joints and can fail in completed models.

Generally, hot glue is more useful in adhering materials to presentation boards than in assembling scale models. Glue guns range in size and in temperature. High-temperature glues work best for fabric, some plastics, glass, wood, and ceramic. Lower-temperature glues are often used for Styrofoam, paper, and more delicate materials.

X-Acto knives and blades are commonly used in model building, as are snap-off cutters and utility knives. A wide range of blades are available for use with X-Acto (or similar brand) knives. The range of blades provides for specialized cutting uses, although the classic fine-point blade (#11) is most useful in cutting paperboards. Cutters with snap-off blades also work well because they allow for easy changing of blades.

The key to using all types of knives and blades is to work with a sharp blade and make many cuts through the paperboard or wood. Foam board, mat board, museum board, bristol board, and cardboard all require at least three cuts through their surfaces. The three-cut method is the only way to achieve neat and tidy cuts, and it requires absolutely sharp blades.

A specially designed polyvinyl cutting pad is very useful for cutting all types of material. Most cutting pads have a grid pattern that allows for alignment. These pads protect table surfaces, provide a nice measured cutting surface, and seem to make blades last longer.

A cork-backed metal straightedge is an excellent cutting edge for model making. In addition, steel straightedges are available with knob holders that protect fingers from cutting accidents. Plastic rulers and triangles are not to be used for cutting edges because they are easily damaged and do not work well.

Professional model makers sometimes use heavy angled plates, as well as clamps, to hold pieces together while glue sets up. These are necessary for detailed and complex models and are not used as often by students for study models.

One busy professional model builder has stated that the six most important items for model making are a steel triangle with knob holder (to protect fingers), a polyvinyl cutting pad with a horizontal wood edge attached (for use in conjunction with the triangle), an X-Acto knife, white glue, double-stick tape, and Long-Mask tape (see Figure 6-11).

CONSTRUCTION AND USE OF MODELS

As stated, all types of model building require patience and time. The first step in model construction is careful consideration of the purpose of the model. If the purpose is for the designer(s) to study spatial relationships and proportions, a very quick study model can be constructed. Quick

FIGURE 6-11

Helpful tools for student paperboard models.

1. Transfer tape

2. Painter's tape (blue)

3. Elmer's white glue

4. X-Acto knife

5. Steel straightedge with knob (a metal triangle with knob also works well)

6. Cutting board with wood permanently attached to use with straightedge or triangle

study models are most often constructed of chipboard, cardboard (corrugated board), mat board, museum board, or foam board.

As a project is refined, a more refined model may be used to study design details and finishes; in this case the study model must be more detailed and may be shown to a client for approval. Refined study models are often constructed of illustration board, mat board, museum board, foam core, or wood (or some combination of these materials). Refined study models may also include plastic or acrylic, for indication of glazed surfaces.

A common method of constructing a quick study model involves gluing orthographic drawings to chipboard, corrugated board, or foam core. This is done by first gluing the floor plan in place on the model-making material, such as foam board. The interior elevations are then glued onto foam core, chipboard, or corrugated board,

attached to the plan, and glued in place. It is advantageous to use scaled human figures in study models. These can be drawn by hand and glued to foam core.

When gluing orthographic drawings, it is important to consider the eventual thickness of the walls and to plan accordingly. Figures 6-12a, 6-12b, and 6-12c illustrate the steps in constructing this type of study model. Figure 6-13 depicts a model constructed similarly, with the exception that the orthographic drawings are attached to a building section, creating a sectional model. Figures 6-14a, 6-14b, 6-15a, and 6-15b show student study models constucted to examine spatial relationships. A more complex model constructed by attaching foam core to orthographic projection drawings can be found in Figures 6-16a through 6-16d.

The materials selected for a model must relate to its scale. For example, a model constructed in ¼" scale requires exterior

FIGURE 6-12a
Quick study models are often constructed by first attaching the floor plan to foam board, then attaching the elevations. It is best to plan ahead and leave extra room at either side of the appropriate elevations in order to attach the adjacent walls.

FIGURE 6-12b
The walls are glued into place on the plan. Notice that the extra room at each side of the first wall elevation allows for gluing and joining the adjacent wall.

FIGURE 6-12c
An overview of the steps of construction.

FIGURE 6-13
A sectional model (a section fragment model) of the Unité d'Habitation, designed by Le Corbusier. This model was part of a demonstration of quick and efficient model building for students.
Model by Thomas Oliphant

6-14a

6-14b

6-15a

FIGURES 6-14a AND 6-14b
This study model, constructed
early in the design process,
was used to study spatial
relationships and scale issues
on a retail project. The model
is constructed in the manner
described in Figures 6-12a,
6-12b, and 6-12c.
Design and model by Denise Haertl

FIGURES 6-15a AND 6-15b
This study model was used for
an in-class presentation and
is constructed in the manner
described in Figures 6-12a,
6-12b, and 6-12c.
Design and model by Tiffany Baca

6-15b

6-16a

6-16b

6-16c

6-16d

FIGURES 6-16a, 6-16b, 6-16c, AND 6-16d
This foam board and paper model was built
to depict the design of a small two-story
building. Due to the nature of the design
and the scale of the project, the model was
designed in two parts, the top of which can
be removed for better viewing of the first
story. Special care was given to accurately
portray specially designed cabinetry and
millwork details.

Design and model by Siv Jane Refsnes

walls that scale to roughly ⅟₁₆"; in this case thin museum board or mat board would be an appropriate choice (see Figure 6-17). In some cases, the paper used in constructing the study model can be rendered.

Some designers prefer pristine mono-chromatic models. In such cases simply gluing an elevation onto paperboard is not appropriate. A model like this requires that measurements be taken from orthographic drawings and transferred to paperboard. The paperboard is cut to the correct dimensions, and the model is then glued in place. Figure 6-18 illustrates a study model

FIGURE 6-17
A model built to study wall heights, constructed of museum board mounted on black foam board. The museum board is the appropriate size for use in a scale model.
Design by Courtney Nystuen. Model by Leanne Larson and the author

FIGURE 6-18
Study model constructed of illustration board.
Model by Eric Zeimet

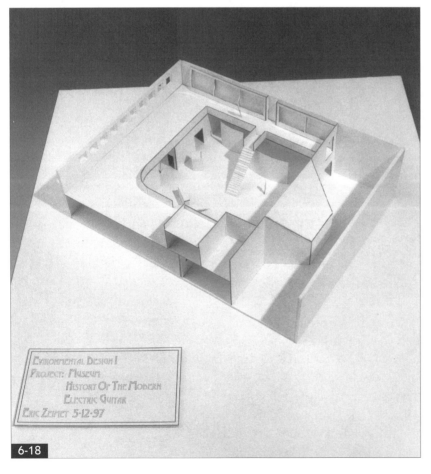

constructed by transferring dimensions instead of attaching elevations.

For the most part, it is best to avoid using manufactured dollhouse products in study models. Such items tend to be too busy and distracting. Instead, abstracting materials to simple forms is useful and less distracting. However, some milled wood items such as paneling and interior moldings can be used to good effect in study models. Figures 6-19a and 6-19b are simple models with abstracted finishes. Figures 6-20a and 6-20b depict a presentation model made using a range of materials with abstracted versions of finishes applied in a visually successful manner.

Very simple, square or rectilinear spaces can be illustrated with FLIP-UP models. These models use floor plans and interior elevations that are rendered and glued onto a paperboard surface. The elevations are then attached to the plan with a single strip of tape placed on both back surfaces. The tape serves as a hinge and allows

FIGURE 6-19a
A vignette model built to study wall finishes, constructed of foam board, rendered mat board, basswood veneer, and basswood dollhouse moldings.

FIGURE 6-19b
A vignette model built to study wall finishes and design, constructed of mat board, rendered mat board, ripple wrap (metallic finish), and basswood veneer.

the elevations to flip up into place. The elevations can be taped into place as needed for study and review (see Figure 6-21).

Creating flip-up models is a way to use drawing skills as an aid in model making, and these models can be stored flat for inclusion in a portfolio. The limitation of flip-up models is that they work only for very simple floor plans and are less realistic spatially than standard models.

Scale Models in Professional Practice

Some design firms use scale models a great deal; others use them rarely. Highly refined presentation models take hours to build and are very costly. For this reason some designers do not use them. However, many designers have a commitment to study projects fully during the design process, and this requires the use of scale models. It

FIGURES 6-20a AND 6-20b
This model was constructed as part of a final design-development presentation for an exhibition-space project and is made of wood, plastic, paperboard, and metal.
Design and model by Melanie Deeg

FIGURE 6-21
A rendered flip-up model.
Constructed of rendered bond
paper on black foam board.
Model by Ardella Pieper

FIGURES 6-22a AND 6-22b
Two views of a large study
model built for a professional
project, constructed of bond
paper, foam board, plastic, teak
veneer, metal screen, and fabric.
Design and model by Meyer, Scherer
& Rockcastle, Ltd.

also requires that design contracts include the costs of model building.

Larger firms often have a fully equipped model shop where a range of models are constructed for study and presentation. In many firms, designers build only study models, and professional model builders are hired to build presentation models.

Firms that use models as a fundamental part of the design process often construct

6-22b

many in the course of a project. This means that a series of models are constructed that reflect the levels of refinement of the design. Figures 6-22a and 6-22b, 6-23a and 6-23b, 6-24a and 6-23b, and 6-25 illustrate a series of models built for one design project.

On very large design projects, such as hotels and entertainment facilities, full-scale mock-ups may be constructed. It is not unusual for large hotel projects to employ full-size room mock-ups for viewing by investors or owners. Unusual design details may also require full-scale mock-ups as a means of study prior to construction.

Industrial designers (also known as product designers) create a number of study models throughout the design process. These models are made of a variety of materials, ranging from foam board to styrene and Balsa-Foam. In an ongoing

process of refinement; industrial designers often create many models for each project, ending with absolutely accurate presentation models that can be mistaken for the real thing.

In the specialized process of designing furniture, it is necessary to construct many models and mock-ups. Furniture study models are often constructed of corrugated board, chipboard, foam board, or styrene. As a design becomes refined, it is often necessary to move to large-scale mock-ups or prototypes as a means of studying form as well as working out construction issues. Prototypes are required to perform as the actual products will, so they are often constructed of materials very similar to the actual final product (see Figures 6-26a and 6-26b). Additional models and mock-ups for a professional project may be found on page 92 of the Color Plates section.

FIGURES 6-23a AND 6-23b
Two views of a smaller study
model built for a professional
project constructed of bond
paper, foam board, plastic,
basswood, teak veneer, and
fabric.
*Design and model by Meyer, Scherer
& Rockcastle, Ltd.*

6-23a

6-23b

6-24a

FIGURES 6-24a AND 6-24b
Furniture models for the project
featured in Figures 6-22a
through 6-23b, constructed of
assorted wood.
Design and model by Meyer, Scherer
& Rockcastle, Ltd.

6-24b

FIGURE 6-25
Presentation model for the
corporate headquarters
featured in Figures 6-22a
through 6-24. Basswood.
Design and model by Meyer, Scherer
& Rockcastle, Ltd.

FIGURE 6-25
Presentation model for the
corporate headquarters
featured in Figures 6-22a
through 6-24. Basswood.
Design and model by Meyer, Scherer
& Rockcastle, Ltd.

FIGURE 6-26a
Chair prototype constructed
of wood and steel.
Designed and made by Thomas
Oliphant. Photograph by Kathy Fogerty

FIGURE 6-26b
Chair prototype (on right)
shown with actual finished
chair (on left).
Designed and made by Thomas
Oliphant. Photograph by Kathy Fogerty

REFERENCES

(Contains both works cited and recommended reading. Annotations where appropriate.)

Mills, Criss. *Designing with Models*. New York: John Wiley & Sons, 2000.

Shimizu, Yoshiharu. *Models and Prototypes: Clay, Plaster, Styrofoam, Paper*.
    Tokyo: Graphicsha Publishing Company, 1991.

7 PRESENTING MATERIALS AND FINISHES

Most professional interior design projects involve study, review, and refinement of interior architectural finishes and materials, as well as furnishings, fixtures, and equipment. Finish materials, furnishings, and fixtures must be studied individually and also be viewed as parts of a whole. All of these items must be evaluated in terms of life-safety issues and performance as well as from an aesthetic standpoint. This chapter focuses only on the presentation of these items and does not cover the important issues of life safety, performance, and specification.

A formal materials presentation is not of particular importance to the individual designer early in the project as an aid in the design process. It is most common for designers to gather a variety of samples and make preliminary decisions without pinning anything down. Most designers can work from large samples kept loose (unmounted) while in the preliminary stages of a design (see Figures 7-1a and 7-1b). Large projects, or those with many team members, may in rare cases require a materials presentation as an early communication and design aid. These cases are the exceptions, not the rule.

Early in the space-planning process, many designers begin to consider architec-tural finishes and materials. After careful study, preliminary selection of finishes, materials, and furnishings can be made. These preliminary selections are presented to the client or end user in a way that reflects the preliminary nature of the selections.

Often, preliminary selections of materials are presented at the same time as preliminary plans, elevations, perspective or axonometric drawings, and perhaps study models. All of the elements used in a particular presentation must be consistent graphically, and they work best if they contain unifying elements. For example, if it is used in a preliminary presentation, a materials board may incorporate the graphics found in the title block of drawings. Or perhaps the format of a materials board can be consistent with the format used to present renderings. In many cases, materials boards are keyed graphically to floor plans and serve as an aid in understanding elements of the design presented.

Some designers prefer to keep the preliminary materials presentation casual, with all elements remaining loose and unmounted. Providing loose items allows the presentation audience to touch and easily examine the samples. Keeping things loose also allows the client to understand

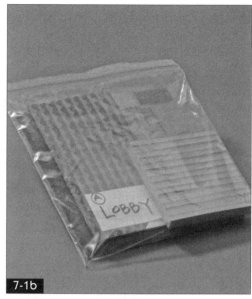

7-1a

7-1b

FIGURE 7-1a
Many designers prefer to keep materials loose and unmounted, especially in preliminary presentations.

FIGURE 7-1b
Loose samples can be kept organized in clear plastic bags.

clearly the preliminary nature of the selection and imparts a sense that there is plenty of room for decision making.

Many designers mount preliminary selections on presentation boards so that the client or end user gets a sense that decisions have been made and are being communicated. Another method of preliminary presentation calls for pinning samples down on a board with pushpins so that they can easily be removed for examination by the client (see Figures 7-2a, 7-2b, and 7-2c).

As a project moves forward, it is important that materials presentations clearly reflect the given stages of the design. Many designers create a materials presentation as part of the final visual presentation, which takes place at the end of design development phase of a project. Large and complex projects often require several materials presentations, which occur at key points in the design development process. Some projects, however, may require no formal materials presentation during the entire design process.

One extremely successful residential designer never mounts materials onto boards for any project. He keeps all sam-ples loose and arranges them on a work-table for his clients' review. Several designers interviewed prefer to drape fabrics on full-size furniture samples and keep all finishes unmounted for client approval—this may vary based on project size, type, and timing.

Clearly there is variation in the manner in which finalized selections of materials, furnishings, and finishes are presented to clients. Many designers pride themselves on consistent, well-crafted materials presentations, whereas others prefer to keep samples loose and informal. Many firms have standards for the way presentation boards are prepared. These standards include preferred board size, color, graphics, and methods for attaching samples, as well as the level of formality conveyed in the presentations.

The standards employed by an individual firm allow presentations to distinctly reflect the concerns and focus of the firm and at the same time clearly convey the selections for a particular project. Final presentations often include drawings, renderings, models, and materials boards, all of which must appear visually cohesive and

7-2a

7-2b

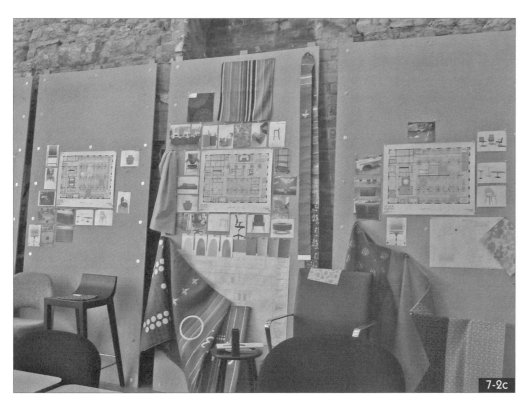

7-2c

FIGURES 7-2a, 7-2b, AND 7-2c
This presentation of finishes makes use of simply mounted samples and includes small finish samples as well as larger fabric samples, full scale furniture, and project drawings. Figures C-50a through C-50i on pages 91 and 92 are additional color images from this project.
By Meyer, Scherer & Rockcastle, Ltd.

FIGURE 7-3

In this example samples are mounted directly to light-colored mat board that is secured on a larger piece of black foam board. The project title is also mounted on the black foam board, while sample titles are printed on paper that is mounted directly on samples.
By Laura Purcell

logical. Information and examples of complete presentations may be found in the following chapter.

On some projects, all of the elements for a final presentation, including materials boards, must be packed for travel. This means that all necessary items are included, and everything of importance must be packed and organized for the designer's arrival in a strange city. Organizing a final presentation for travel can take weeks of preparation. There are large projects that include more than 50 materials boards that must be packed for travel and presentation to large audiences. Presentations of this sort must be organized in a clear and logical fashion that leaves no margin for error.

The variation in practice and presentation of interior design projects requires that design students develop a range of skills in preparing materials presentations. Fortunately, internships often provide an excellent opportunity for students to become involved in creating many types of design presentations, including materials presentations, thus allowing the students to see particular office standards as they relate to these presentations.

Although there is great diversity as to formality of presentation and office graphic standards, there are numerous factors common to all materials presentations. These have to do with legibility, organization, graphic cohesion, quality of craftsmanship, techniques, and tools, and appropriateness. All design students can benefit from a clear understanding of these factors in developing visual skills and creating meaningful presentations.

MATERIALS AND MEDIA

Many of the materials used in presentation boards are discussed in previous chapters. Information on types of paper and drawing tools can be found in Chapter 1, page 2; additional information on paper and rendering media is found in Chapter 5, page 144. For descriptions of paperboards, adhesives, and cutting tools, refer to Chapter 6, page 183.

Most materials presentations require sturdy backing materials, most often a type of paperboard. Foam board is often used in such presentations because it is sturdy yet lightweight and easy to work with. Samples, titles, and notes can be applied directly to be top paper surface of the foam core. In some cases white foam board is used as the surface to which all samples are applied; a mat board border is also added to the surface of the foam board This type of presentation has the added feature of resisting warping, making it useful for student portfolios, which otherwise fall prey to warping and wrinkling. While many prefer white foam board, others favor black foam board for more dramatic presentations and in some cases a portion of the black foam core is left visible to serve as a visual border (see Figure 7-3). Figures 7-4a and 7-4b depict attractive, well-organized professional presentations mounted directly on white foam-core board.

In some presentations foam board is covered with mat board, illustration board, bond paper, or Canson paper. Samples and titles are then mounted to the top paper surface (see Figures C-39a, C-39b, C-40a, and C-40b on pages 80-81). When thinner papers such as bond paper or Canson paper are used, the entire surface can be laid out with titles and notes and plotted using CAD or printed on a large-format copy machine; samples are then added to the appropriate locations as shown in Figures 7-5a and 7-5b. Some words of warning about the use of lightweight paper applied to boards: warping and wrinkling are huge problems if spray adhesive is used; two-sided tape is far superior as are products such as StudioTac.

Smaller or lightweight materials may be mounted on lighter-weight boards such as mat board, illustration board, or museum board. However, lighter boards can appear flimsy and will not support heavy materials such as tile or stone samples. Mat board and museum board are sometimes cut with windows; samples are mounted behind the windows just as artwork is matted (for further information, see the discussion regarding window matting later in this chapter, pages 221–222).

Materials presented in professional practice are often large and quite heavy. Full size ceramic tile, glass, and stone samples are particularly heavy. For this reason Gatorfoam board or wood panels are used as a mounting surface in some professional presentations. Large pieces of Gatorfoam board can be used with minimal warping, as can wood panels. Gatorfoam board and wood also allow for the mounting of very heavy samples.

Professional practice also requires very large-scale sample mock-ups to be provided on some jobs. For example, it is not uncommon to create 3-inch-by-3-inch ceramic tile sample mock-ups for large projects such as retail malls and airports. The appropriate subcontractors on a project often provide these large-scale samples. However, in some cases, design firms create them.

Nontraditional projects often require nontraditional materials presentations. One designer uses galvanized sheet metal, with magnets holding samples in place, for nontraditional presentations. A recent presentation made use of chain-link fencing panels as a mounting surface. For student projects designed to be viewed in a gallery setting, I have seen clear acrylic rectangles taken from inexpensive photoframes and used as sample containers as shown in Figure 7-6. For thesis-type projects, top students have been known to fabricate custom sample holders as shown in Figure 7-7. In some instances sketches of custom elements work to good

FIGURES 7-4a AND 7-4b
Professional presentation board mounted on foam board with titles on plastic label tape and hand-drawn ink borders.
Projects: Laurel Gardens of Avon, Avon, CN and Lourdes Nursing Home, Waterford, MI.
By Arthur Shuster, Inc.

7-5a

7-5b

FIGURES 7-5a AND 7-5b
Student design presentations with related
samples mounted on photocopied Canson
paper that contains printed drawings and titles.
By Kelly Urevig

7-6

FIGURES 7-6
These samples are contained
in a clear acrylic box typically
used as part of an inexpensive
photoframe.

PRESENTING MATERIALS AND FINISHES **211**

FIGURE 7-7
These samples are contained in a custom box fabricated in steel by the student for use in a senior thesis presentation.
By Ciarah Coenen

FIGURE 7-8
This nontraditional board consists of rendered illustration board and draped samples.

effect included on sample boards as shown in Figure 7-8.

A variety of adhesives are used to mount samples, and a variety of mounting techniques is employed in materials presentations (see "Techniques and Methods of Presentation" later in this chapter).

ORGANIZATION AND COMPOSITION

Successful materials presentations may vary greatly in terms of placement of samples and materials, yet designers generally agree on the importance of planning the arrangement of presentation graphics.

Stylistically boards may vary greatly. However, regardless of style or method of sample organization, some basic principles of graphic design should be employed in laying out presentation boards. For example, the use of a grid can do wonders for any presentation (see Chapter 9, page 245, for more information about grids).

FIGURE 7-9
Boards look best with some type of border.

1. Borders may be implied (dashed lines), with no items displayed beyond the implied borders.

2. Borders may be defined with a window mat.

3. Borders can be drawn onto the board surface or applied with graphic tape.

4. Borders may be defined with a sheet of colored paper mounted on foam board (also shown in Figure 7-3).

Traditionally, presentations with multiple boards should have a consistent compositional orientation: all boards should be formatted vertically, all horizontally, all square, and so forth.

Regardless of the presentation style, materials boards should have actual or implied borders. A border may be drawn, printed, or created with graphic tape (plastic or vinyl tape is available in a range of thicknesses and colors), or the border area may be left blank, with no samples or titles placed within a given area. Figure 7-9 shows thumbnail sketches of border arrangements.

There are distinct, diverse opinions regarding the organization of samples for presentations (see Figure 7-10). One school of thought calls for materials to be laid out in relation to their actual physical location. This means that all flooring is placed at the bottom of the arrangement, furnishings are placed above flooring, wall finishes are placed above flooring, window treatments and ceiling materials are placed at the top of the arrangement.

It is also common for designers to place items that relate to one another in close proximity on the presentation board. For example, a picture of a chair will be mounted adjacent to the wood finish and upholstery samples for that chair. This method is useful for clients who are not accustomed to viewing presentation boards, such as corporate officers or homeowners.

Another school of thought calls for materials to be placed according to their visual impact within the composition. For example, on a project with hundreds of yards of rubber floor tile and very little carpeting, the presentation may show large samples of rubber flooring and smaller samples of carpeting.

Some designers place samples of exactly the same size on the board and lay them out in equally spaced horizontal bands. Others

FIGURE 7-10
Board organization.

1. Materials applied in relation to their location in the environment: flooring at the bottom, walls above flooring, ceiling materials at top of board.

2. Materials applied in relation to proximity or physical contact; for example, flooring adjacent to related furnishings and finishes.

3. Materials placed according to their visual impact on the composition; for example, large areas of flooring represented by large samples.

4. Materials placed in relation to a graphic element or design parti; in this example, the materials form a collage relating to the floor plan.

place important items in the center of the presentation and spin additional samples out from the center. A few designers use the floor plan of a given space as an abstract diagram for laying out the materials on a presentation board.

There is a bit of controversy in regard to whether samples should physically touch one another on presentation boards. For years designers were trained to lay out samples with blank spaces (negative space) between samples. In current practice some designers, who think that items that will touch in reality should touch on boards, no longer consider this important.

Many designers place black or white cloth tape on the edges of materials boards. The tape can hide the several layers of material that would otherwise be exposed at the edge and creates a near, clean look. A black taped edge creates a distinct border, whereas a white taped edge is less visually dominant. Certain designers find a taped edge unnecessary if the boards have been cut cleanly.

On occasion clients require that materials boards be framed and placed behind glass. This is most common when presentations will be viewed by investors or hung in the sales or leasing office of a developer of commercial real estate. In these cases the particular needs of the audience must be considered in the titling and layout of the boards.

Titles, Keys, and Legends

It is imperative that all materials presentations clearly communicate the items selected. This means that samples must be titled, referenced, or keyed. There are two basic systems of referencing samples and images on presentation boards. One method requires that all items be titled or labeled directly on the front of the board, adjacent or very close to the appropriate sample. Another method allows for samples to be keyed and referenced with a legend on the front or back of the board or on an accompanying document. Designers and firms most often have office standards

FIGURE 7-11
Board titles.
  1. Materials may be titled directly on the board.
  2. Materials may be titled using a code system, with a legend or key placed on the back of the board or coded to the floor plan and elevations (as also shown in Figures 7-3 and 7-12).
  3. This example employs no titles on the face of the board; instead a coding system and legend are used on the back of the board.
  4. Legend on the back of board shown in Step 3.

that call for some form of one of these methods. Figure 7-11 shows thumbnails of some methods of titling and keying boards.

There are many board-titling methods. Some designers prefer labels to be kept simple; for example, a carpet sample may simply be labeled "Carpet—Master Bedroom" or "Carpet." Other designers prefer that actual specifications be included in the title; for example, the carpet would be labeled "Carpet—Master Bedroom, Wool Berber, 42 oz., Helios Carpet Mills." Some designers prefer simple titles on the front of the board with full specifications keyed to the back of the board or keyed to a floor plan. Figure 7-12 shows a board with samples keyed to a floor plan, as does Figure 7-3.

Systems for keying or referencing samples vary as well. Some designers prefer a letter or number code that relates to the type of sample used. For example, carpet may be listed as "C-1," wallcovering as "WC-1," and both are then fully referenced on the back of the board. Other designers prefer a simple numbering or lettering system starting with "1" or "A," running through all of the samples and referenced on the back.

Some designers prefer a system that employs no titles or codes on the front of the presentations. Instead a duplicate image of the board appears on the back with samples specified or referenced. It is also common to key materials to related floor plans or elevations and use the orthographic drawings as part of the reference system. For example, a materials board may have the code "C-1" for a particular carpet; the locations for the carpet are then shown on an accompanying floor plan.

There are many ways to create the actual titles used on boards. The simplest titles are created by hand lettering. In some cases

FIGURE 7-12
Materials sample board making
use of titles keyed to a floor
plan.
By Anne Cleary

FIGURE 7-12
Materials sample board making use of titles keyed to a floor plan.
By Anne Cleary

FIGURE 7-13
A clear ruler allows for accurate clean cutting of titles and symbols and for accurate placement on boards.

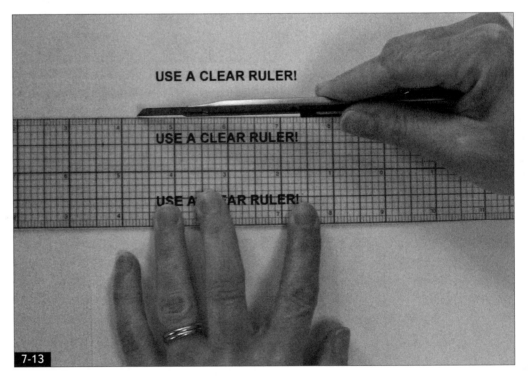

lettering is drawn directly on the top surface of the presentation board. A more professional look is created by using machines that print type onto plastic tape, such as Kroy or Merlin machines. After the machine expels the printed tape, a plastic backing is peeled away and the tape is mounted to the board surface or raised mat board title plates, much as in hand lettering. It is imperative that the tape lettering is neatly cut and applied to boards with the use of guidelines. Figures 7-4a and 7-4b show tape titles used in a presentation.

Appliqué film (sticky back) is commonly used in titling boards and drawings for presentation. Almost any graphics may be photocopied onto sticky back. The film is then cut to size and the backing surface removed, allowing the graphic to be applied to any paper surface. Sticky back works well in creating neat titles and unusual graphics, such as logos for boards and drawings. Sticky back can be found at most commercial photocopier supply stores and is available in a range of finishes from matte to glossy. Designers often select a matte finish for titling materials boards. It is imperative that appliqué film is measured and cut neatly (an X-Acto works well). In applying film to any surface, vertical and horizontal guidelines are required. For more information on appliqué films, see Chapter 1, page 4.

Most computer word-processing software will allow for printing a range of type styles. This means that students and designers with computers can create beautiful titles by simple computer generation of the appropriate words. The titles may then be mounted directly, or first applied to paperboard and then mounted (with the use of guidelines).

When cutting the paper or adhesive tape for titles care must be taken to cut the titles in straight, parallel lines and to avoided crooked, messy cuts. One means of accomplishing this is through the use of a clear ruler. The ability to see through the ruler at the guidelines and type allows for accurate, clean cuts to be made (see Figure 7-13).

As discussed previously titles, borders, notes, and additional information can be created using CAD (or other software) and

FIGURE 7-14

plotted or laid out on a large sheet of paper and photocopied using a large-format copier (or a standard copier for boards 11 inches by 17 inches, and smaller). The large copy is then mounted on paperboard and samples are attached. This method allows titles and logos to be printed on colored papers that accept photocopy toner. The colored paper is then mounted on paperboard, and samples are applied to the colored paper. Figure 7-14 is a presentation board with drawings, titles, and borders copied directly onto colored paper, with surface-mounted samples.

FIGURE 7-14
Board with drawings and titles printed or plotted on kraft paper with samples surface mounted on the top of the paper.
By Daniel Effenheim

FIGURE 7-15

In wrapping fabric samples, first allow an appropriate amount of material for wrapping. Then pull the ends firmly in place and secure with glue or tape. Adding a piece of paperboard to the back of the wrapped sample allows for easy mounting and gluing.

TECHNIQUES AND METHODS OF PRESENTATION

Currently, given the time constraints of professional practice, most designers mount or attach samples to the front surface of a presentation board. This method requires samples to be neatly mounted with all edges trimmed or wrapped.

Fabrics are often wrapped around cardboard (or mat board) and taped or glued in place. This treatment produces neat, uniform samples with no unraveled edges. Figure 7-15 illustrates the construction of these samples. The same wrapping method can be used on formal boards for paint samples (see Figure 7-16). When it is necessary to save time, fabric samples can be neatly trimmed and placed on mat board, which is then glued to the presentation board. In

appropriate circumstances, fabric samples may be draped and glued in place.

Pictures or photocopies of furnishings and equipment look best if they are mounted (with double-sided tape, Studio Tac, or spray mount) on mat board, which is then trimmed and mounted directly on the presentation board. Placing these items on mat board allows them to sit on the surface of the presentation board, creating a shadow line and adding a professional finish to the board; it also can prevent warping. The fastest method of trimming photos that are mounted on mat board is to use a large paper cutter with a sharp blade (see Figure 7-17). This is quicker than cutting with a utility knife or X-Acto. Replacement blades are available for paper cutters and should be replaced as necessary.

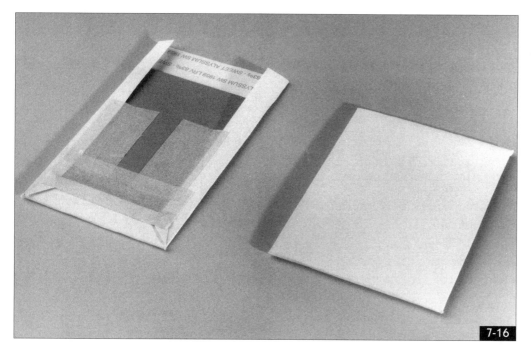

FIGURE 7-16
Paint samples can be wrapped
around a cardboard form and
held in place with tape.

7-16

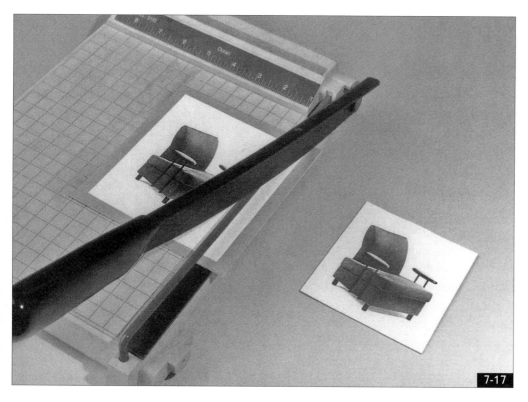

FIGURE 7-17
Photographs look best mounted
on mat paperboard and then
trimmed and glued onto a
board. A paper cutter makes
quick work of trimming.

7-17

Many designers find that mounting samples using Velcro® is useful (see Figures 7-18a and 7-18b). This allows clients to remove samples in order to examine them closely and can allow for later replacement. While this adhesive method can work quite well in the appropriate situations, it may allow samples to droop and become uneven-looking.

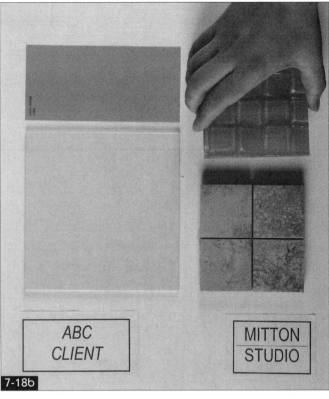

FIGURES 7-18a AND 7-18b
The use of Velcro allows samples to be removed for examination and replacement. However, this type of attachment may allow samples to become uneven looking.

When mounting heavy objects such as tile, stone, or metal panels, it is sometimes necessary to score the mounting board surface prior to applying glue. Scoring the surface adds texture to the board and increases the bonding capacity of most glues. This is especially necessary if Canson or another art paper is applied on top of a mounting board. Often, the paper must be cut away to reveal the mounting surface, so objects are glued directly to the backing board. This prevents the sample from pulling the Canson paper from the backing board. A consistent, thin application of white glue can often bond heavy samples to boards. In rare cases, contact cement is used, but because it is toxic and rather unpleasant to work with, it should be used as a last resort.

Especially large or heavy samples may require two layers of foam board to be used as backing. This allows one layer of the foam board to be cut away so that the sample may be recessed into the opening. Some designers find that heavy-duty carpet-tape—this is a type of heavy-duty double-sided tape—can work well to bond heavy surfaces to boards. However, carpet tape comes in a range of adhesive types and can have mixed results dependent upon the type used. Therefore, it is best to test for adhesion prior to using these tapes.

Plastic laminates and other samples may have product numbers printed on them. These printed numbers can often be removed with an electric eraser. Bestine or another solvent can also be used to remove stubborn printed information.

Designers use a variety of adhesive products in mounting samples and materials. A relatively thin application of white glue works beautifully in adhering lighter and medium-weight samples. However, white glue will cause light papers (tracing paper, vellum, bond) to wrinkle. In mounting these papers, double-sided tape, rubber cement, or spray-on adhesive (for small areas) can work well. Studio Tac works well in adhering paper and light samples to board surfaces.

Hot glue can work well in creating materials presentations if it is used on light- to medium-weight items with large flat surface areas. Heavier samples will *not* bond well with hot glue. A fairly thin, consistent application works best. Big globs of glue are not only messy, but do not create enough surface area of glue for a good bond. It is imperative that care is taken to prevent the hot glue from spilling onto the presentation board surface.

Sometimes it is necessary to remove an item that has been glued permanently in place. Handheld hair dryers may work to warm and loosen a variety of adhesives, such as spray-on adhesive, StudioTac, hot glue, rubber cement, and sticky back. A warm setting is usually best because a hot setting may cause melting or warping.

There are some technical issues to consider in mounting a presentation. It is generally a mistake to use spray adhesive to mount large bond or print paper drawings to foam board or mat board. Boards mounted in this fashion will wrinkle or warp—or both. It is far superior to use Studio Tac or rubber cement to mount these lightweight drawings. In some cases, drawings may be mounted on Canson or other art papers, which creates a thinner presentation format that can be inserted into a portfolio.

Some designers prefer to use large black clips (available at office supply stores) to attach drawings to foam board or precut plywood sheets (the exact size of the drawing's surface). This allows drawings to be easily removed and replaced with revised drawings.

Some designers and educators prefer formal boards with samples placed behind neatly cut window mats. Clearly, window mats create tidy and clean presentation boards. However, cutting a window for each

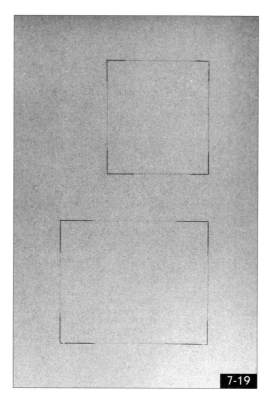

7-19

sample is time-consuming. Because time and budgets are constant factors in design practice, some designers have forsaken this presentation method, and others use individual window mats only for very formal presentations or those that will eventually hang in sales rooms or developers' offices. Some design firms continue to employ window-matted presentation boards.

Window matting requires that the board be designed and laid out with all of the samples and items in place. Window locations are drawn on the surface of the mat board and then cut in the marked locations. If a beveled edge is required, I recommend using a commercially available mat cutter. Mat cutters range in price from about thirty dollars to more than one thousand dollars. Mat cutters generally provide a housing for a cutting blade that slides along a metal straightedge, providing a beautiful beveled or straight cut. Most mat cutters create a beveled edge by making cuts from

FIGURE 7-20
Window mats can allow items to project from the windows. Photograph

FIGURE 7-21
The nature of some materials requires items to be recessed beneath window mats.

FIGURE 7-22
Interior view of matted flat artwork. The drawing is taped to the back of the window, and the backing board is hinged at the top with tape. To preserve artwork, only archival materials should come in contact with the artwork.

the back of the mat board surface; this can become quite confusing when many windows are to be cut.

When cutting windows by hand, it is imperative to use a very sharp blade. It is also important that the cutting blade is used to make a minimum of three cuts: one through the top, one through the middle, and one through the bottom paper surface. Making three cuts will create clean, sharp edges. It is also a good idea to use a fresh blade for each window. To avoid overshooting the corners of windows with the blade, try to precut corners (see Figure 7-19). A nail file can be used to smooth ragged cuts when necessary.

In window matting, samples and/or other elements are attached to the backing board, and then the front board with windows is placed on top (see Figure 7-20). In some cases, the mat board lies on top of the samples to create a presentation where the samples are recessed behind the windows (see Figure 7-21). It is common for boards with window mats to have taped edges that conceal the many layers of material involved. In presentations employing window mats it is also common to include window-matted drawings. In these cases, a window is cut in a board and that board is hinged (using tape) to a backing board. The flat drawing is then taped over the back of the window (see Figure 7-22) or attached to the backing board. Archival mat board, backing board, and hinge tape are used for matting drawings that should be preserved. Figures C-41a, C-41b, C-42a and C-42b on page 82 shows a materials presentation in which some elements are window matted and others are surface mounted.

Digital Technology

Increasingly, designers are relying on digital technology when preparing materials presentations as well as documenting various selections and options. Currently, digital cameras and scanners are used to capture materials, samples, and product imagery. Many firms scan all samples for use in specification books. Additionally, firms also scan all components of visual presentations to preserve images and retain accurate records. Firms working on long-distance projects use scanned versions of presentations as a means of communicating. In many cases, digital files containing visual presentations are sent via e-mail for client review. In other cases, the actual presentation boards are sent or are left with the client while the designer retains digital files. Discussion of elements of the presentation can thus be conducted over the phone or via e-mail.

Current methods of documenting finish selections include scanning actual materials and importing them directly onto design drawings such as orthographic drawings and three-dimensional views generated on CAD or drawn by hand (see Figures C-38b and C-38c on page 79). Additionally, many

suppliers and manufacturers of of materials and furnishings offer online digital images available for downloading for use in digital presentations.

Once digital images of materials and furnishings are obtained, Photoshop imaging software is used to create digital design presentations. Using this software, drawings can be imported via scanning, as can all of the desired finish materials. The various finish materials can then be imported directly onto the appropriate places on plans, elevations, and three-dimensional views as described in Chapter 5 (see Figures 5-9a through 5-9h and 5-10a through 5-10h).

Complete virtual boards can be created by scanning materials and adding text. In a few hours, most students can develop the basic skills required for creating digital renderings and materials boards using this Photoshop or similar software. It is also worth noting that these virtual sample presentations lack the textural quality available with true finish materials; they are nonetheless worthwhile, especially in terms of setting a conceptual direction or being used in conjunction with the actual samples.

The Internet has become a powerful tool for obtaining design and building product information and related visual imagery. When items are not available in firm or school product libraries, many people seek images of them via the Internet. Specification information, visual information, and product guides can be found online. There is a range in terms of the accuracy of the visual imagery found on the Internet: Some excellent digital images are available and the best of these are designed to be printed at accurate scale with decent color rendition and are of a high enough resolution to work well when directly downloaded and printed (for physical boards) or when used in digital presentations. On the other hand, some of the visual imagery for materials, furnishings, and equipment are not of a high quality and requires some digital manipulation for use in presentations—or they are not useful for anything other than determining which actual samples should be ordered for a specific project.

While technology allows designers to use digital images rather than actual physical samples, some people (designers and clients) may find such samples off-putting due to their lack of textural quality. In other words, some designers and clients simply prefer the look and touch of the actual project and, therefore, many designers continue to use real samples rather than digital samples.

It can be difficult for students to obtain current samples for use in student presentations because manufacturers and their sales representatives are often unwilling to give away free, current product samples to students. In such cases, students may find it worthwhile to order samples for a relatively low fee plus shipping. When actual samples are not available for free or for a fee, students often choose to work with digital images of products. However, educators seem split in their willingness to allow digital versus "real" samples. Therefore, a student should clearly discuss this situation with an instructor prior to completing a presentation. Luckily, samples for professional design products continue to be relatively easy to obtain.

There are some online resources for obtaining digital samples and some of these allow students to order product samples. Tectonic Studio is an online resource library that allows for sample imagery downloads as well as free samples for students that pay for a special student membership; the references section of this chapter contains the web address for this service.

The following chapter contains additional information about putting complete design presentations together including information on organizing and incorporating materials, finishes, and furnishings into larger presentations. Additional information about the inclusion of digital imagery may also be found in the following chapter.

REFERENCES
(Contains both works cited and recommended reading. Annotations where appropriate.)

Leach, Sid Delmar. *Techniques of Interior Design Rendering and Presentation*. New York: Architectural Record Books, 1978.

Tate, Allen. *The Making of Interiors*. New York: Harper & Row, 1987.

Tectonic Studio. http://studio.bluebolt.com/bbnplain.sph/BlueboltStudio.class/ com.bluebolt.backend.communication.ControllerServlet/848/BBX

8 MAKING THE COMPLETE PRESENTATION

The previous chapters were intended to serve as an introduction to some of the drawing and presentation methods used throughout the various phases of the design process. Drawings, renderings, models, and materials sample presentations were covered separately for purposes of clarity and so that students might develop the distinct skills required to complete these items successfully. However, these items are generally presented together as part of a complete design presentation, both for student and professional presentations. Therefore, an understanding of how to bring these elements together as part of a total, unified presentation is essential.

The successful design presentation combines multiple elements in a way that is by some measure consistent, or unified. Creating a unified presentation from many disparate elements can be more complex than it may sound. For example, a presentation may include sheets of orthographic drawings or construction documents, renderings, models, and materials presentation boards. Creating unity among such varied formats can be a challenge.

The key is to meeting this challenge is to seek a unifying element or elements that will hold the presentation together—visually and conceptually. Specific project graph-ics, including title blocks, logos, and conceptual diagrams, may be employed as unifying elements. For instance, the graphics found in the title block on a sheet of ortho-graphic drawings may be used on materials sample boards and mounted renderings to unify the presentation. In some cases, the actual format of the boards serves as a unifying element. For example, all of the two-dimensional elements of a presentation can be mounted on boards with consistent horizontal bands at the bottom or side, in a consistent color or design (see Figures 8-1a, 8-1b, and 8-1c).

Most professional design firms have an "office standard" presentation board design and drawing sheet layout. These may include a standard title block or graphic band placed in the same or a similar location on all boards and sheets. Use of a consistent or standard format allows all projects for the firm or office to have a uniform look, which can relate to the firm "brand." This also makes the design of the presentation take less time in that the major graphic devices need not be rethought for each project. In contrast to professional use of a standard presentation format, students most often select a new for-mat, layout, or unifying graphic device(s) for each project, as the student has done in Figures 8-1a, 8-1b, and 8-1c.

FIGURES 8-1a, 8-1b, AND 8-1c
These boards for a student retail design project employ a consistent graphic border in order to create consistency for the three boards that contain a variety of imagery and samples. All boards were composed using Photoshop and include CAD drawing, manual perspective drawing, and surface-mounted materials.
By Tina Bucher

B/3   WEST ELEVATION   SCALE

C/3   ELEVATION SKETCH   SCALE   D/3   ELEVATION SKETCH   SCALE

Beautiful Lips

Beautiful Eyes

Beautiful You

8-1c

Certainly, there are no hard-and-fast rules in bringing together the many visual aids used in design presentations. However, consistency, clarity, legibility, and craftsmanship are worthy goals for all projects. In all cases, it is important to carefully consider the presentation audience. An audience familiar with design drawings will require far fewer visual aids than one unfamiliar with viewing floor plans and elevations. Moreover, an unfamiliar audience requires far clearer titling and greater graphic consistency than a group of design professionals.

The foregoing considerations point to the need for design presentations to be *designed*. Students must see unity of presentation as a *design problem*, rather than an afterthought. In designing and developing a presentation, it is worthwhile to follow the steps of the design process. The presentation should be analyzed, a list of criteria created, and research regarding the audi-

ence and available materials undertaken. Synthesis is achieved by the creation of thumbnail drawings and design sketches. The design of the presentation must be evaluated, and only then should the presentation be created.

My ongoing discussions with design professionals consistently point to the need for students to consider the need for a project presentation to clearly "tell a story"—the specific story of that project. Another way of stating this is that student presentations must clearly *communicate* the *design intent*. including the conceptual basis for the projects as well as the most important design elements. This requires a bit of an editing process, in that including too much information in a student presentation can be confusing and overwhelming to someone viewing it for the first time, such as in a job or internship interview.

The process of editing and sorting out the elements of a student presentation

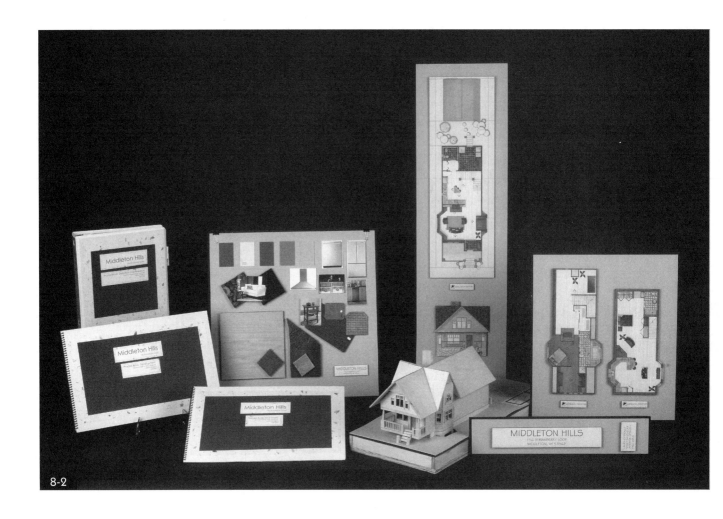

FIGURE 8-2

This complete final student presentation illustrates the editing process that must take place in designing the presentation. The final design solution is presented using formal boards and a scale model, with design-process information and construction documents presented in binders and booklets. Elements are designed in manner that is graphically consistent.
By Laura Eysnogle and Vicky Salzsieder

requires that students consider a way of clarifying and including the finalized design elements within the major elements of the presentation and yet also provide some process documentation (perhaps in an accompanying binder). Therefore, the major presentation "boards" or elements must be clear, concise, and easy to follow, whereas the in-process sketches, inspirational material, and research documentation may be collected into an accompanying book or folder—this allows those items to be readily found if necessary, but not to overwhelm the final design solution.

The previous paragraph points to an interesting fact: student design presentations must often convey the final design solution as well as in-process design decisions made along the way. This combination of information is required by many instructors and is useful to include in the student's final design portfolio. This situation lies in contrast to most professional presentations, which often contain only items presented at a certain point in time for a particular phase of the design process. For example, a final professional design presentation may contain some early conception imagery but generally focuses on final design development level images and samples. On the other hand, a student making a final design presentation will often be required to include process imagery and research. This is why selection and organization of imagery is vital to the student design presentation as illustrated in Figure 8-2.

Process and Presentation

In preparing and organizing most design presentations, it is important to consider the stage of the design process that is to be communicated. As described previously, preliminary presentations are quite different from final design development presentations. Often, designers wish to convey the preliminary nature of the design and this can be conveyed using unmounted drawings—those that are simply clipped to a backing board or pinned to a wall, as well as unmounted materials samples, and study models. Whereas a more finalized design solution—such as one being made toward the end of the design development phase of a project—may include formally presented (mounted or framed) drawings, formal presentation boards for materials and furnishings, and lavishly created scale models.

The need for the presentation to reflect the particular stage of the design process is true for professional presentations as well as for student presentations. It is not uncommon for a student's preliminary design solutions to be presented quite informally using tracing paper, pushpins, and loose material samples. Such informal presentations should still be of a quality that makes design intent clear with some type of unifying element(s) employed to convey underlying concepts and the general direction the project will take as it is being refined. As stated, students are often asked to include some portion of this preliminary work in their final design presentation as well—making for some additional challenges.

As a design progresses through the various stages of the design process, presentations may be said to "tighten up" in terms of refinement and representation of specific finishes, materials, and design details. For example, presentation of a project in the schematic or preliminary design phase will often include a general sense of the aesthetic direction of the project such as a palette of colors, basic materials direction, and some indication of architectural details, as well as plans, elevations, and perspective sketches. This lies in contrast to a presentation of a project in the final stages of design development, which may include very specific finishes, furnishings, hardware, and finalized architectural and millwork details, plus highly detailed plans, elevations, and perspective drawings. Presentations for both phases of the design process may include scale models; however, the more preliminary presentation would typically include study models to convey basic massing and spatial relationships whereas the presentation made at the end of design development may include highly finished models that clearly indicate all materials, finishes, and, on occasion, furnishings.

ORGANIZATION AND COMPOSITION

Designing a presentation requires that an analysis must be made that includes the relative sizes of elements, the number of components presented, and the various formats to be employed. The size of the audience and the layout of the room used for the presentation influence its relative size and format. Time as well as budgetary constraints must be considered. Students are often under both time and budgetary constraints and should keep this in mind when planning presentations. In other words, students must be realistic in terms of time and money.

As one moves forward in the design of a presentation and the important issues are analyzed, several thumbnail sketches can be made of possible presentation formats, and these should be reviewed and evaluated. The most successful sketches can be taken to a higher level of refinement by doing additional drawings, quick mock-ups or by

These thumbnail sketches illustrate a consistent organizational structure used to unify the various presentations elements. The dashed lines indicate alignment locations, which means that some items align with these while other items simply relate to them. Dotted areas indicate a consistent implied border that contains all objects—notice that the bottom of boards have a taller borders and contain the board titles. There are many ways to lay out boards; these figures simply illustrate possible examples.

using digital layout software. Creating thumbnails first and then refining these allows one to make sure all of the parts and pieces fit prior to any actual cutting and pasting of elements—which can save money and time.

In sketching and refining any presentation, attention to the graphic design of individual elements as well as the total package is essential. Some information about graphic design is presented in the following chapter and is worth reading prior to the beginning of any presentation design.

One of the key components to consider in terms of the graphic design of interior design presentations is the notion of using a consistent format or layout from board to board. This may require using a consistent graphic border or edge treatment as dis-

cussed in Chapter 7, page 213, as well as using an organizing grid or some organizational structure that graphically unites the various components. In addition, consistent location of titles and consistent use of text from board-to- board and sheet-to-sheet is helpful. Figures 8-3 and 8-4 depict thumbnails and organizing principles for presentation design and formatting. Figure 8-5 employs a consistent border and some consistent graphic elements to create a successful student presentation.

TECHNIQUES AND METHODS OF PRESENTATION

Possible presentation formats include renderings and materials formally mounted on boards. On some occasions, drawings, renderings, sketches, and materials are left unmounted and are simply pinned up in

8-5

the design firm's conference room (or in some appropriate viewing area), and the client is invited to view the work (as previously shown in Figure 7-2c in Chapter 7. In these instances, full-size samples of furnishings and equipment may be placed in the viewing area as well. Images highlighting methods of visual presentation used in two professional design projects are illustrated in pages 89 through 92 of the Color Plates section. Some projects and situations call for nontraditional boards such as those shown in Figures 8-6a, 8-6b, 8-7a, 8-7b, and 8-7c.

Increasingly projects are presented using "digital" boards. This is done using software such as InDesign, Quark, or Photoshop (or other graphic imaging software) and importing drawings and graphics while composing the board digitally as

shown in Figures C-44a, C-44b, C-45a, and C-45b. These presentations are created digitally, often using unifying graphics as shown in Figures C-46a, C-46b, C-47a, and C-47b, and are then printed and either left unmounted or mounted to foam board or Gator Board. In some cases, all project graphics—including orthographic drawings, sketches, and preliminary or inspirational graphics are printed on digital boards—with the only nondigital presentation component being materials samples as shown in Chapter 8 (see Figures 8-1a through 8-1c). In other cases, the entire project is presented digitally, including materials and finishes as shown in C-38a through C-38c.

Digital boards may consist of images created using only digital means such as CAD drawings, computer models, and digital

FIGURE 8-5

This presentation employs a consistent implied border and consistent titling and graphics applied in a mirrored manner; this nicely unifies a range of diverse elements.
By Jenna Michels

8-6a

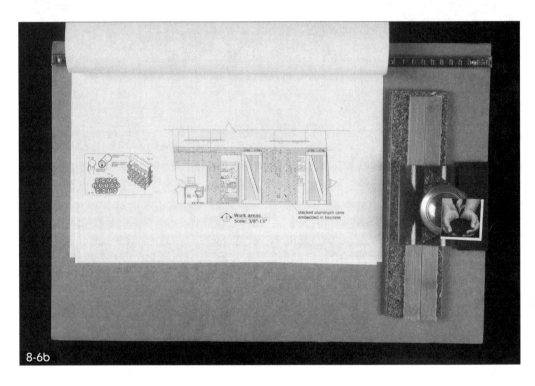

8-6b

rendering. Hand-drawn elements may also be included by simply scanning the items and importing them into the digital file as shown in C-48a through C-48c on page 88.

In creating digital boards important project graphics such as preliminary or ideation sketches, diagrams and conceptual imagery can be copied or scanned and incorporated into a presentation background. Orthographic drawings and other presentation elements may then be added "on top," creating an interesting and unified

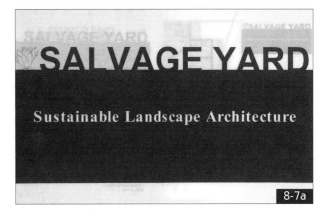

Figures 8-7a, 8-7b, AND 8-7c
This booklet-based presentation combines drawings on transparent and opaque papers, and makes use of consistent, concept-inspired graphics.
By Megan Gruen

FIGURES 8-8a AND 8-8b
These boards contain drawings
and materials mounted on an
intermediate layer of mat board
affixed to a bottom layer of
board.

By Vicky Salzsieder

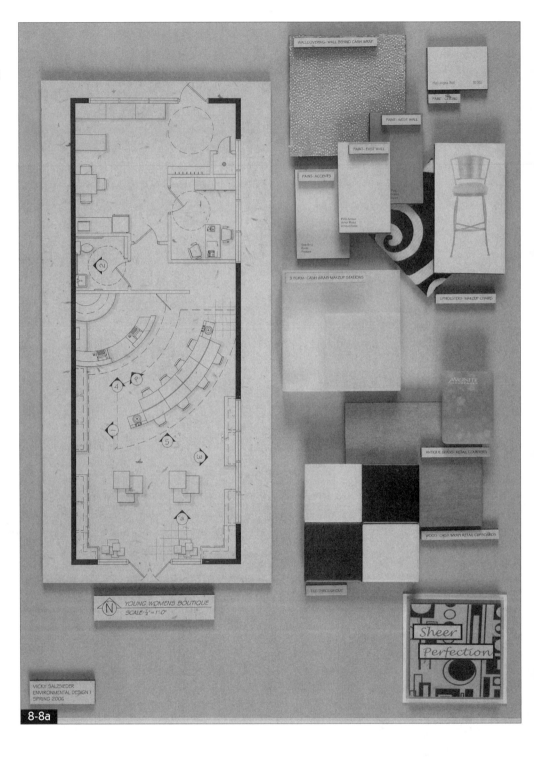

presentation that speaks to the origin of the design concept as shown in Figures C-47a and C-47b on page 87.

Successful design presentations may be made using traditional boards. These are created much like the material sample boards discussed in the previous chapter. Typically drawings and additional items are created and attached directly to the surface of the board as shown in Figures 8-8a and 8-8b and illustrated in Figures C-40a, C-40b, C-40c, C-42a, and C-42b and as

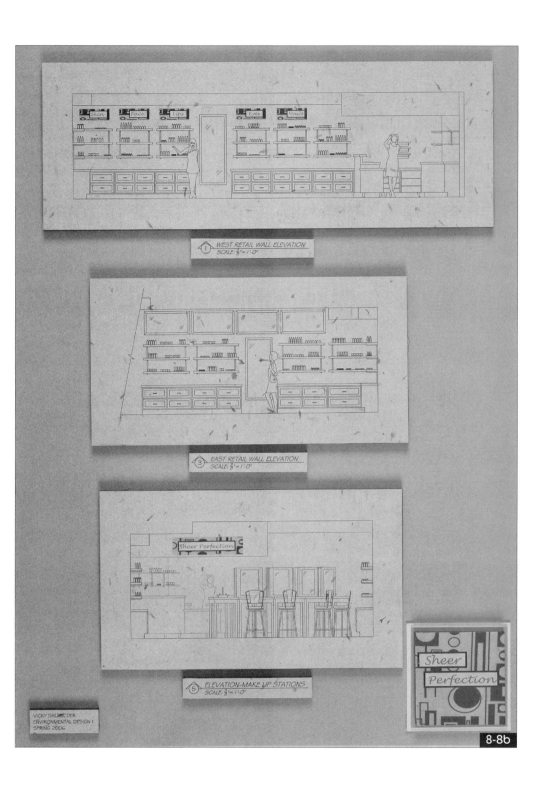

WEST RETAIL WALL ELEVATION
SCALE: 3/8" = 1'-0"

EAST RETAIL WALL ELEVATION
SCALE: 3/8" = 1'-0"

Sheer Perfection

ELEVATION-MAKE UP STATIONS
SCALE: 3/8" = 1'-0"

VICKY SALZEDER
ENVIRONMENTAL DESIGN I
SPRING 2006

Sheer Perfection

8-8b

previously shown in Figure 8-5. In another approach drawings are set behind carefully cut window mats as shown in Figures 8-9a through 8-9c, and in Figures C-41a, C-41b, C-43a, and C-43b on pages 82-83.

When mounting items directly to the top surface of the presentation board. it is helpful to set those items on a primary mounting surface before attaching them to the larger board; this allows them to sit up a bit and to create shadows on the surface of the board. Mounting drawings behind a

FIGURES 8-9a AND 8-9b
This presentation includes
drawings set behind window
mats with material samples
affixed to the board surface.
By Laura Blanchard

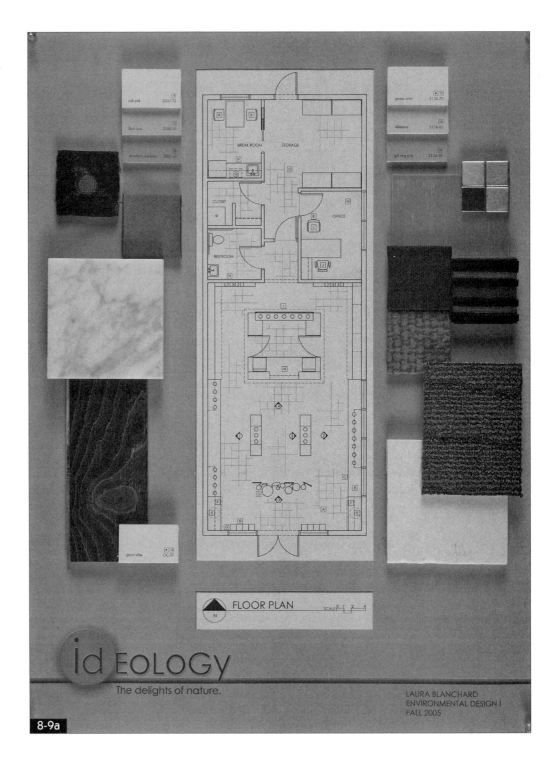

window mat may employ a series of small windows for each individual drawing or may format the series of drawings so that they can sit behind a single window.

Professional project presentation may make use of many of the items covered in this and previous chapters. Figures C-49a through C-49g and C-50a through C-50i beginning on page 89 illustrate some of the many elements used in the communication of two professional projects.

The discussion to this point has been

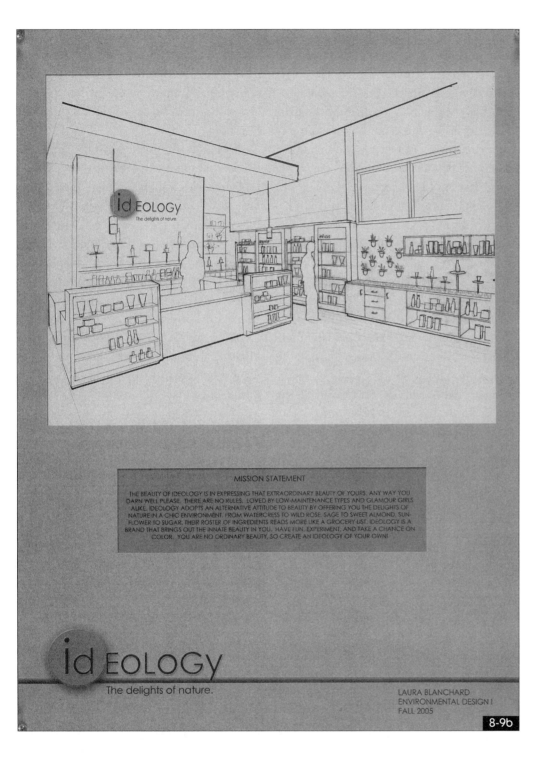

MISSION STATEMENT

THE BEAUTY OF IDEOLOGY IS IN EXPRESSING THAT EXTRAORDINARY BEAUTY OF YOURS, ANY WAY YOU DARN WELL PLEASE. THERE ARE NO RULES, LOVED BY LOW-MAINTENANCE TYPES AND GLAMOUR GIRLS ALIKE, IDEOLOGY ADOPTS AN ALTERNATIVE ATTITUDE TO BEAUTY BY OFFERING YOU THE DELIGHTS OF NATURE IN A CHIC ENVIRONMENT. FROM WATERCRESS TO WILD ROSE, SAGE TO SWEET ALMOND, SUNFLOWER TO SUGAR, THEIR ROSTER OF INGREDIENTS READS MORE LIKE A GROCERY LIST. IDEOLOGY IS A BRAND THAT BRINGS OUT THE INNATE BEAUTY IN YOU. HAVE FUN, EXPERIMENT, AND TAKE A CHANCE ON COLOR. YOU ARE NO ORDINARY BEAUTY, SO CREATE AN IDEOLOGY OF YOUR OWN!

id EoLoGy
The delights of nature.

LAURA BLANCHARD
ENVIRONMENTAL DESIGN I
FALL 2005

8-9b

confined to the creation of the actual physical embodiment of the presentation—either traditional or digitally crafted "boards." However, presentations are increasingly "virtual" in that they are created for digital display—most typically on a computer monitor or projection screen. This type of presentation can be made in person or sent electronically to the viewer. The notion of a purely digital presentation, one that is created and viewed digitally, is not a new idea—it is merely becoming more and more commonplace in an increasingly global economy.

Ways of creating a purely digital presentation include using page layout software such as InDesign or QuarkXPress to create the individual presentation "pages" or "boards." Much like traditional boards, these may be designed using similar graphics, formatting, and text, in a templatelike fashion, with each page or board containing differing drawings, sketches, and materials (scanned or captured digitally).

Such digital presentations tend toward huge file sizes due to the inclusion of many graphic images and this, as well as software compatibility issues, may require that the presentation be saved in a smaller more accessible file format such as a PDF (Portable Document Format). Saving digital presentations as PDF files allows them to be viewed by those with Adobe Acrobat, which is readily available. It's worth noting that PDF files that are to be used for viewing by display only—such as on a monitor or projection screen—may be of a rather low resolution. This is not the type of file to be used when a presentation is meant to be printed because the low resolution will result in very poor print quality.

Designers and students also use Microsoft PowerPoint, Apple Keynote, and other similar software in creating digital presentations. Rather than using the stock templates available, most design presentations are best with a visual quality very similar to standard design presentation boards. This can be achieved by importing images and composing the presentation as has been discussed for digital boards (using Photoshop, Illustrator, InDesign, or similar software), which allows for selection of a range of background and text colors as well as a range of typefaces. Additionally, logos, title blocks, or some type of unifying graphic may be imported and used in a similar manner on each slide, creating a custom template for the presentation. In professional presenta-

tions, this slide design often mirrors the standard presentation board and sheet design used as an office standard, whereas student presentations vary project to project as shown in Figures 8-10a, 8-10b, and 8-10c.

Presentations created using PowerPoint that contain many images also tend toward large file sizes, which can make the presentation difficult to send electronically. Much like other software, PowerPoint presentations can be saved as a PDF file so that the presentation may be sent electronically and viewed on a range of computers. The specifics of saving presentations as PDF files on PowerPoint require selecting "PDF" from the print window under the "Print" command—with this command, rather than printing, the file is saved in the new PDF format.

PUBLIC SPEAKING AND DESIGN COMMUNICATION

Clearly, this book has as its focus the *visual* presentation of information rather than the *verbal* communication of the presentation, and while a thorough and detailed description of public speaking falls outside of the scope of this book, some worthwhile basics can be described in this section as a means of rounding out the information provided to this point.

Before covering those basics, it is worth noting that an understanding of public speaking and solid verbal presentation skills are important tools in professional design practice as they are keys to creating complete and successful design presentations. Public speaking is a worthy area of study for designers; in fact, for some design students, an undergraduate minor in communication or speech is a worthwhile consideration. In cases where such study is not possible, taking speech communication courses and reading books covering verbal presentations are recommended—some

8-10a

FIGURES 8-10a, 8-10b, AND 8-10c
These are "slides" from a student's PowerPoint presentation for a thesis project. The imagery was created using a range of software (for modeling, rendering, and image manipulation) and imported into PowerPoint. The presentation clarifies project concepts, and gives a slide-by-slide "walk through" of the space and is more interesting visually than what a standard template would provide.
By Ilka Schnelle

8-10b

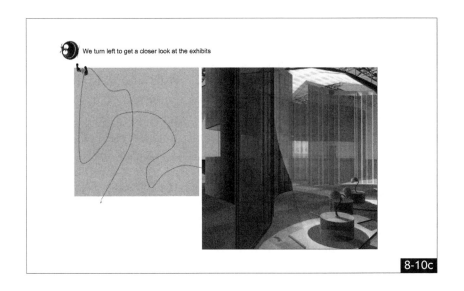

8-10c

related references may be found at the end of this chapter.

Many of the available references covering public speaking and verbal communication relate to creating "persuasive" or "winning" presentations, and in some ways these fall short as aids in preparing for design communication for one simple reason—in some cases the goal of design presentations is to uncover information or to clearly communicate aspects of a design, rather than to persuade the client. Therefore, a key in organizing verbal design presentation is to ask a simple question: What is the exact purpose of this particular presentation? Design presentations can be said to do one of three things. These are: (1) uncover information; (2) sell or market design services; and (3) communicate design solutions (this can be combined with uncovering information in some instances where client or end-user feedback to is required).

Understanding more about these possible presentation purposes allows for the proper tone, appropriate organization, and content of the verbal presentation. Therefore, each of the listed purposes will be discussed in further detail in order to clarify how the presentation may be created most successfully.

Presentations meant to *uncover* information—which must occur early in the programming phase of the project and often continues throughout the project—require that the designer or design staff craft appropriate questions and *listen* carefully to answers during such presentations and meetings. This is often done by means of standard programming documents such as forms, questionnaires, and inventories that are either given to the clients and discussed later or completed by the design staff during or after the meetings or presentations. This type of information-seeking meeting or presentation has "listening"

as its focus rather than "selling" or "persuading" a client. Therefore, the entire presentation should be developed around the notion of listening and clarifying.

Presentations intended to *market* a design firms services fall into the realm of "persuasive" presentations. Here, one may find it helpful to study ways of making "winning" presentations, which often call for absolute clarity of purpose, simple and effective visuals, and a great deal of preparation and research about the possible client. Interestingly, although this type fits most into the realm of making a sales "pitch" or "winning" a client, one idea that is often stressed in design marketing is the notion that the client will be listened to as the design process progresses—so in many ways listening is a constant in design presentations. This is far more often the case in professional practice than it is in most student presentations (because students do not always have a living client to listen to).

Design *communication* presentations employ the visuals that have been discussed in this book as well as a clear plan of how these items should be presented. Many design communication presentations require client or end-user feedback. This means that as items are covered, the presenter seeks to make sure that the audience clearly understands what is being discussed. Putting this another way, the client must approve the design or aspects of the design being presented so that the project may move forward. For this to occur, the presenter must seek feedback and input and ask questions of the audience in order to make sure there is understanding and agreement.

The previous paragraphs in this section are intended to clarify various purposes of presentation in order to provide clarity of purpose and an ability to tailor presentation appropriately. For example, in an early programming meeting where gaining information is the purpose, the presentation should be designed around the give-and-take of questions, discussion, input, and answers rather than around a formal persuasive speech. This is contrasted by a presentation that is intended to communicate the final design details of a project, which may necessarily require forcefully making a point that the design is complete and that it is time to move into construction documentation.

A word to students about making presentations intended to communicate design projects: It is very important to have a strategy for covering all of the necessary components of the design clearly and in the appropriate amount of detail. For example, in a student presentation, it is possible to begin with a discussion of the general concepts involved or the design problem selected and then to follow with a discussion of the floor plan, moving from each room to the related drawings that cover that room. Clarifying the main locations on a plan and then returning to the lobby and at that point communicating all of the related elevations, details, sketches and related materials and finishes can work well. In contrast, one may completely cover the plan and related drawings, and then handle materials separately. In either case, a consistent method should be developed so that the student is not jumping back and forth between rooms and drawings or materials—this is not only confusing but has the potential to cause the presenter to forget important elements of the design.

One additional issue related to student presentations includes a common error stating only minimal information about design intent, such as, "Here is my project . . . here is the lobby and that's the reception desk." While this may seem reasonable, the verbal presentation should not only contain more precision and clarity, it also requires an appropriate

introduction. Rather than stating, "This is my project," something that introduces both the project and the design intent should be mentioned, such as, "I would like to present my design for a corporate headquarters for the XYZ Company. My design is based on the concept of teamwork because . . . " After such an introduction, the actual design may be presented and will tend to be engaging and of interest to the audience. Some students do not do this because they find it corny or uncool; however, this is the way professionals tend to present projects, so early practice will put students ahead in both interviews and entry-level work.

Verbal Presentation Basics

While the types of presentations vary greatly in terms of purpose and style there are some elements that they may share and these must be considered as well. What follows are some general guidelines about making clear, easy-to-follow presentations, which are worthy goals for all situations.

The Audience

Understanding the audience has been discussed as it relates to the level of finish of graphic elements covered previously. However, the discussion here relates to understanding the level of sophistication or subject knowledge of the audience members. For example, when one is making a design communication–type presentation to a large public gathering, the audience may consist of people that have not learned how to read a floor plan. Therefore, making such a presentation would require careful consideration of which images to share with the audience in which order so that the design will be clear and understandable. In contrast, when making a presentation to a group of design professionals, detailed technical drawings may be shared and readily understood requiring little background information.

Similarly, understanding the audience will allow the presenters to gauge the level of technical detail and jargon to use in the presentation. Experts in a given field are comfortable using and understanding certain terms, whereas the general public may be lost when acronyms or technical terms are used. Clearly gauging the audience for their knowledge about specifics is required in the preparation of any presentation.

Structure and Flow

While the purpose of the presentation may vary from information gathering to clear design communication, a careful consideration of the structure of any presentation is required. Most presentations will benefit from the inclusion of a clear *introduction* and *conclusion*. Absolute clarity about the purpose of the presentation should be included in the introduction, and, a clear and concise summation of the most important elements should be included in the conclusion. It is absolutely reasonable to say, "Today we are going to cover X, Y, and Z" in the introduction and to say, "In covering X, Y, and Z, we hope you take away these important aspects of this presentation as you leave today."

Creating a clear introduction and concise conclusion is not as easy as it may sound due to the danger of repeating too much detail or information. Careful thought should be given to the true *core* information being disseminated, and this is what should be covered at the beginning and the end of the presentation. Besides helping to create clarity, doing this has an added benefit of allowing an audience member to question whether they comprehend the information as the presentation is concluded, and thus can allow for successful questions to be raised when information is unclear.

As stated in the previous discussion about student design presentations, thought should be given as to how drawings, models, and samples are presented in terms of structure. Will the plan be shown first, followed by details that relate to each room or space? Or will more time be spent initially describing the concept and how design elements relate to this concept? Many designers find it helpful to consider the presentation as a "walk through the space," whereby each element is discussed as one might find it on the first journey through the building. Regardless of the structure that is selected for the presentation, it is important that each element is clearly covered in a consistent manner so that the audience can remain focused on the information rather than thinking, "I'm lost . . . what part are they talking about right now?"

An additional method of keeping the audience on track is to occasionally remind them as to what area or item is being discussed. This may seem repetitious; however, in a long and complex presentation the audience may begin to drift a bit, so it can be highly worthwhile to occasionally state, "Again as we enter to the Research Area we find . . ." or "Here in the Research Department the workstations . . . ," as a way to reinforce exactly what area is under discussion. Asking for questions is another way to restate and refocus the presentation, such as "Are there any questions about the Research Area before I move on?"

Creating presentation thumbnails has been discussed in terms of project graphics and these may also be used to clarify the order and structure of the verbal presentation. In doing this, the thumbnails are organized to determine the order in which the graphics should be presenated and to ascertain the timing of additional information that should be presented.

Keep It Simple in Content and Graphics

Many books on presentation and public speaking describe the need to keep content and graphics as simple and straightforward as possible. The need for simplicity relates to understanding the audience, because what is simple for a group of experts may be over the head of the general public. However, the concept of simplicity goes beyond audience identification in that all presentations should be kept as simple and easy to follow as possible. This notion of presentation simplicity relates to the need to boil the elements down to their most condensed attributes and to state them in the simplest manner possible.

Seeking simplicity may be most important in creating PowerPoint–type presentations where it's key to keep text variation to a minimum and to avoid information overload. Keeping the amount of text minimal, especially headlines and bulleted information, can lend to clarity. Avoiding the use of large amounts of data or numerical information is also helpful. Images should have a clear relationship to the information being conveyed and should serve as clear illustrations (such as drawings and models) or simply as a means conveying simple design intent, inspiration, or context.

In some ways, design presentations are easier to keep simple than are other forms of business communication due to the use of consistent graphic elements such as drawings and models. Putting this another way: Our pictures tell a story. Therefore, we must seek the way to convey this story as simply and clearly as possible, which often involves letting the project graphics serve as the imagery for the presentation, with the verbal portion seen as supporting the graphics.

Rehearse

Good presentations require practice and rehearsal; the entire presentation should be rehearsed in advance when possible. This means actually saying the words and going through the visuals in front of other people. Taking a quick look at some notes is not rehearsing—it is reviewing. However, taking the time to practice saying the words at the same time as one moves through project graphics allows one to understand pacing, possible weaknesses, and to develop a solid feel for the material—it is the only way to become completely comfortable with the totality of the presentation.

Rehearsal is required in preparation for professional presentations as well as student presentations. Even those professionals with many years of experience continue to practice and rehearse. Professional firms have been known to hire presentation coaches and to require designers to make presentations to community members and schools as a means of developing skills in this area. The level of rehearsal for a presentation relates directly to the type of presentation being made and the level of polish of the presentation requires. For example, a student desk critique does not require much rehearsal, whereas a final design presentation made to support a long-term project may require extensive rehearsal. In the professional realm presentations made to stakeholders and those made to market a firm's services may require extensive practice. When in doubt, practice—it will only serve to enhance the presentation.

REFERENCES

(Contains both works cited and recommended reading. Annotations where appropriate.)

Burley-Allen, Madelyn. *Listening: The Forgotten Skill*. New York: John Wiley & Sons, 1995.

Reynolds, Garr. *Design Basics*. http://www.garrreynolds.com/Design/basics.html

Tufte, Edward. *Beautiful Evidence*. Chesire, CT: Graphics Press, 2006.

——. *The Cognitive Style of PowerPoint: Pitching Out Corrupts Within*, 2nd edition. Chesire, CT: Graphics Press, 2006.

Weissman, Jerry. *Presenting to Win: the Art of Telling Your Story*. Upper Saddle River, NJ: Prentice Hall, 2006. *While notions of "winning" are not necessarily always applicable to design presentations, this book has some excellent information on organization and presentation design.*

9

PORTFOLIOS AND RESUMES

The mere word *portfolio* can strike fear in the heart of a soon-to-be design graduate. This is because in representing a student's body of work, the portfolio is often the key to getting an excellent entry-level job or internship. And often the portfolio becomes symbolic of a student's fears about graduation and employment.

Yes, portfolios can be scary business. They require planning and organization, an expenditure of money, excellent design skills, and a huge amount of effort. Working on your portfolio also signifies that the next step is interviewing, followed by working. This is the goal of many individuals pursuing an education in design. Therefore, working on a portfolio is a commitment to working in design. And, of course, anyone who will hire you without looking at your work is probably not really hiring you to do design.

Creating a portfolio along with a resume, cover letter, and other related items is a necessary step in moving forward as a designer. This is true whether one is searching for an internship, an entry-level job, or a new job within the design community after years of experience. The graphic design of one's portfolio, resume, and cover letter must be appropriate to the intended audience, most often a design director, managing designer, or human resources director of a firm or corporation. These professionals are busy people who will be reviewing a great deal of information. As a result, economy and organization are key factors in the design of one's employment-generating tools. A basic understanding of the principles of graphic design and general hiring practices can help in creating employment-seeking materials. Some of those principles and concepts are covered in this chapter.

Although some basics are covered here, it is most useful for interior designers and design students to enroll in an introductory graphic design course (more advanced courses are also highly beneficial). Graphic design is a fascinating discipline with a rich history and vast application in the practice of interior design.

GRAPHIC DESIGN COMPONENTS

Grids

Good graphic design allows for good communication. Organization and composition lead to clear communication and are important principles of graphic design. For years graphic designers have employed grids as a means of composing and organizing information. Grids provide the frame-

FIGURE 9-1a
Grids provide the framework for page design. These are examples of simple multi-column grids and columns divided into blocks.

9-1a

FIGURE 9-1b
Text and images can be structured using grids.

9-1b

work for the design of any page or two-dimensional surface. Writing in *Grids* (1996), André Jute states, "The primary purpose of the grid is to create order out of chaos." He goes on to say, "Of all the tools available to help the designer to present a concept in a thoroughly professional manner, none is more powerful than the grid."

Grids offer structure and aid in the organization of data, allowing the reader to easily locate and comprehend information. In addition, grids are very helpful for individuals with little experience in graphic design and page layout. Components of a grid include the actual page size, the margins at the four edges of the page, and the printed area. The printed area is often divided into columns, further dividing the grid structure.

In many areas of graphic design, such as book and magazine design, margins are set according to printing and publication constraints. In resume and portfolio design, however, margins are set rather arbitrarily, based on individual preference. Margins may be equal and uniform or asymmetrical, focusing attention on a particular portion of the page. With the margins established, the total print area is defined and columns can be created within the print area. Columns are useful because most people prefer to read short lines of text rather than long lines. Simple grids employ a limited number of columns to carry data. Some occasions call for many columns and further division within columns (usually into blocks). Regardless of the number or width of columns, it is essential that spaces between columns are left blank for ease of reading and clarity of communication. Figures 9-1a and 9-1b depict some simple grids.

Thumbnail sketches are helpful in laying out the elements of a grid. Thumbnails may be drawn by hand or quickly generated by computer. When drawing thumbnails by hand, it is best to work in scale. This means that the thumbnail sketches of an 8½-by-11-inch resume should be drawn in a workable scale.

Grid thumbnails are constructed easily with the use of appropriate computer software, such as PageMaker® and QuarkXPress. Margins and columns are quickly indicated, allowing the designer to evaluate the layout immediately. In creating hand-drawn or computer-generated grids, it is important to experiment with a range of options. When one creates thumbnails, it is also essential to estimate the amount of text required for the document, with important headings or areas of text identified.

Type

According to Jute (*Grids*, 1996), the main purpose of the grid is to organize various typefaces and integrate type and illustrations of varying format and origin. This means that type and illustrations become part of the grid and are significant elements of composition. Understanding basic information about typography is essential for successful graphic design.

Typefaces can be divided into two main categories for purposes of classification: serif and sans serif (Figure 9-2). Serif typefaces have main strokes that end in cross strokes or accents. Sans serif typefaces do not have these cross strokes or accents. Serif typefaces are thought to work best for long passages of text, in that the serif leads the eye across the page. Sans serif typefaces are considered highly legible for a word or group of words that stands alone, such as a headline. Within the two classifications there are many varying typefaces. For example, Avant Garde, Gill Sans, and Helvetica are sans serif typefaces. Garamond, Bodoni, and Palatino are serif typefaces.

Most word-processing or page-design programs allow for the creation of a number of style choices within a typeface.

SERIF
Serif

SANS SERIF
Sans Serif

9-2

FIGURE 9-2

Examples of serif and sans serif type.

Underline, *Italics*, **Bold**, ALL CAPS, SMALL CAPS, Shadow, ~~Strikethrough~~, and Outline are generally available. Very often these styles are overused by those without graphic design experience. Overusing underline, bold, outline, or shadow style can destroy consistency and legibility. To add emphasis within lines of text, it is often best to use the italic style in place of bold or underline. Writing in *The Non-Designer's Type Book* (2005), Robin Williams states, "Rarely should you use all caps and never should you underline. Never. That's a law." Williams continues to describe only headings, headlines, and subtitles as benefiting from the use of bold style.

Williams goes on to discuss other options for emphasizing type, such as using a bold italic version of the same typeface or a completely different bold typeface. There is much agreement with Williams's admonishments against using all bolded type in the world of professional graphic design; however, many resume writing guides call for their use. This points to the fact that professional graphic designers are trained to create emphasis through the use of various design elements rather than simply relying on bold type, caps, or other styles.

Word-processing and page-design programs allow for the size of type to be altered instantly. Text is easiest to read when set at 9, 10, 11, or 12 points. Most text used in resumes and business correspondence is set at 10, 11, or 12 points. Many graphic designers insist that smaller type, such as 10 or 11 points, is actually easier to read than 12-point type for text. Titles for portfolio elements are generally larger. The size of type selected affects column width. In general practice, column width is limited to fewer than 65 characters. Therefore, when small-size type is used, columns are generally narrow, which is often easy to read at a glance.

Jute (*Grids*, 1996) sets forth a useful rule of thumb regarding type selection—a designer should remain limited to "sixteen fonts as follows: two typefaces, in two sizes, in two weights, in two styles." It is important to note that Jute is referring to an entire unit of design, such as a book or magazine; clearly a resume or brochure should employ fewer fonts. In graphic design, restraint will consistently produce the best results for those with limited experience.

The alignment of type in a column has an influence on the composition of the page and the legibility of the document. ALIGNMENT refers to the way type is aligned in columns. Word-processing and page-design software allow for a range of alignment. Left-aligned (flush left) type is aligned to the left column margin. Right-aligned type is aligned to the right column margin. Center alignment centers text in the column. Justified alignment creates type that is aligned to both the right and left margins (see Figure 9-3).

Left-aligned text is considered very readable and is the standard setting (default) for most word-processing programs. Center-aligned text can appear quite formal; however, centering large blocks of text can diminish legibility. Right-aligned text is somewhat unusual, but in some cases it is useful. Although justified text creates blocks of type with crisp margins, it can become heavy compositionally.

Proper spacing between letters, words, and paragraphs is important. Most word-processing and page-design programs automatically establish spacing between characters. However, in certain cases there appears to be too much space between characters, and the spacing requires adjustment. Adjusting the space between pairs of letters is called KERNING. The amount of space between lines of type is called LEADING. Leading can be adjusted in most word-processing or page-design programs. For purposes of legibility, it is common to increase leading as line length increases.

The preceding discussions of grids and typography are related to the design of resumes, personal identity systems, and business correspondence. Although grids are very useful in the design and layout of portfolios, most portfolios do not require extensive text. Therefore, portfolios will be discussed separately in this chapter.

Most individuals seeking design-related jobs should create the following: a resume, cover letters or letters of application, a thank-you letter, an acceptance letter, and a refusal letter. In addition, most recent graduates find that a promotional mailer sample portfolio can help in getting one's foot in the door for interviews. Most firms receive cover letters and resumes constantly, and it is often the graphic strength of resumes or promotional mailers that gives potential employers a glimpse of what sets special applicants apart from the crowd.

THE RESUME

In *Your First Resume* (1992), Ron Fry defines a resume as "a written document that attempts to communicate what you can do for an employer—by informing him what you have already done—and motivate him to meet you. However, content alone cannot do that job; presentation is almost equally important."

The resume is an essential tool in finding work in design; it is a means of illustrating one's strengths and opening doors to interviews. With the cover letter and the appropriate samples of work, it is an introduction to potential employers. This means your resume must be well considered and professional.

Most individuals responsible for hiring new employees are very busy and must wade through large numbers of resumes and cover letters. For this reason, a resume must clearly illustrate one's attributes in an eye-catching manner. It must be brief and legible, and at the same time elevate one above other applicants.

Designers' resumes are different on the whole from those of many other business professionals. Because we do creative work, our resumes may be presented in a creative manner. In fact, many of those hiring design professionals look for creative (yet concise and legible) resumes. Burdette Bostwick states in *Resume Writing* (1990), that creative resumes do not follow a formal patterns or standard format. Burdette goes on to describe the necessity of including only relevant, condensed information in creative resumes. In designing and writing a creative resume one must meet all of the requirements of a traditional resume, yet do so in a creative manner.

Where I teach, we often have successful professional designers discuss resumes with our senior students. I must say that the students are always amazed that the visiting professionals never agree about resume and portfolio styles and formats. Typically professionals involved in facilities management of office planning and furniture dealerships are looking for more restrained traditional resume design. Designers engaged in retail, hospitality, or exhibition design seem to look for extremely creative, nontraditional resume designs.

The disagreement among design professionals points to a key in resume writing. It is necessary to analyze carefully your own personality, strengths, weaknesses, and employment objectives prior to writing and designing your resume. It is only after you figure out who you are, what you are comfortable with, and what your objectives are that you can create a resume that reflects these issues. The creative

This is aligned flush left, ragged right.

This is aligned flush right, ragged left.

This is justified and is aligned both left and right.

This is centered

9-3

FIGURE 9-3
Examples of alignment.

resume must reflect you and illustrate who you are.

If you are comfortable with a simple, straightforward resume, that is what you must use. If, on the other hand, you are most comfortable with a dynamic or non-traditional resume, you must undertake to create one. These differing resume styles will clearly appeal to different employers and will set you on your way to making the appropriate employment connection.

One caveat about the creative resume: Do not go overboard with poorly refined designs or an unstructured, ill-conceived resume and use the excuse of "creativity" to get away with it. Resumes must necessarily be professional-looking and legible, and work within standard business practices.

There are some basic guidelines for the design of creative resumes. The use of a grid is highly beneficial for all resumes; designers should employ some form of grid to provide graphic structure. Generally, employers will find it easiest to deal with a standard letter-size paper format. Most business correspondence is formatted this way. I have found that resumes printed with a horizontal orientation may become lost in files; using nonstandard paper sizes can present problems because odd sheets of paper also tend to get lost. In Western countries most readers move their eyes from left to right and this should be considered in developing headings and clusters of text.

In designing your resume, it is important to show restraint in type selection (most often, no more than two different typefaces). It is also important to use restraint in kerning and leading. The paper selected should allow for legibility. Very dark or highly decorative papers may present problems; they can be distracting and can thwart photocopying. It is also best to avoid folds and staples, both of which can be problematic in filing.

Additional guidelines for resumes include careful consideration of the location of your name. Although there are a number of appropriate locations, it is never a good idea to make the name hard to locate. Some employers prefer the name to be placed close to the top margin for filing purposes. Generally speaking, your name, address, and phone number should be presented in a straightforward manner. Do not confuse creativity with unduly clever complications that can frustrate potential employers. Remember, the goals are to attract attention, sell yourself, and allow employers to find you (see Figures 9-4 through 9-10).

Creative resumes can be organized in a *chronological* or in a *functional* format. A chronological resume describes work experience in a reverse chronological (last first) order. This type of resume often lists employers' names, position titles, and the dates the positions were held as a means of organizing information. Short statements relating to activities, duties, and accomplishment are clustered with each position. Chronological organization makes it easy for an employer to quickly determine work history and education. Chronological resumes are most commonly used by designers with several years of experience in design and by those remaining in a given field.

Functional organization groups work experience by function and job duties. Functional resumes highlight related work experience and focus attention on the type of job held rather than chronology. The organization of a functional resume allows for emphasis on particular experiences by organizing relevant skills into skill group paragraphs. This type of resume organization is useful for designers who may have held non-design-related jobs but wish to focus attention on design experience. This may be particularly true for recent design

Nina B. Bruss

Campus Address
1721 S. Broadway St., Apt. 220
Menomonie, WI 54751
Cell: (612) 229-6389
Email: brussn@uwstout.edu

Permanent Address
8906 Telford Crossing
Brooklyn Park, MN 55443
Phone: (763) 425-0896

Education

University of Wisconsin-Stout, Menomonie, WI
Bachelor of Fine Arts: Art
Concentration: **Interior Design** (FIDER-accredited program)
Grade point average: 3.7/4.0
Anticipated graduation: May 2004

Objective

An internship position in a commercial design firm where I can utilize my creative
and technical skills and obtain a greater knowledge of the interior design field.

Courses & Skills

Commercial and residential interior design studios, courses in design, construction,
lighting, and fine arts.
Proficiency in Mac and PC applications including word processing, AutoCAD 2004,
Illustrator 10, and Photoshop 7.

Work Experience

Intern, May-August 2002
Marshall Field's Rosedale Home Store, Roseville, MN
Organized resource center, drafted floor plans, ordered and priced fabrics, assisted
designers with material selections and accompanied them on house calls.

Receptionist, 2002-Present
Marshall Field's Rosedale Home Store, Roseville, MN
Utilizing communication skills by directing customers and telephone interaction
and operation of switchboard.

Banquet Server, 2001-2002
Lancer Catering, Brooklyn Park, MN

Hostess, 1999-2000
Cattle Company, Maple Grove, MN

Other Experience

UW-Stout London Summer Art Program, 2003
Fine arts and travel in England, Scotland, and France

Honors & Activities

Chancellor's Award for Academic Excellence, 5 semesters
ASID Student Chapter Events Coordinator, 2003-present
ASID Student Chapter Secretary, 2002-2003
ASID Student Chapter Member, 2000-present
IIDA Student Chapter Member, 2003-present
Participated in BASF 8 hour Student Design Competition, fall 2003

References & Portfolio

Available upon request

9-4

FIGURE 9-4
Student resume by
Nina Bruss Bouten

9-5

education
university of wisconsin-stout, menomonie, wisconsin
bfa • art • interior design concentration
3.5 cumulative gpa
5.02 - 12.05

university of wisconsin-lacrosse, lacrosse, wisconsin
9.01 - 5.02

objective
to obtain a job in the field of interior design in order to gain
knowledge + experience

experience
interior design intern 6.05 - 8.05
smart associates - minneapolis, minnesota
prepared construction documents
corrected red lines
organized resource library
assisted in making finish selections
prepared presentation boards

resident advisor 8.03 - 5.05
university of wisconsin-stout, menomonie, wisconsin
antrim froggatt hall
planned monthly programs
advised hall residents, staff + guests

marketing representative 5.04 - 8.04
spanarele industries - waukesha, wisconsin
assisted in preparing the corporate website
prepared computer version of image library

customer service representative 5.02 - 8.02
a designer's view - waukesha, wisconsin
assisted in preparation for store opening
assisted design professionals

organization + activities
newh student representatives 8.05 - present
iida student member 8.04 - 11.05
resident advisor council 8.03 - 5.05
resident advisor + hall director hiring committees 8.03 - 5.05

exhibits and honors
deans list
uw-marshfield student art exhibit 10.04 - 2.05
uw-stout computer imagery student show 3.05

computer skills
microsoft word
microsoft excel
autocad 2006
rhinocerous 3-d modelling
adobe photoshop
adobe illustrator
adobe indesign
dreamweaver

references available upon request

ciarah coenen
permanent address
1814 enterprise street
waukesha, wisconsin 53189
telephone 262.617.2176
coenanc@uwstout.edu

9-6

601 8th Ave. So.   Email sederstroma@uwstout.edu
South St. Paul, MN 55075   Mobile 651.269.3150

Andrea Sederstrom

Objective: To obtain a position in a commercial design firm in which I will be able to use both technical and creative skills to enhance all aspects of design in relation to the interior design field.

Education: University of Wisconsin - Stout
CIDA Accredited
Graduation Date: December 2007
BFA in Interior Design
Minor in Business Administration

Related Courses:
Commercial Design II	Architectural Design
Commercial Design I	Architectural Graphics
Residential Design II	Construction Documentation
Residential Design I	Lighting Design

Computer Skills: AutoCAD 2006
Photoshop
Illustrator
Microsoft Word
Microsoft Powerpoint
SketchUp

Work Experience: May 2005 - present
Ropes Course Lead Student Manager
Supervise and schedule staff and act as a primary contact
between customers and coordinator. Conduct routine
maintenance and training on the course.
Ropes Course Facilitator
Facilitate groups on the ropes course and tailor events to
the goals of the group while ensuring proper safety measures
are taken.
Stout Adventures Specialist
Enforce climbing wall and rental center policies and procedures,
monitor climbers for safe technique, assist customers whenever
necessary with a friendly, enthusiastic, and helpful attitude.

Awards Recieved: Three time recipient of the Chancelor's Award
(For recieving a GPA of 3.5 or higher)

*References and portfolio available upon request.

FIGURE 9-5
Student resume by
Ciarah Coenen

FIGURE 9-6
Student resume by
Andrea Sederstrom

FIGURE 9-7
Student resume by
Ardella Pieper

9-7

education
university of wisconsin-stout, menomonie, wi
bfa • interior design concentration • 5.98
GPA • 3.7/4.0

winona state university, winona, mn
associate of arts degree
graduated magna cum laude

experience
internship • 5.97-8.97
shea architects, minneapolis, mn
responsible for generation of construction documents created on autocad 13
selected finishes and composed project presentation boards
interacted with clients and reps throughout project design phases

art director • 6.96-8.96
girl scouts of the milwaukee area, milwaukee, wi
planned weekly art activity schedule
created art activities for entire camp
supervised campers during art sessions

lab supervisor • 9.95-5.97
uw-stout interior design lab, menomonie, wi
organized and maintained lab references and materials
implemented efficient organization ideas for lab facility

desk supervisor • 9.95-present
uw-stout antrim/froggatt hall, menomonie, wi
advised hall residents, staff, and guests with questions or concerns
maintained positive customer relations

floral designer • 6.95-9.95
dj campus floral, winona, mn
experimented with a variety of floral mediums
designed floral arrangements

organizations and activities
asid student chapter liaison • 1997-98
asid newsletter chairperson • 1997-98
asid junior representative and publicity committee member • 1996-97
art and design student advisory council member • 1997-98
participated in asid regionals, minneapolis, mn • 1996-97
participated in asid student chapter career day • 1996-98
participated in the frank ching drawing workshop • 1996

exhibits and honors
work exhibited in best of design shows, uw-stout • 1997,1998
work featured in interior design visual presentation by maureen mitton
to be published by john wiley & sons • new york, new york
chancellor's award for academic excellence • 1995-present

computer skills
autocad release 13
photoshop 4.0
illustrator 7.0
freehand 7.0
quark xpress 3.3

references and portfolio
available upon request

ardella pieper
school address
436 froggatt hall
menomonie, wi 54751
telephone 715.232.1738
piepera@post.uwstout.edu

permanent address
rural route one, box 139
rushmore, mn 56168
telephone 507.478.4324

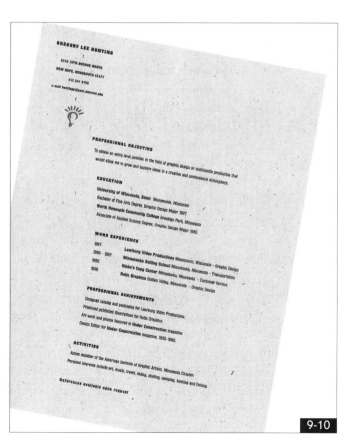

FIGURE 9-8
Student resume by
Anne Cleary

FIGURE 9-9
Student resume by
David Winkler

FIGURE 9-10
Student resume
by Greg Bunting

graduates who have held a nondesign job but wish to focus attention on a previously held successful internship. The functional resume also provides an opportunity to describe skills that may transfer to a design position from another profession, such as project management.

Burdette Bostwick (*Resume Writing*, 1990) has identified a basic resume, appropriate for those entering the job market with little experience. A basic resume focuses attention on career objectives and education and may include extracurricular activities, useful skills such as languages other than English, summer jobs, volunteer work, and interesting hobbies. For those seeking a design-related position, computer skills and specialized class work should be emphasized in the resume and highlighted in the portfolio. In writing all types of resume it is best to use action words to describe experience. Words such as *accomplished*, *achieved*, and *created* work well to insert energy into the described activities.

Many employers look for an employment objective as part of an entry-level resume. If included, this should be a briefly stated objective for the immediate future—the next two to three years. A well-stated objective can tell an employer a great deal about you and your communication skills. A vague, poorly stated objective can land your resume in the trash. Some employers find objectives trite and tedious. Therefore, if you do not have a genuine objective, it may be best to omit this feature. It is also worthwhile to review and edit the objective for a particular job application so that it is in keeping with the position.

Recent graduates should assess the strengths of their educational programs and highlight them in their resumes. Course work in construction and construction documents, business, specialized computer software, human factors, universal design, and related fine arts activities should be noted. This does not mean that you should list every course taken. Instead, focus on what made your education extraordinary. Student membership in design organizations and service projects should be included as well. Remember, your resume must set you apart from the competition.

Recent graduates with prior nonrelated education and work experience often employ a combination of the functional and chronological resume formats. This can be done by clustering related activities chronologically and emphasizing skills and experiences. It is exceedingly important that individuals with multiple life experiences seek interesting and appropriate ways to communicate them in resumes. It is also important for those with a few years of design experience to alter the basic resume to clearly communicate experience.

Currently potential employers may request that a resume be sent via e-mail. This is worth doing because it lands the resume in the correct hands, often immediately. To preserve the graphic integrity of the resume it is best to send it as an attachment rather than as lines of text to the e-mail message. Prior to sending a resume in this fashion it is worthwhile to send a test message to be sure that the resume document can be opened. Saving the resume as a PDF file allows for it to be opened and to be viewed easily by most computers. As discussed previously in Chapter 8, page 238, saving most types of file in the PDF format is generally done by making a selection of "PDF" in the Print window.

Some large corporations use computer-tracking systems to search through hundreds of applicant resumes. Although design firms do not generally use these systems, companies that may hire interior designers use them. It can prove worthwhile to inquire whether or not a particular large corporation or governmental agency makes use of such a tracking system because a creative resume may prove less than ideal in these situations. Because tracking systems rely on scanning resumes and creating a database through the use of key words, certain graphic nuances may be lost, to say the least. If documents are to be scanned, it is useful to simplify the resume and perhaps use less italicized type and more bold type.

Spelling and grammatical errors will land a beautifully designed and produced resume and/or cover letter in the garbage can or shredder. Check, check, and check again prior to mailing anything to potential employers.

Additional Correspondence

It is customary to send a cover letter with a resume as means of stating your interest in a job. In addition, a thank-you letter, letter of acknowledgment, and letter accepting or declining an offer are useful. One of the reasons to design an original, creative resume is that you can use graphic elements included on all correspondence used for your job search. A cover letter using design components found in the resume is an attractive and enticing promotional item. Following up an interview with a similarly designed thank-you card is an excellent idea that says volumes about a designer's skills and professionalism. When creating these various elements it is important to use similar paper and printing processes so that the elements are visually consistent.

There are varying circumstances encountered in applying for a job. For example, a position may be advertised or communicated by word of mouth. In other cases a resume and cover letter may be sent to a huge number of firms and companies (this is known as broadcasting or generalized mailing). Because there is a range of circumstances, a cover letter must be sent with the resume as a means of introducing yourself, describing your interest in a position, and briefly listing your qualifications.

A successful cover letter generates enough interest for the reader to turn the page and review your resume. In most cases a brief cover letter is best—everyone's time is valuable. Although there are significant variations, most cover letters include an introductory paragraph. This is where you describe your interest in the company and state that you are answering an ad or that a mutual acquaintance links you to the employer. In a generalized mailing it is common to simply introduce yourself, whereas in a letter targeted for a particular position you may lead with why you are interested in working for the particular firm or company.

The cover letter then continues with a partial list of your qualifications (including information about your recent degree or job). The final paragraph should recap, with interest and enthusiasm, the points stated. Be clear and brief; do not waste the reader's time by going over in detail what is covered in your resume. Some applicants find it useful to include a stamped postcard with the resume and cover letter. The postcard can be preprinted with responses such as "We are not hiring at this time," to be mailed back to the applicant.

All forms of business correspondence discussed require accuracy and correct spelling and grammar (do not rely on spell-check alone). By being brief and to the point, you demonstrate business acumen and professionalism. Although a resume can be quite nontraditional and creative, other forms of correspondence should follow standard business conventions. A good book on resume writing and job seeking can be worth the cost.

Employers are often deluged with resumes and cover letters from recent graduates. An excellent resume and cover letter go a long way in getting the door

FIGURES 9-11a, 9-11b, AND 9-11c

Sample portfolio ready for mailing, as well as opened with contents displayed.
By Jill Stifter

9-11a

9-11b

9-11c

open. However, in some cases more is required. It may be necessary to actually include samples of work with a resume and cover letter. Most often this entails creating a mailer or sample portfolio (see Figures 9-11a through 9-17c).

A sample portfolio is an interesting means of offering a quick look at your work. I have found that recent graduates with well-designed sample portfolios, also known as "mailers," cause quite a stir with employers and are often called for interviews. In designing sample portfolios, careful consideration must be given to items for inclusion and the overall cost of mailing. Sample portfolios are expensive, time-consuming, and should be used only for targeted firms or known job openings.

The most inexpensive sample portfolios contain reduced black-and-white copies of design projects and student work. These may be photocopies or images scanned into a computer and used in conjunction with page-design software. Reduced color photocopies are also an option for sample portfolios.

Sending samples of work along with a resume and cover letter creates the need for a well-designed package to house the items. When designing a sample package it is important to consider mailing regulations and ease of opening and review. In some cases the package can be designed for return, with postage and return instructions enclosed. However, the party who receives the documents has absolutely no responsibility to return them. Digital portfolios can work in a manner similar to sample portfolios, and those are covered in detail at the end of this chapter.

FIGURES 9-12a AND 9-12b

Sample portfolio, closed as
well as opened for view.
By Mercedes Thauer

9-12a

9-12b

9-13a

FIGURES 9-13a AND 9-13b
Sample portfolio, closed as well as
opened to reveal a "chain set."
By Kathryn Pertzsch

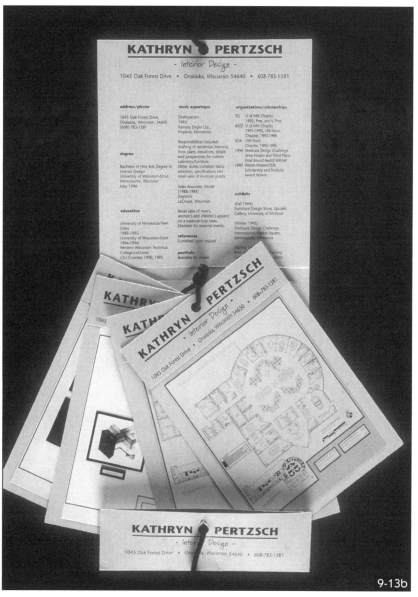

9-13b

FIGURE 9-14

Professional brochure for
firm owned by the creator
of Figures 9-13a and 9-13b.
Firm: Pertzsch Design Inc.
Design by Susan C. Schuyler of the
Creative Edge

9-14

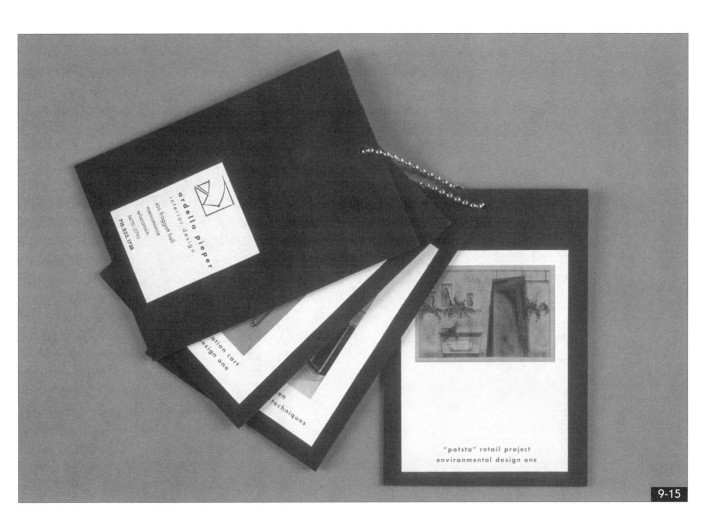

FIGURE 9-15
Sample portfolio on a chain.
By Ardella Pieper

9-16a

9-16b

9-16c

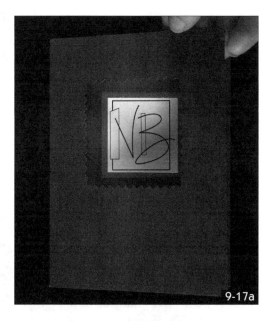

9-17a

FIGURES 9-16a, 9-16b,
AND 9-16c
Resume, related business card,
and sample portfolio created
by a graphic design student.
By Rachel Eidet

Construction Documents

A set of construction documents for a large
office space.

9-17b

FIGURES 9-17a, 9-17b,
AND 9-17c
Sample portfolio—notice the
consistent graphic relationship
to the resume in Figure 9-4.
By Nina Bruss Bouten

Office Design

n.b.b. design is a small hospitality design firm with
a layout promoting work in team settings. The space
is designed for comfort for both employees and clients
with warm finishes and inspirational elements.

9-17c

THE PORTFOLIO

Putting together a design portfolio requires the selection of appropriate items for inclusion, the selection of a format (or grid) for the items included, the selection of an actual portfolio case to house the contents, and some practice in presenting a portfolio.

The selection of items is a primary step in creating a portfolio. This requires taking an inventory of all student projects and assignments, as well as items completed during an internship or specialized study. It is important to assess the items honestly and decide which projects are excellent and ready for inclusion, which items require reworking, and which should be tossed out.

In selecting items, it is essential to include a range of project types. Residential, commercial, small and simple, large, concrete, realizable and highly conceptual projects all have a place in a portfolio. It is also useful to include a range of types of presentation. Currently, it is important to include CAD drawings and additional computer-generated imagery, as well as construction documents, if possible.

Many soon-to-be graduates wonder whether all projects should be presented completely consistently, or whether projects should be treated individually in terms of graphics and format. Unfortunately, there is no hard-and-fast answer to this question. Like resumes, portfolios reflect the tastes and personality of the individual. This means that for some a portfolio that is completely consistent graphically is the only possibility; for others a diverse portfolio with a range of project formats, sizes, and styles is best.

Creating a portfolio that is completely consistent means that all items must be exactly the same size, similar in color, and consistent graphically. This often requires that all projects be redone for inclusion in the portfolio, an expensive and time-consuming proposition. Another drawback is that this type of portfolio presentation does not show projects as they were done for class assignments and therefore may not indicate growth or improvement.

Portfolios that present projects with a range of graphic styles require some element of unity to tie the projects together. In these portfolios the quality must be consistent, so often a few projects are redone for greater legibility or graphic unity. It is also useful to limit, to some degree, variation in the size of boards and sheets presented because too much variety in size can be confusing and messy.

Regardless of the level of consistency of format, all portfolio presentations benefit from elements that add unity and cohesion. The best way to create graphic unity is to use a consistent or similar grid for all projects presented. When this is not possible, a consistent typeface, title block, or logo may be employed. In some cases, perhaps the only possible unifying element is the size of items presented.

Students often ask how many projects to include, and that is difficult to answer. The best way to decide on quantity is to take an inventory of the projects you wish to present, then do a mock-up presentation or run-through and check for time. It is best to limit the presentation to a half hour or 45 minutes (for entry-level jobs). Although many interviews go on for longer than an hour, some are cut short, and you must make sure all the best work is presented in the time allotted. First interviews often take between a half hour and a full hour. When setting up an interview, it is reasonable to ask how much time will be allowed. Knowledge about the interview time combined with knowledge about the potential employer can allow you to edit items in the portfolio.

Questions often arise as to sequence or organization of projects. Much like resumes, portfolios may be organized chronologically or functionally. Generally one's best projects are completed in the last two years of school, with the finest completed in the last studio courses, with the most in depth project typically being a thesis project, which should most often be presented first in entry level interviews. Regardless of the presence of a thesis project, there is merit in presenting the most recent projects first and working backward.

Grouping projects in terms of scope and function also has merit because it allows one to target certain areas for certain interviews. For example, if hospitality projects are clustered together, one can focus on them in an interview with a hospitality-oriented firm. When clustering projects functionally, it is common to lead with the strongest projects and work backward.

Organizing projects purely in terms of quality also has merit. Presenting the strongest projects first can generate excitement. This allows for weaker projects to be seen as building blocks. I think it is a mistake to lead with weak projects in the hope that you will build excitement as quality increases. Weak projects seen too early will generally put off a potential employer. Moreover, there is always the possibility that the potential employer will be called away in the middle of the interview, not having seen the best work.

One of the biggest problems for interior designers in creating entry-level portfolios is the size and weight of many presentation boards. It is difficult to include many thick boards of mounted materials in a standard zipper portfolio case with plastic sleeves. One way around this problem is to include all drawings, renderings, and graphics simply mounted or copied onto paper, held inside sleeves. Only materials presentations are then mounted on paperboard. The materials boards can be removed from the portfolio and presented as the employer reviews the project drawings in the sleeves.

Some recent graduates opt for a thin

FIGURE 9-18
Portfolios and presentation cases.
1. Zippered presentation case with binder, sheets, and sheet protectors
2. Zippered portfolio for use with individual boards (no binder)
3. Hard-sided portfolio (no binder)
4. Attaché case (individual boards, no binder)
5. Handmade box (individual boards, no binder)
6. Small presentation case with binder, sheets, and sheet protectors (excellent for photographic and smaller images)
7. Inexpensive coated paper or fiber portfolio (no binder)
8. Easel binder with sheets and sheet protectors (usually no larger than 18" x 24")

boxlike portfolio and present all projects mounted on boards or plates, in many cases this involves taking high-resolution photographs of the original presentation in order to reduce overall size. The boards are carried to the interview in the portfolio or presentation case, then removed and handed in stacks to the interviewer. Some students decide that they wish to have a very compact portfolio and choose to reduce all project documents to fit a smaller case. This creates a manageable portfolio; however, reducing all student work can be time-consuming and expensive. Some potential employers may ask to see original project boards, while others may be perfectly happy to view reduced photographic images of the original.

FIGURES 9-19a AND 9-19b
Student project booklet
(exterior and interior pages)
created for a furniture design
class.
By Sarah Amundsen

FIGURES 9-20a AND 9-20b
Student project booklet
(exterior cover and in use)
created for an interior design
studio project.
By Ardella Pieper

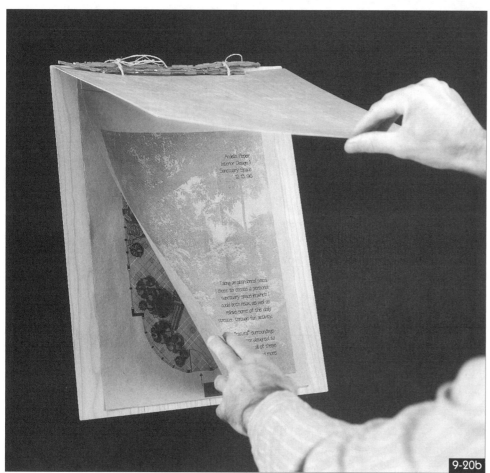

Practicing designers usually have photographs taken of built projects and combine these with sketches and reduced working drawings. Photographs, sketches, and reduced drawings can be included in small, very manageable portfolios or binders. Figure 9-18 illustrates some popular portfolios and presentation cases.

Some design graduates manage the size problem by presenting multiple portfolio cases. This is most often done with special projects, such as a thesis or long-term project. Putting special projects into separate portfolios can add interest to the presentation. However, it may be a mistake to use more than two individual portfolios because they can become difficult to handle if the applicant is nervous. Figures 9-19a, 9-19b, 9-20a, and 9-20b are samples of project notebooks. Additional examples of project notebooks may also be found in the preceding chapter.

In the case of technical drawings, it is perfectly appropriate to hand them to an interviewer as flat stapled sheets, rolled drawings, or a small booklet. These drawings, such as construction documents and CAD drawings, are important to bring to interviews and are often presented outside the traditional portfolio case. It is worth practicing arriving in the room for the interview with a portfolio case and rolls of drawings. Remember, you will need to shake someone's hand at the same time you are setting down your portfolio, drawings, and perhaps a coat or bag.

It is important to include design-process documents with finished presentation drawings in the portfolio, Employers often wish to see how a potential employee thinks and the nature of his or her design process. The best way to document the design process in student projects is to save everything—all research, notes, doodles, schedules, bubble diagrams, sketches, and so forth. At the end of the project these process documents and sketches can be photocopied and bound into a project process booklet. The project booklet is then available for discussion during the interview. Retaining sketches, notes, and drawings is also important for practicing designers, who should keep these items for reference (and for interviews).

THE DIGITAL PORTFOLIO

Digital portfolios provide an excellent vehicle for relaying the types of visual imagery and project information found in standard interior-design portfolios. There are significant issues involved in creating digital portfolios, and these relate to the use and selection of software, organizing and obtaining digital images, and the decision about whether to create a Web-based portfolio or a portable portfolio (using a CD or DVD). These issues can present something of a roadblock to some students and designers, which is unfortunate, because despite having to deal with these issues, digital portfolios can be easier than one might think to create.

The information provided in this section is an overview of some basics related to preparing a digital portfolio. For detailed information about use of specific software and tools, I recommend consulting a book that focuses on digital portfolios. Understanding issues such as color management, file size and compression, and image interpolation are required should one seek to create a well-refined digital portfolio. Information about resources that contain this material may be found in the References section at the end of this chapter.

Initial digital-portfolio development involves many of the same steps as a developing a "real" or physical portfolio. Decisions about what to include and the manner in which to include it must be made well in advance of sitting down to the computer with Web-authoring software or a CD to burn. Consistency between the digital portfolio and the actual physical portfolio is a worthy goal and can be accomplished with some thought and planning. Very often, digital images of the actual pages of the physical portfolio are used to create the "pages" of the digital portfolio. When possible, it is helpful to select background colors or type styles consistent with the elements of the physical portfolio.

Therefore, while the remainder of this chapter covers some of the technical issues related to creating a digital portfolio, it is worth emphasizing again and again the following important concept: Technology and graphics should not overwhelm the information contained in a digital interior design portfolio. Instead, the technology should be used to support, clarify and enhance the original work contained in the portfolio. It's about the work, the projects, and the telling of your unique story, not about the bells and whistles of the digital design.

In *Designing a Digital Portfolio* (2004), Cynthia L. Baron writes, "A digital portfolio is a collection of creative assets distributed via computer-based media. This broad definition covers a range of forms: PDF attachments, CD presentations, DVD demo reels, work housed on laptops and websites." Currently, interior designers are using various forms of digital portfolios as components of a complete package, which often includes a physical portfolio, a resume, and perhaps a sample mailer. While the digital portfolio has not replaced the physical or traditional portfolio with all employers, it is certainly a viable element to have available for potential employers. My informal discussions with firms hiring designers have shown that some prefer only a well-designed cover letter and resume be sent via digital means, while other firms prefer that the letter, resume, and a digital portfolio be available for

review prior to an interview. Most prefer that the portfolio contains, to some degree, real or physical examples of projects rather than completely digital representation—although this seems to be evolving.

Before going further with this discussion it is important to make a clarification. The term *digital media* can be used to refer to elements created using electronic media. Therefore, any design presentation produced using digital photographs, CAD, imagining software, or modeling and rendering software can be said to be created using digital media. This means that one could create all of the pages of a printed portfolio using various forms of computer-generated imagery, yet it would still have the feel of a tradional portfolio because it would have printed pages that exist within a physical portfolio. This lies in contrast to a completely digital portfolio, which would be one that was both generated and viewed via computer, and which is referred to by Cynthia Baron when she describes the "creative assets" being "distributed" via computer based media. Therefore, the term *digital portfolio* is used here to describe a portfolio that is meant to be viewed *via computer* rather than in its printed form.

The notion of viewing a digital portfolio *via computer* is important as it relates directly to a number of technical issues such as the color system used (RGB) as well as a lower-resolution (72 dpi for the Web) graphic files that may be used, whereas portfolio elements generated via digital media but intended for eventual *printing* use CMYK color and require higher resolution graphic files (a minimum of 300 dpi). These important differences require that a decision needs to be made while the portfolio is developed: Will it be a true digital portfolio, viewed only via digital means? Or will it be designed to be printed with a secondary version available via electronic delivery?

These distinctions and related issues are illustrated in Figure 9-21.

Digital portfolios present two distinct choices: the portfolio may be Web based or portable (typically saved to a disk such as a CD or DVD). Web-based portfolios may require a bit more time to prepare and require ongoing server space but they have the advantage of being readily available (when done properly) for prospective employers and clients. CDs can be relatively easy to prepare, are viewable without a Web connection, and do not require server space. Another portable option is the use of a laptop with a preset portfolio presentation readily available for view.

Because many employers who hire interior designers continue to require a review of a physical or traditional portfolio, with at least some actual materials samples included, we are not quite at the point where the digital portfolio suffices as a complete survey of student and prior work. For this reason, most interior designers do not arrive for a portfolio review with a laptop ready to show a completely digital portfolio. However, while we are not quite there yet, it is not uncommon for some multimedia and graphic designers to choose this approach. In the future, doing so could help designers avoid some of the issues raised in creating Web-based and portable portfolios such as compatibility and ease or control of navigation.

FIGURE 9-21
Digital portfolios may be Web based or portable, with each option having various advantages and technical considerations.

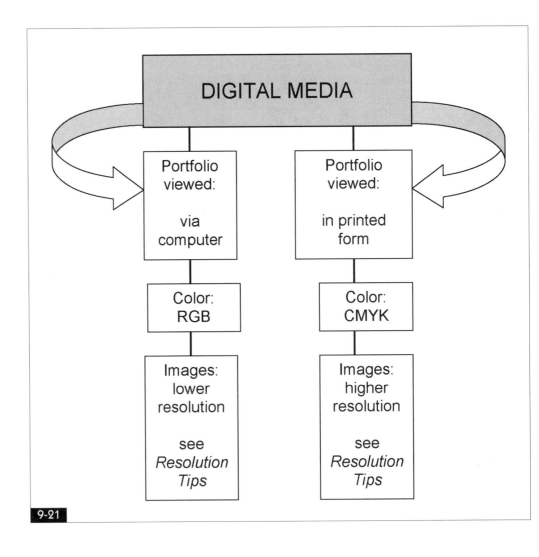

Web-Based Portfolios

Creation of a Web site requires use of some type of web-authoring program; these allow text, links, digital images, and often audio and video to be imported and viewed. Adobe Photoshop, Macromedia Dreamweaver®, GoLive®, and Microsoft FrontPage are commonly used among students with whom I come in contact. Most Web-based portfolios, which typically start with a home page, provide some sort of introduction as well as links to the various pages of the portfolio. Each page or slide should then link back to the main page or provide some form of navigation. Photoshop, Dreamweaver, and FrontPage all provide standardized templates that allow for quick-and-easy generation of digital portfolios. Working with standardized templates is useful for those with little experience using Web-authoring software, but it can be limiting in terms of font selection, layout, and background colors and styles (see Figures 9-22, 9-23a, and 9-23b).

I agree with Robin Williams, writing in *The Non-Designer's Web Book* (2005), "It's easy to make a Web page; to make a well-designed web page, however, is not so easy." Web-authoring software allows those of us who do not know HTML (Hypertext Markup Language) or *anything* about the design of Web sites to create Web pages and digital portfolios easily by using templates. This means that one must consider the amount of time available and to use standardized templates if time is short due to the learning curve involved in going beyond the template. However, it's worthwhile to spend time developing a more well-designed digital portfolio as time allows. For those interested in spending the time necessary to move away from standardized templates, I recommend reading Williams's book, which is easy to understand and covers all aspects of Web site creation. Additionally, *The Web Style Guide: Basic Principles for Creating Web Sites*, by Sarah Horton and Peter Lynch (2002), is useful.

FIGURE 9-22

A simple Web-based portfolio page, created using a standard Photoshop template.

Architectural photograph by Ed Gohlich

9-23a

9-23b

FIGURES 9-23a AND 9-23b
Screen shots of the home page
and a single portfolio page for
Web-based portfolio created
using Macromedia
Dreamweaver.
By Anne Harmer

FIGURES 9-24a AND 9-24b
A portfolio title page (9-24a)
created using Photoshop can
serve as the home page for a
Web-based portfolio, with the
individual linked pages created
from the individual pages of the
portfolio (9-24b). These files
could also be used to create a
CD that either runs to preset
timing or consists of PDFs
selected at the discretion of the
viewer. This student portfolio
page shares unifying features
with the resume in Figure 9-4
and sample portfolio in Figures
9-17, 9-17b, and 9-17c.
By Nina Bruss Bouten

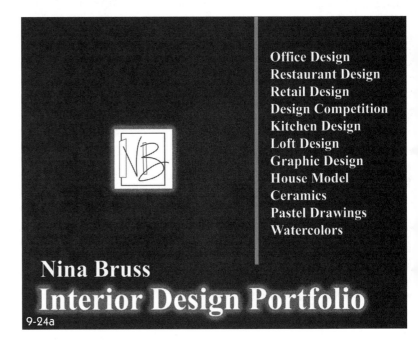

Office Design
Restaurant Design
Retail Design
Design Competition
Kitchen Design
Loft Design
Graphic Design
House Model
Ceramics
Pastel Drawings
Watercolors

Nina Bruss
Interior Design Portfolio
9-24a

Because Web-based portfolios require a home page or introduction that allows for navigation into the various links or pages of the portfolio, thought must be given to the organization of the home page and descriptions given for the individual project pages and links. As with many forms of visual presentation, the creation of a series of thumbnails or a storyboard with various well-sketched-out pages aid in the design process. In addition, giving serious thought to titles and descriptions that will be found on the home pages is highly worthwhile.

Options for the home pages include creating a format that is graphically consistent with the person's physical portfolio—this allows for the individual linked pages to be uploaded versions of the actual portfolio pages. This is particularly easy if the portfolio has been designed using software such

Restaurant Design

9-24b

as Photoshop or Illustrator or InDesign as shown in Figures 9-24a and 9-24b. It can also be done using digital photographs of the physical portfolio boards or pages, as discussed at the end of this chapter.

Portable Digital Portfolios (CDs and DVDs)

As stated, the digital portfolio can also be saved to a disk (CD or DVD, with more options on the horizon) and sent to potential employers. CDs are available in CDR versions, which are "read only" disks, which means that they cannot be altered and cannot be written over. (CDRW disks allow for the disk to be read and rewritten.) Typically, portfolios are produced on CDR versions as these are the least expensive and there is no need to pay extra for the rewriting capabilities. DVDs hold more data than CDs, allowing them to handle intensive graphics, motion, and sound.

While CD-based portfolios have advantages, they have a disadvantage related to issues of computer-platform compatibility, meaning that a disk created on a Mac is not readily opened on a PC. To ensure that the disk can be opened on either platform, a hybrid disk must be created. It is worth testing a CD on both platforms to ensure compatibility. Furthermore, CDs do not automatically translate the software application they were created with to any computer they are inserted into. Therefore there are two options to chose from: First, the CD can simply be loaded with portfolio pages saved as a single or multiple PDFs, which will open easily on computers loaded with Acrobat viewers (which is highly commonplace).

Another option is to set the CD up similarly to a Web site with a system of navigation that allows the viewers to move from image to image as they desire. This requires that

FIGURE 9-25

Screen shot of a CD-based portfolio gallery and a single portfolio page created using Portfolio by Extensis. The sketch shown is based upon a Brunschwig & Fils advertisement.
By Randi Steinbrecher

the necessary software is embedded in the disk, an example of which is shown in Figure 9-25.

A simple CD with all images saved as PDFs is by far the easiest and most straightforward type of digital portfolio to create. These are not flashy but they can be opened on most computers avoiding the problems mentioned in the previous paragraph. This type can also be created in a short time, making them ideal for many interior designers—who are, after all, not typically trained in Web authoring. Figures 9-26a through 9-26c illustrate the use of PDFs to display portfolio pages. Most graphic imaging software allows for saving as files as PDFs and Photoshop allows one to save a series of files in the desired order by choosing "File"—"Automate"—"PDF Presentation," and selecting the desired files or folder.

In cases where a designer wants the CD to be experienced more like a Web portfolio or to create a preset visual experience more (like a slide show), the CD must have special files loaded onto it. Because CDs are read by browsers using the "file system protocol" and Web sites are read using "hypertext transfer protocol"(http), one cannot simply put the HTML pages created by Web-authoring software onto a CD—it won't automatically "run" and open to the main page. Creating a self-starting CD on a Windows-based computer involves adding one or two small files to the root directory of the CD during creation. One file is called "autorun.inf," which is required to auto-launch a program with an ".exe" extension. If the file that is to be auto-started is not a program (Web pages, for example), then a second intermediary .exe file should also be added to the root level. One such file is "ShelExec.exe," which associates the Web page file with a default browser and launches the page in that program. ShelExec.exe can be downloaded as freeware.

It is important to note that the previous paragraph describes creating a CD that operates like a Web site or preset slide show. Some designers and students are perfectly content with simply creating a CD containing a gallery of images with minimal text, in which images can be selected and enlarged. This is done easily by saving the files as PDFs as discussed previously.

9-26a

9-26b

9-26c

FIGURES 9-26a, 9-26b, AND 9-26c
Screen shots of a portfolio with pages created in InDesign saved as PDFs to a CD.
By Shelley Pecha

One last word or two about creating a CD-based portfolio: this can also be done quite easily using PowerPoint. Because PowerPoint is presentation software based on a slide show format it is quite readily used for the creation of a preset or guided slideshow type portfolio. One simply creates "slides" with images and descriptions of projects—or imports portfolio "sheets" from Photoshop, or other imaging software. The slides can be organized as any presentation would be with a careful eye on the order and editing of projects as well as checking for accurate spelling and graphic consistency (of text, and heading sizes and color) and then saved and burned to a CD. Because these tend to be huge files, saving the PowerPoint as a PDF prior to burning it

to the disk is a good move (this is done in the Print window in PowerPoint).

There are, however, two problems with the PowerPoint approach. First, some employers may find the use of PowerPoint less than sophisticated, and second, even with files saved as PDFs, the show will require PowerPoint is installed to run. In a pinch, PowerPoint may work well; veering away from the stock templates is vital in these cases, as is double-checking that the person viewing the portfolio has the software available for viewing.

CDs are easily included in an attractive package that also includes a cover letter and resume. When doing this, it important to create an attractive CD labels that is consistent with the accompanying graphic

FIGURE 9-27
CD labels are created easily and are best handled in a manner graphically consistent with the resume or mailer.
By Anne Cleary

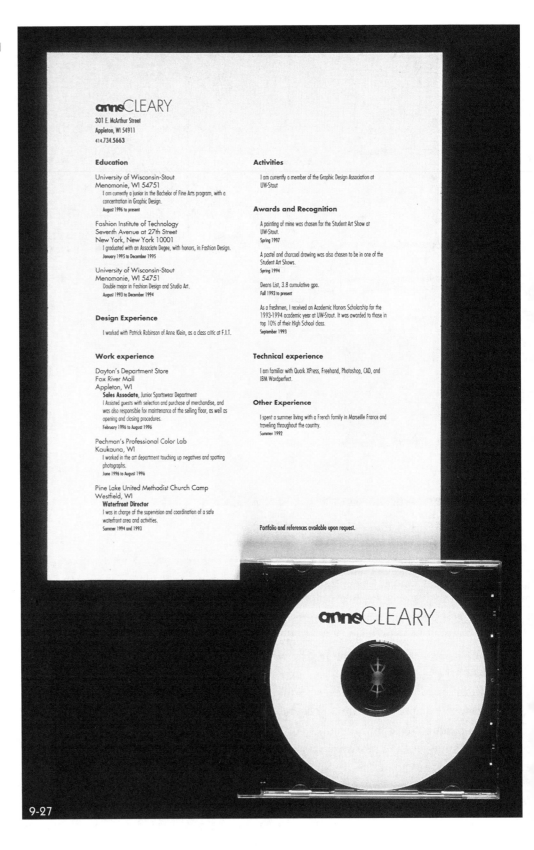

elements as shown in Figure 9-27. CDs are labeled using labeling software as well as printers that can print directly on the surface of the disk.

Preparing Work for the Digital Portfolio

Interior designers and design students often produce large presentation boards containing items and elements created by hand. This means that in order to include this nondigital material, it must be scanned, or photographed with a digital camera, to prepare it for inclusion in a digital portfolio.

Many colleges and universities provide digital-photography services as well as use of high-quality scanners. In cases where this type of service is not available, students can photograph their own work using digital cameras or have this done by professionals. High-quality cameras must be used to avoid distortion, poor color rendition, and generally poor quality results.

Photography of three-dimensional items such as scale models, furniture, and sculptural elements requires adequate lighting and selection of some type of appropriate background. For those of us who are not professional photographers, it is worthwhile to photograph projects with a range of light sources in order to have some success. Shooting projects both indoors with electric lights (perhaps) supplemented by daylight and outdoors offers the more opportunity for success than does one setup. For outdoor photography scale models may be placed with or against a sky or landscape background to good effect. When set indoors selecting a neutral background on a table or against a vertical element (a wall some foam board) can work well. Lighting the project as well as possible usually with a range of light sources is useful as is trying a number of different lighting set ups.

Photography of flat work such as presentation boards and drawings can be more challenging than one might think. Lighting and distortion are the typical problems inherent in such photography. Many presentation boards and drawings have some glossy surfaces that cause can reflections, especially when the flash feature is used. If possible, turning the flash off and lighting with a variety of electronic lights can be beneficial. In some cases, taking the photographs outside in a cloudy day can reduce glare and reflections. A copy stand, which is a flat surface with attachments for cameras and light, is useful in photographing smaller boards and other flat work.

Distortion in photography of flat work can make the edges of boards and drawings look as though they bow out unnaturally. One remedy to this situation is to overshoot the edges of the boards by a wide margin and to crop the photographs using electronic media. Distortion and difficulties with focusing on large boards may require that they are photographed in sections and brought together using graphic-imaging software. In some cases, elements from large presentations may be scanned separately and composed in a new manner using graphic imaging software.

Professional designers are well served by photographing their projects as soon after construction is as complete as possible. When possible, hiring a professional photographer—particularly one with a specialty in architectural photography—is ideal. While it may be expensive, it is generally well worth the price (within reason) for purposes of firm marketing and eventual project publication.

Scanners may be used for project boards and sheets, freehand drawings, and sketches, as well as preliminary project doodles. This, of course, depends upon the size of the project and that of the scanner. In most cases scanning the original at a

Resolution Tips

Scan images at a higher resolution than the suggested final use size. This allows for files to be re-sampled at a lower resolution later if needed. In cases where the original resolution is too low —do not rescale up— instead scan again at the appropriate resolution.

Line drawings and sketches should be scanned at a very high resolution so that lines show up clearly. Scan these at least double the final resolution required and then scale them down as needed later (scaling down is required when lines appear jagged) or to use them for web based images. In preparation for scanning, drawings should be cleaned up with extraneous marks and lines erased.

For web images, scan at a scale where pixel dimensions are roughly double what they will be on the screen —this means different sizes of work will be scanned at different ppis. In doing this, a small object (like a business card or postcard) might be scanned at 300ppi and a larger object (such as an 11 X 17 inch image) might be scanned at 72ppi.

Suggested Image Resolution

Web graphic	72ppi
Printed (non line art)	300 dpi
Line art	300 to 600 dpi

File Types

Digital files are created in the application file type they are made in, requiring that they are later saved or copied into a more universal format. Various types of images require varying file types for later use and manipulation.

File Type	Recommended Use
EPS	Illustration, conversion of CAD (such as .dwg) files
TIFF	Photographic images

The following file types are compressed (often for use on the web) and not recommended for image editing or manipulation, which will result in a loss of image quality:

JPEG	Compressed file for photographic and graphic images: 24-bit color depth supported by most web browsers
GIF	Compressed file for graphic images: 8-bit color depth (less quality but smaller than JPGs) supported by most web browsers, useful for simple items like logos.
PNG	Compressed file for graphic images: intended as a replacement for GIFs, increasing web browser support
PDF	Used for primarily for publication and/or type intensive documents reduces file size for a range of uses. Can be generated from CAD files for later manipulation (such as rendering in Photoshop) but EPS offer greater options. NOTE: PDF can be saved at higher resolutions than the standard of 72 dpi (this requires the proper software/driver installation)

9-28

high resolution is a good idea. High-resolution files are easily reduced in image editing software for a specific use at a later time. Line drawings are best scanned at an extremely high resolution (above 600 dpi) so that detail is crisp and clear. Unlike line drawings, hand-rendered drawings elements such as wood grain and tile grout lines that look beautiful to the human eye can look messy when scanned above 300 dpi; the high resolution seems to "explode" pencil and marker lines.

In preparing manually created drawing, renderings, and doodles for scanning, it is imperative that the drawings are very clean. This means erasing all messy lines and smudges as these all look much worse when scanned and it is inefficient to try to clean these items up digitally. In many cases, it's worth crafting a final version of a beautiful crisp, clean line drawing so that the scan is crisp and clean. Cleaning the scanner glass helps to create perfectly clean scans.

More information about resolution and file types for creating Web and printed portfolios can be found in Figure 9-28.

Presentation elements that are too large to be scanned as one element may be scanned in sections and "put together" visually using editing software. This can allow for a new, better version of the project as elements can be edited that were less than successful. It is also a way to create a new presentation from elements previously included in a group project. In addition, preliminary elements can be saved and scanned and incorporated into final project presentations (see Figure C-48b on page 88).

For some, it is easy to become bogged down in the technology of creating a digital portfolio. For others, the technology comes easily but the big picture of determining a way to "tell one's own story" is difficult. Currently, the digital portfolio is not the only key to being offered a fulfilling job in design; it can, however, be a part of a successful package. In the future, with the ongoing evolution of technology and concerns about use of resources, there is the potential for digital portfolios to gain more complete and widespread use in interior design practice.

Clearly, developing a successful resume and portfolio takes work, talent, and time. The graphic design and organization of these elements deserve careful consideration and a serious look inward. By taking an honest inventory of your objectives, work, interests, talents, and skills, you can design a system that communicates your identity to potential employers. Developing a schedule and budget for your portfolio system in your final semester at school is extremely helpful. Researching potential employers and firms early in your last year of school is highly advisable. Practicing professionals are well advised to save everything (make copies!) for inclusion in a future portfolio—because in a designer's life, learning never ends.

FIGURE 9-28

Resolution and file types for creating Web and printed portfolios.

REFERENCES

(Contains both works cited and recommended reading. Annotations where appropriate.)

Baron, Cynthia. *Designing a Digital Portfolio*. Berkeley, CA: New Riders, 2004. *This is a well-organized book that contains helpful technical and design related information intended primarily for graphic design.*

Benun, Ilise. *Self Promotion Online*. Cincinnati, OH: North Light Books, 2001.

Berry, Wayne. *15 Seconds: Creating a CD-ROM from a Web Site [online]*. Available at www.15seconds.com/issue/990708.htm, 1999.

Berryman, Gregg. *Designing Creative Portfolios*. Menlo Park, CA: Crisp Publications, 1994.

———.*Designing Creative Resumes*. Menlo Park, CA: Crisp Publications, 1990.

Bostwick, Burdette. *Resume Writing*. New York: John Wiley & Sons, 1990.

Eisenman, Sara. *Building Design Portfolios: Innovative Concepts for Presenting Your Work*. Gloucester, MA: Rockport Publishers, 2006. *An exquisite book with beautiful examples of graphic design related portfolios.*

Fry, Ron. *Your First Resume*, 3rd edition. Clifton Park, New York: Thompson Delmar Learning, 2001.

Horton, Sarah, and Lynch, Peter. *Web Style Guide: Basic Design Principles for Creating Web Sites*. New Haven, CT: Yale University Press, 2002.

Jute, André. *Grids*.New York:Watson-Guptill, 1996.

Kirby, J. Douglas. *Educational Technology: Digital Portfolios*. Available online at www.dkirby.com/edtech/digitalportfolio.htm, 2002.

Linton, Harold. *Portfolio Design*, 3rd edition. New York: W. W. Norton, 2003.

Marquand, Ed. *Graphic Design Presentations*. New York: Van Nostrand Reinhold, 1986.

Oldach, Mark. *Creativity for Graphic Designers*. New York: McGraw-Hill, 1998.

Rich, Jason. *Job Hunting for the Utterly Confused*. Cincinnati, OH: North Light Books, 1995.

Swan, Alan. *The New Graphic Design School*. New York: John Wiley & Sons, 1997.

Williams, Robin. *The Non-Designer's Web Book*, 3rd edition. Berkeley, CA: Peachpit Press, 2005. *Highly recommended reading for those interested in learning more about building a Web site. Williams's books are clear and easy to follow.*

———. *The Little Mac Book*, Tiger edition. Berkeley, CA: Peachpit Press, 2005.

———. *The Non-Designer's Type Book*, 2nd edition. Berkeley, CA: Peachpit Press, 2005.

DIRECTORY OF
FEATURED PROFESSIONALS

Craig Beddow, AIA
Beddow Design • Digital Architecture
225 9th Street East, #303
Saint Paul, MN 55101

Melissa Brewer
Illustrator
melissadbrewer@yahoo.com

Cuningham Group Architecture, P.A.
St. Anthony Main
201 Main Street SE, Suite 325
Minneapolis, MN 55414

CNH Architects Inc.
7300 West 147th Street, Suite 504
Apple Valley, MN 55124

Ellerbe Becket
800 LaSalle Avenue
Minneapolis, MN 55402-2014

Kathy Fogerty
1070 Ashland
Saint Paul, MN 55104

Ed Gohlich
P.O. Box 180919
Coronado, CA 92178

Peter Lee
1331 North East Tyler, Studio 232
Minneapolis, MN 55413

Robert Lownes
Design Visualizations
www.designvisualizations.com

Meyer, Scherer & Rockcastle, Ltd.
710 South 2nd Street, 7th Floor
Minneapolis, MN 55401

Courtney Nystuen
P.O. Box 111
Menomonie, WI 54751

Thomas Oliphant Studio
tomo@thomasoliphant.com

Matthew Saunders
Illustrator
Msaunders77@yahoo.com

Arthur Shuster, Inc.
1995 Oakcrest Avenue West
Saint Paul, MN 55113

Smart Associates
119 North Fourth Street, Suite 506
Minneapolis, MN 55401

Bill Wikrent
Learning Technology Services
University of Wisconsin–Stout
Menomonie, WI 54751

BLANK CRITERIA MATRIX

This blank matrix can be photocopied and used as necessary.

"Project Name" Room	Criteria	Adjacencies							Comments	
1										
2										
3										
4										
5										
6										
7										
8										
9										
10										
11										
12										

Legend

①	Major Adjacency	○	Secondary Requirement
1	Minor Adjacency	Y	Yes, See Comments
●	Mandatory Requirement	X	Undesirable

A-1

APPENDIX 3

DRAWING ELEVATIONS: A RESIDENTIAL CASE STUDY

Many students find drawing interior elevations confusing at first. This is due to the fact that interior elevations convey spatial information using specific drawing conventions. These conventions often cause elevations to look very different from a perspective drawing of the same space.

Reviewing the interior photographs of an actual house and the related interior elevations provides a clearer understanding of the standard drawing conventions employed. In reviewing the drawings and photographs, it will be helpful to make special note of the lack of perspective lines found in elevations. Additionally, the location of each elevation reference symbol on the floor plan and its influence on the manner in which the elevation is drawn is of significant importance.

FLOOR PLAN- SECOND LEVEL
SCALE: 1/4"= 1'-0"

A-2

FIGURE A-2
An AutoCAD-generated floor plan for a multilevel residence with standard interior elevation symbols shown in locations viewed in the photographs and elevations.
Residence feature designed by Kristine Recker-Simpson
CAD drawings by Randi Steinbrecher

A-3

⬡1 ELEVATION- SECOND LEVEL
SCALE: 3/4"= 1'-0"

A-4

A-5

⬡2 ELEVATION- SECOND LEVEL
SCALE: 3/4"= 1'-0"

A-6

A-7

⌀3 ELEVATION- SECOND LEVEL
SCALE: 3/4"= 1'-0"

A-8

FIGURE A-3
Photograph of the view referenced in elevation symbol 1.

FIGURE A-4
AutoCAD-generated interior elevation drawing of the view referenced in symbol 1. Note that given the location (in plan) of the reference symbol, the base cabinets on the left and the base and upper cabinets on the right have been cut through and shown with a bold line weight.

FIGURE A-5
Photograph of the view of the kitchen similar to that referenced in elevation symbol 2.

FIGURE A-6
AutoCAD-generated interior elevation drawing of the view referenced in symbol 2. Note that given the location (in plan) of the reference symbol, the base cabinets on the left and the base have been cut through and shown with a bold line weight.

FIGURE A-7
Photograph of the view of the sitting area referenced in elevation symbol 3.

FIGURE A-8
AutoCAD-generated interior elevation drawing of the view referenced in symbol 3.

COLOR THEORY FOR RENDERING

Color rendering requires a basic understanding of color theory, especially the properties of color and how to approximate these with various media or pigments.

Hue. What we often call a color should actually be referred to as a *hue*. Green and orange are both hues. Hue is changed only when mixed with another hue. Green mixed with blue changes the hue to greenish blue.

Value. This term refers to lightness or darkness. Adding white lightens a color without changing the hue; this is also true of adding black to darken a color. *Value* also refers to the manner in which light falls on an object illuminating its surface.

Chroma. Also referred to as intensity or saturation, *chroma* describes the purity or level of brightness of a color. Describing something as being dull or bright is a way of referring to chroma.

Hue, value, and chroma are all properties of color and are part of color rendering. Consider the following example. When rendering a faded red chair, we must select the correct hue—red. The red must be not bright, but faded; this mean the chroma is not highly saturated. The chair must have light, medium, and dark values applied to various locations based on the light source—these values are necessary in rendering.

When using markers, the following can be done to achieve properties of color:

Hue. Sometimes a desired marker hue does not exist. Layering two marker hues can sometimes produce the appropriate hue. For example, red-orange is often created by layering orange and red. In some cases the hue can be altered with the application of colored pencil over the marker color. Hue is also altered by making a pool of color on tracing paper and "picking it up" with a colorless blender; the blender is then dabbed on in the desired locations.

Value. The best way to create value with markers is to lay gray marker in the appropriate locations prior to the colored marker application. This is done by locating the light, medium, and dark areas of the form, then light, medium, and gray markers can be underlaid. Colored marker is then applied on top of the gray, and the values are complete. Sometimes the complementary color may be under laid in place of gray. A wash of gray or complementary colored pencil may also be applied on top of marker in the appropriate locations.

To create highlights or light areas, it is sometimes necessary to wash over marker with light-colored pencil, especially white or beige. Washes of dry pastel may also be used to lighten or darken areas and to achieve value gradation. Small amounts of white gouache or white-out pen (pen only—not liquid from a bottle) also work for highlights.

Chroma. Marker chroma is often dulled by the application of a layer of complementary-hued marker, colored pencil, or dry pastel. Chroma may be brightened with the application of a similar hue of marker, pencil, or pastel. For example, to brighten dull green marker color, apply a brighter green colored pencil layer on top of the marker.

It is worthwhile to experiment with multiple layers of markers, washes of pencil, and pastel to vary hue, chroma, and value to enrich a rendering.

SCALE FIGURES AND ENTOURAGE

Adding scale figures to orthographic projections, perspectives, and paraline drawings provides a touch of realism and clarifies relative proportions. Adding plants, animals, and other elements of everyday life can also enliven drawings. It is also helpful to trace figures or cut and paste photographs onto CAD-generated drawings.

A number of books are available with scaled figures and entourage elements such as plants, cars, boats, and sports equipment. These books contain hundreds of images, free of copyright restrictions, that are easily traced onto transparent paper. Images from magazines can also be traced into drawings. Many designers prefer to draw their own scale figures, reflective of personal style. Figure A-9 shows a step-by-step creation of stylized human figures.

Human figures must be placed at the appropriate height and locations in a drawing. In orthographic projections and paraline drawings, most adult figures should be drawn with eye levels at about five to six feet. In perspective drawings, most adult figures should be placed with eye level at about five to six feet, which is the standard horizon-line location. In perspectives drawn with nonstandard horizon lines (those above or below eye level), scale figures are placed at five to six feet, which may be far above or below the horizon line. Figure A-10 shows placement of human figures in two-point perspective.

I recommend keeping a file filled with entourage elements such as plants, window coverings, and decorative objects. Mail-order catalogs, plant catalogs, equipment catalogs, and magazines provide excellent images for entourage elements. Items from a clip file can be drawn or traced using a quick stylized approach that allows for elimination of details. These traced items should be simplified to speed the drawing process and to avoid overwhelming the composition. Photographs and drawings can also be scanned and imported into digital drawings and models following the placement rules covered in Figure A-10. Figures A-11, A-12, and A-13 are simplified drawings of human figures and plants that may be traced.

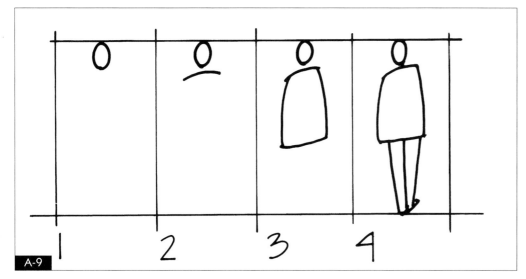

FIGURE A-9
Step-by-step drawing of human figures.
1. Draw a small oval head.
2. Draw curved shoulders slightly below head.
3. Draw torso extending downward from shoulders.
4. Draw legs below torso; legs can be slightly uneven.

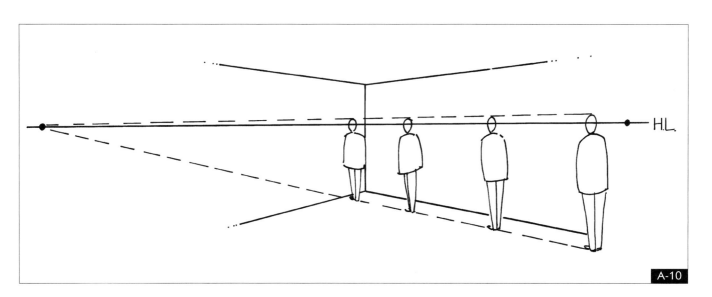

FIGURE A-10
Figures and other scale elements diminish in size as they recede from the viewer. A standard adult figure will diminish in size in accordance with the location of the horizon line.

FIGURE A-11
These simplified scale figures can be copied, reduced, or enlarged as necessary and traced for inclusion in drawings, as shown in Figure A-10. The horizon line is shown at a standard five to 6' above floor level.

FIGURE A-12
These simplified scale figures can be copied, reduced, or enlarged as necessary and traced for inclusion in drawings, as shown in Figure A-10. The horizon line is shown at a standard five to 6' above floor level.

FIGURE A-13
These simplified plants can be copied and traced for inclusion in drawings.

TWO-POINT PERSPECTIVE GRID

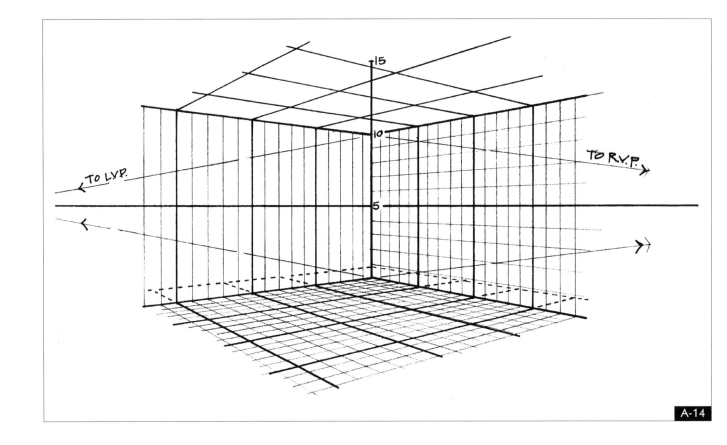

A-14

FIGURE A-14
This basic two-point perspective grid can be copied and used as an aid in constructing drawings, as shown in Figures 4-12a through 4-12e on page 131. Note that the horizon line or viewer's eye level is at 5' above the floor.